To God be the Glory.
the Best is Yet to Come!"

J. Bronson Haley

THE DEPTH OF GRACE

Finding Hope at Rock Bottom

J. BRONSON HALEY

Copyright © 2011 Bronson Haley

All rights reserved. No part of this book may be used or reproduced by any means, graphic, electronic, or mechanical, including photocopying, recording, taping or by any information storage retrieval system without the written permission of the publisher except in the case of brief quotations embodied in critical articles and reviews.

WestBow Press books may be ordered through booksellers or by contacting:
WestBow Press
A Division of Thomas Nelson
1663 Liberty Drive
Bloomington, IN 47403
www.westbowpress.com
1-(866) 928-1240

Because of the dynamic nature of the Internet, any Web addresses or links contained in this book may have changed since publication and may no longer be valid. The views expressed in this work are solely those of the author and do not necessarily reflect the views of the publisher, and the publisher hereby disclaims any responsibility for them.

Any people depicted in stock imagery provided by Thinkstock are models, and such images are being used for illustrative purposes only.
Certain stock imagery © Thinkstock.

ALL SCRIPTURE QUOTATIONS, UNLESS OTHERWISE INDICATED, ARE TAKEN FROM THE HOLY BIBLE, NEW INTERNATIONAL VERSION®, NIV®. COPYRIGHT © 1973, 1978, 1984, 2010 BY BIBLICA, INC™. USED BY PERMISSION OF ZONDERVAN. ALL RIGHTS RESERVED WORLDWIDE. WWW.ZONDERVAN.COM. SCRIPTURE QUOTATIONS MARKED NIV 1984 ARE TAKEN FROM THE HOLY BIBLE, NEW INTERNATIONAL VERSION®, NIV®. COPYRIGHT © 1973, 1978, 1984 BY BIBLICA, INC™. USED BY PERMISSION OF ZONDERVAN. ALL RIGHTS RESERVED WORLDWIDE. WWW. ZONDERVAN.COM. SCRIPTURE QUOTATIONS MARKED KJV ARE TAKEN FROM THE KING JAMES VERSION OF THE BIBLE. (PUBLIC DOMAIN.) SCRIPTURE QUOTATIONS MARKED NCV ARE TAKEN FROM THE NEW CENTURY VERSION. COPYRIGHT © 1987, 1988, 1991 BY WORD PUBLISHING, A DIVISION OF THOMAS NELSON, INC. USED BY PERMISSION. ALL RIGHTS RESERVED.

Author's Note: To protect the identities of the individuals mentioned in the stories I relate in this book, I have chosen to change the names. Only the names of public figures and my immediate family members have not been changed. Thanks for your understanding.

ISBN: 978-1-4497-1046-0 (sc)
ISBN: 978-1-4497-1047-7 (dj)
ISBN: 978-1-4497-1048-4 (e)

Library of Congress Control Number: 2011921081
Printed in the United States of America
WestBow Press rev. date: 2/7/2011

And our hope for you is firm,
because we know that just as you share in our sufferings,
so also you share in our comfort.
2 Corinthians 1:7

CONTENTS

Introduction	The Life and Death of Jackson Hunter	1
Chapter 1	Growing Up … Too Fast	9
Chapter 2	A Walk on the Violent Side	13
1st REST STOP: Simon Peter		24
Chapter 3	Trips over the Tracks	29
Chapter 4	Burglary	33
2nd REST STOP: Jacob's Journey: Part 1		39
Chapter 5	House Arrest	49
3rd REST STOP: Jacob's Journey: Part 2		54
Chapter 6	Not Dead Yet	61
4th REST STOP: Follow Me		64
Chapter 7	Saved	73
Chapter 8	Free Beer and Cigarettes	77
5th REST STOP: License to Sin?		80
Chapter 9	A Confused Alien	83
Chapter 10	Telephone Pole	87
6th REST STOP: Darkest Hour		90
Chapter 11	Bricktown	97
7th REST STOP: The Sacrifice		102
Chapter 12	Transcripts	105
Chapter 13	SOS (Sold-Out Saturday)	109
8th REST STOP: Breath of God		113
Chapter 14	Streets of Gold	119
Chapter 15	Silent Struggle	125
9th REST STOP: Most Glorious Hour		128
Chapter 16	Sniper	141
Chapter 17	Mexico	153

10th REST STOP: Reconciliation of the World	158
Chapter 18 Officer "Abuse"	173
Chapter 19 "Stoned" Cop	181
11th REST STOP: Rightfully Insecure	184
Chapter 20 The Word "Restore"	189
Chapter 21 Sniper: Part 2	193
12th REST STOP: The Mountain of the Lord	199
Chapter 22 Facing the Wind	207
Chapter 23 The Road to Emmaus	217
13th REST STOP: Flesh Seekers: Part 1	224
Chapter 24 Mike Mertle	231
14th REST STOP: Flesh Seekers: Part 2	241
Chapter 25 Bullet	251
Chapter 26 The Celebration	259
15th REST STOP: Heavenly Sanctuary	269
Chapter 27 Forget as God Forgets	281
A FINAL NOTE FROM THE AUTHOR ...	287

INTRODUCTION

The Life and Death of Jackson Hunter

Jackson Hunter jumped into my pickup and we backed out of his driveway, ready to tackle the Rocky Mountains for some 4x4 action in the middle of winter. As soon as we got on the road, we put our brilliant minds together and decided to stop at the corner store to pick up an eighteen-pack of beer. Hey, I was an experienced off-road driver, having spent my share of time in the backwoods of northwest Louisiana—so a little beer would only add to the night's excitement.

But once we got off the highway, it didn't take much time for me to figure out that my off-road experience in mud and water wasn't going to do much on snow and ice. Fretting about getting stuck in a Louisiana mud hole was nothing compared to worrying about sliding off a mountain to our death. Therefore we drove very, very slowly—and drank really, really fast—to meet the challenge.

After driving up the mountain for about an hour, I noticed we had less than a quarter tank of gas. The sun was quickly falling behind the mountains, and my truck's on-board thermometer told me that the outside temperature was now a balmy seven degrees—a drop of twenty degrees in just twenty minutes. It was definitely time to turn around.

After mastering the art of driving up the mountain, I figured driving back down would be a piece of cake. No doubt the six beers I had ingested added to my confidence. As I picked up a little speed, I noticed we were

1

approaching a curve, so I decided to have a little fun. And, yeah, it sure was fun—nothing like an innocent little fishtail to land us in a ditch, on an abandoned road, in now zero-degree weather.

After trying to back up and drive forward without moving a single inch, I grabbed another beer. I didn't say anything for the next several minutes, but I was sure that Jackson was waiting to hear my solution to the problem. In the back of my mind, dark thoughts began to nag at me … *We have less than a quarter of a tank of gas.* … *Who knows how low the temperature will drop in the middle of winter after nightfall on this remote mountain?* … *We are not prepared to hike anywhere and survive the trek.* … *Will the gas we have left last us all night sitting here running a V-8 engine?*

I didn't communicate any of these fears to Jackson, but I did brilliantly summarize the solution to our problem for him: "Whatever we have to do to get out of this ditch is what we are going to do." Jackson nodded but didn't ask any questions.

The ditch we were in wasn't too deep—just deep enough to shift the bulk of my 7,500-pound 4x4 *away* from the road. Plus the factory tires on my truck were not designed for snow and had created an extremely slick surface on the snow as they spun. Pushing the truck anywhere was out of the question.

But I was somewhat relieved when I remembered grabbing three towropes before leaving home. Granted, towropes are not a whole lot of good without a large piece of pulling equipment to do the actual towing. But I figured that we were in a situation where it was definitely going to be a combination of little things that might get us safely back on the road.

After unloading my toolbox and laying everything on the road, we came up with a plan. We had three towropes, two 1x6x10-inch steel plates, a 3-foot wooden 2x4, and a jack. Two of the towropes were ratcheted for use in securing large loads to tractor trailers. The ratchets were not strong enough to pull my truck out of the ditch, of course, but they were strong enough to shift the weight of my truck into the direction we needed to go. We secured both ropes to my front bumper and fastened the other ends to a tree on the opposite side of the road. After tying the remaining rope to my rear bumper, we secured it to another tree across the road. I wasn't sure if it would help, considering it wasn't ratcheted, but I didn't care. Maybe it would help keep us from sliding farther into the ditch, given a worst-case scenario.

By now I noticed that Jackson was getting extremely nervous. The temperature was still dropping fast, and the chances of someone driving

The Depth of Grace

down this particular road anytime soon were slim to none. I'm sure he was asking himself the same question that was in my mind: *What happens if we don't get out of this ditch?*

We continued to work and didn't talk about it, jumping into the truck every few minutes to get warm and then hopping back outside to work a bit more.

It was now time to place the two steel plates under the front and rear tires of the driver's side. As we continued, our work stints were getting shorter and shorter. We started at around three minutes of work before taking a warm-up break, but due to the extreme temperature, we were now working in one-minute intervals while spending more time in the truck getting warm. It took us around forty-five minutes to clear the snow with the 2x4, jack up the tires one at a time, and place the steel plates underneath.

Realizing we were approaching the "do or die" point, I asked Jackson if there was anything else he could think of that might increase our chances. He shook his head and said nothing. My truck was still doing a great job drinking up the remaining gas, and our fears increased every second that we came closer to our attempt at freeing ourselves.

After deciding we had done everything we could, I got one last idea … out of desperation, no doubt. After jacking up the front right tire, I asked Jackson to retrieve the owner's manual of my truck from the glove box and hand it to me so I could put it under the tire. He gave me a funny look, but when he realized I wasn't joking, he did as I said. I quickly placed it under the tire, and upon releasing the hydraulic pressure in the jack, my truck lowered onto the manual.

After climbing back in the truck, I realized that Jackson's weight probably wasn't helping at all, so I told him to get out. He jumped out, gave the towrope ratchets a couple more tugs, then walked about a hundred feet up the road. By now the wind had picked up and the temperature had dropped well below zero.

Right before I hit the gas, horrible thoughts began to flood my mind …

I was the one driving tonight.
It was my idea to get the beer.
It'll be my fault if Jackson dies out here.

My brain also kindly recalled for me all the times I'd heard of stories like this having a tragic ending. It would have been different if I had been by myself. But, at the time, I was looking up the road at my friend,

3

thinking that he didn't deserve this. I didn't think God would hear me, but I asked Him for help anyway as I shifted my truck into low four-wheel drive.

When I punched the accelerator, my truck jumped out of the ditch like a tyrannosaurus rabbit. After pulling to a stop, I quickly jumped out and took off running toward Jackson, seeing right away that he was sprinting toward me. We jumped and met in midair, clutching each other in arms pumped full of adrenalin. After dancing around together for a few seconds, we had one of those humbling moments: you hug a man like he's a man and a woman however necessary to make her feel good, but you don't ever hug another dude like that no matter what the case may be.

After realizing what we were doing, we stopped, looked at each other in embarrassment, then walked toward the truck, confessing our fears to one another and enjoying our breakthrough.

The ride back to Jackson's home will forever be implanted in my mind. After finally experiencing the security of a full tank of gas, we relaxed a bit. Jackson began to open up to me for the first time. He had a drug problem and it had been defeating him for seven years.

Jackson told me that, just a couple of months back, he had been arrested in Colorado because of a warrant. He had failed to take care of a drug charge in Shreveport, Louisiana, and was extradited back to his hometown as a result. He described the feelings he experienced while chained to several other people who were also being hauled to court. It took three weeks to arrive because they had to make several stops on the way to pick up other criminals. Jackson mentioned that the first couple of days were not so bad. The officers were nice, and they got three meals a day. He didn't like the idea of feeling like some sort of slave criminal, but he was okay.

"It was the next couple of weeks that almost killed me," he said to me.

On the third day of the jaunt back to Louisiana, Jackson began to go through withdrawals from not having drugs. He'd been through withdrawals before but never under such circumstances. He described some of the thoughts that were going through his mind as his journey disintegrated from not so bad to downright miserable.

"You know, Bronson, when you're on the drug, everything seems fine. Life can be pulling you through the darkest of valleys, but somehow you feel like everything is okay, and you continue to move forward," Jackson told me. "When the drugs began to wear off in the van, reality began to

The Depth of Grace

set in, and I was overwhelmed with who I'd become over the years. The people I was chained to were not in as bad shape as I, and they were pretty much lowlifes. Here I am dealing with chronic restlessness, cold sweats, and nausea among other things. I was nothing more than a drug addict, chained to several others being hauled back to Louisiana to face drug charges."

On the tip of my tongue, I had the words "Jesus" and "freedom." However, I kept my mouth shut and kept driving. Why? Because, personally, I was in a place in my life where I was desperate for relief myself.

I had been away from God for around five years. Over the course of that period, I'd lost several friends and acquaintances due to the party scene. Pete Holt was murdered by his roommate after a heated argument. Nate Baldwin was stabbed in the chest after fighting another man over his girlfriend, and he died in her front yard. Cam Barton was blown out of the back of a truck headed south on I-49 as he stood up to relieve himself and died when he hit the concrete. Several others I knew also died living the fast life. These tragedies were difficult to deal with for me, knowing deep down that I knew about Jesus but didn't tell anyone because I didn't have the strength to stay strong in my own faith. I was sure there would be more who would die without me telling them about Jesus—and the guilt was sickening.

But that's not the only weight I had on my shoulders as I spoke to Jackson.

About a year and a half prior to this talk with Jackson in my truck, I had dislocated my shoulder on a biking trip and was prescribed pain medicine for relief. This medicine did more for me than just help my shoulder. The drug made the pain in my heart bearable as well. After just a couple of months, I developed an addiction to the meds and became trapped in a merciless world of darkness equal to death.

After the talk with Jackson that night in Colorado, I decided that I was going to get off the pain medicine. I was going to get off it and somehow get my life right with God. I couldn't imagine how God was going to remove the extent of my shame, guilt, pain, fear, and addiction—or even if He would after all the horrible ways that I had failed Him. But, if He did, I was going to share Jesus with Jackson, my other close friends, and everyone else who needed to hear so that they, too, could overcome the challenges in their own lives.

When I arrived home from Colorado a week later, I quit taking the medicine. I was okay the first and second day, but on the third day,

J. Bronson Haley

my world came crashing down. I began to experience severe restlessness, nausea, and tremors. And just like Jackson had related to me about his own withdrawal experience, reality began to set in for me and I realized who I'd become over the years. I was nothing more than a drug addict who let down everyone who had ever believed in me.

When I was saved in 1997, God restored me and gave me a wonderful home to live in with a great family. However, I subsequently hurt my own family, the family I was living with, and many people in my church. This guilt, along with the deaths of many friends, was the reason I got hooked on the painkillers in the first place. Now I was extremely sick after setting my life back a year and a half. I remember thinking, *I can see why people kill themselves.* I don't have a story where I had the gun to my head, but I did think seriously about it at this time. Strangely enough, I still felt like there was hope for me because of my past experiences with God.

Overcoming the addiction, shame, and guilt was an extremely farfetched idea. While going through the withdrawals, I began to think about my friend Jackson and the story he had told me on that cold night in Colorado. Going through hell is bad enough even knowing deep down inside there is hope with God. I could not imagine what Jackson must have gone through and was continuing to go through without knowing God or His ways. I began to think about the rest of those in the world who, like Jackson, were suffering in unimaginable ways, having never experienced the love of God—at least in a way that radically transformed their lives.

After failing at my first attempt to beat the addiction, I decided to get into shape as an edge against my cravings. So one day I took off out the door of my home for a run—only to soon break down in tears after having to turn around at the end of the block to walk back. I used to be very athletic, and now I couldn't even make it past the stop sign at the end of my street.

Several months later, on my fourth attempt to overcome my addiction, I got a phone call from another close friend of mine named Sam. He and several other friends had gone out the night before to celebrate Jackson's birthday. I was excited to hear that Jackson had turned twenty-four! They went to the casino and had a wonderful time. Then Sam said that Jackson laid his head down early that morning and never woke up. He was found the next day with his phone in his hand and his hand resting on his chest. He had talked to his girlfriend just a couple of hours prior to the time he was found. My friend died of a drug overdose.

The Depth of Grace

When I got the news, I dropped to my knees and begged God for forgiveness. I promised the Lord that, if He would restore me, I would tell the world about His Son. This book is the result of that promise.

I warn you, though, that the stories you'll read here aren't sugarcoated. I was a wild guy (still am a little, I guess), and I pushed it to the limit—and beyond—way too much. That's why these stories have all the blood, sweat, tears, and raw grit that my friends and I really experienced. Even more, though, these stories show one thing: no matter how deep you've fallen into the pit, God's grace can reach down and pull you out.

I'm living proof.

CHAPTER 1

Growing Up ... Too Fast

As a child down home in Louisiana, I remember waking up in a pitch-black room to my mother's screams. My sister, Shannon, was six at the time and I was five. Our room was on one end of our trailer, and my mother and stepfather's room at the opposite end. When I woke, I quickly jumped up on the top bunk with my big sister. This wasn't the first time this had happened, and we knew Mom was in trouble. All we could do was huddle together, listen, and hope she would be okay.

Several minutes later Mom walked into our room, battered and crying with mascara running down her face. After making sure she was all right, I climbed back down into my bed as she climbed up on the top bunk with my sister to sleep for the night. A few moments later footsteps echoed through the trailer. I quickly scurried out of bed and opened the door to see what my stepfather was doing. The image I saw at that moment will be with me for as long as I live. Walking through the kitchen, heading in our direction, was my stepfather—naked, with hatred beaming from his eyes into my own. He was a big man with long, dark, stringy hair. As he entered our room, my sister began to cry. Then my mother screamed as he grabbed her by the feet, dragged her off the top bunk onto the floor, and out of the room. I watched as Mom kicked and screamed while being hauled through the living room, the kitchen, and into the hall that led to their room. I remember wishing I could do something to help her, but I was too afraid and too small. The noise died down after a few minutes, and my sister and I fell asleep. Sadly, I can't say that's the last time something

9

J. Bronson Haley

like that happened; rather, it was just one snapshot from a childhood that forced us to grow up a little too fast.

———

My mother and our biological father had divorced when I was one and Shannon was two. Both parents struggled with alcohol problems, but they always loved us and we never doubted that fact. We went through many difficult times as young children, but kids today go through much worse without the love of their parents.

I do remember one time when Mom boldly stepped in between my stepfather and me in my defense. I was around five years old, just sitting in the bathtub with the water running. Mom left the room for just a moment to check on my sister. When she was gone, the water became very hot and I began to cry while hollering for my mother. My stepfather then walked in, grinning from ear to ear. He knelt down by the tub and began to splash the scalding water into my face, laughing the whole time as I began to scream. My mother entered the bathroom shortly after I started yelling, and I got a clear picture of the "Don't get between momma bear and her cub" scenario. After sinking her claws into his face while hollering and screaming at him, Mom was forced to the back bedroom. Climbing out of the tub, I was embraced by big sister.

This experience proved to me that Mom would do anything in her power to keep me from harm. I often got my feelings hurt growing up, but the battle wasn't against just me. The battle was against my family, and alcohol was to blame.

———

For most of my younger years, my real father lived north of town on Caddo Lake. "The Caddo Club" was the name of this small trailer-park community of around ten families. Some of my best childhood memories were born during the time I spent with my father. My sister, a couple of friends, and I spent hundreds of hours exploring the banks of Caddo Lake and roaming the surrounding woods. I even had the chance to live there from the time that I was around eight to eleven years of age.

Dad married a Native American Indian woman named Jewel, and— not to stereotype anyone in any way—I hate to say that she was a real wild Indian. She was twenty-two and loved to party. Even more, she was always up for a good fight with the neighbors after a healthy night of drinking.

Adding fuel to the fire was the fact that Jewel said she grew up in a haunted house, which led to her fascination with the spirit realm. A late night séance was common for our family on school nights, so I have to admit that Stepmother always kept things exciting.

So I have to ask, do you believe in ghosts? Well, one day my stepmother; a good friend of hers named Deb Hart; Deb's daughter, Millie, who was around eighteen at the time; my sister, who was ten; and I (at nine years old) set out on a mission to penetrate the spirit realm. We all loaded up in the car one afternoon and headed to Waskom, Texas, on a ghost hunt. During the forty-five minute drive, Millie explained our mission in great detail. During the early 1800s, a family of five lived on Concord Road in Waskom: daddy, mommy, a ten-year-old son, a six-year-old girl, and a one-year-old baby. For no apparent reason, the father went mad one night and proceeded to murder his family, and then he committed suicide. Their home was a beautiful two-story house. This had been the largest home in the small town of around one hundred people.

After this tragedy, many families had moved into the home, but none stayed for very long. Some of them mentioned seeing members of the deceased family at various times and claimed that the house was haunted. Thus it was the perfect place for us to have our spiritual—and outlandish—extravaganza. A town cemetery sat right down the street from this haunted house, and this was our first stop. Our mission at the cemetery: find the graves of the deceased family prior to visiting their house.

After several minutes of examining various graves, some of which did indeed date back to the early 1800s, we came upon the graves of a family of five, fenced off from the rest. I stayed close by my sister due to the intensity of the scene (I might have been a bit scared all by myself, but my sister and I were extremely tough together).

And this was one spooky place! A storm was nearing, and dark, heavy clouds loomed overhead. The wind was blowing and the leaves tumbled around us as we stood before the grave site. It was all like some scene from the movies, and fear crawled up our spines.

Many of the grave caskets were above ground, and most were cracked and falling in on themselves. This family's graves were particularly in bad shape. Being the adventurous and most disrespectful of the group, I began to slide open one of the graves to take a peek inside. Looking into the smallest of the five graves, I froze in mock bewilderment. As the others crept closer to witness the source of my delusional facial expression, I hollered at the top of my lungs, tensing every muscle in my body and scaring the poor girls have half to death. That was really funny. I was one bad little nine-year-old.

J. Bronson Haley

A few moments later we loaded up in the car and headed to the home of the murderous father and his victims. The house had a circular driveway and Millie told us that the estate was in the process of being turned into a tourist attraction. From the end of the driveway, we could partially see a second-story balcony that appeared to have its windows all boarded up. Pulling farther into the drive, everyone in the car went silent as we all noticed a little girl standing on the balcony in front of a boarded-up door. She looked to be around six and was wearing an old dress—and in her arms, she was holding what looked like a baby. The girl was frozen in place, just staring at the car, and her eyes were so dark that they seemed to be sunken into her face.

Terror gripped me as I gazed up at the girl, but Millie just started explaining in more detail how the home was a historical site and how the town had decided to turn the house into some sort of museum, which is why it looked to be under construction at the time. She went on to say that many people in town told stories of seeing one or more of the deceased family members at various times, so they had decided to build statues of the family going about their daily routines in the home, with the intent of giving tours to tell the story of the murders.

Thinking it was all beginning to make sense and that we were simply looking at a lifelike statue of the little girl, I began to calm just a bit as I listened to Millie's explanation—until the little girl began to walk across the balcony, still staring at us, and with the baby beginning to move in her arms. That did it for me! I began to scream bloody murder while pulling Deb's hair and kicking the seat in front of me, begging her, "Please leave! Please leave!"

The ride home was very quiet. Every once in a while, someone would ask a random question, obviously expecting no answer in return. After all, what answers could any of us come up with? The balcony had been boarded shut. No cars had been seen at the home, and we had no explanation for the little girl and the baby, with the girl never taking her eyes off of us the whole time.

For several days after that, I rounded corners very slowly and quickly jerked back shower curtains, worrying with fear that I might catch sight of the little girl on the balcony in Waskom. I don't know whether it was a ghost or an evil spirit, but it really opened my eyes to the possibility of another, invisible realm. Whatever the case may be, it was real, and the little girl will not be forgotten.

CHAPTER 2

A Walk on the Violent Side

When I was eleven years old, my mother remarried, and my sister and I enrolled in Broadmoor Middle Laboratory School for my sixth-grade year and her seventh. I made many friends, and I developed a strong bond with one boy in particular. His name was Pete Holt and he wasn't like any kid I'd ever met.

Prior to enrolling at Broadmoor, Pete had attended Hollywood Elementary—an all-black school in the middle of the ghetto. He lived with his mother while attending Hollywood and was very hardened as a result. His mom was one of the sweetest women I'd ever met, and she loved Pete to death. At the same time, though, she had a drug problem, and this addiction was destroying her day by day.

Pete often told me stories about fights he got into at Hollywood Elementary, at the bus stop, on the bus, and on the streets of this ghetto neighborhood. He was one of the only white boys in the area, but was among the toughest kids in the neighborhood. His mom sometimes told me stories of looking out the window of her house toward the bus stop and through all the violence seeing these two little white hands being thrown in every direction. I could only laugh as she told of how she would then run outside, cussing out the other kids while retrieving her son.

Because our childhood experiences were similar in many ways, Pete and I connected quickly. His boyhood had been even tougher than mine, but we understood each other and developed an extremely close bond as a result, which ended up helping us both at our new school.

13

J. Bronson Haley

Broadmoor's student population was about half white, half black. When I began sixth grade at the school, for some reason I was afraid of black people and would sometimes get picked on. This fear didn't last long after I started hanging out with Pete. He explained to me that if you show people you are not afraid, most of the time they will leave you alone. But, if you let them see your fear, they'll run with it, and you'll never hear the end of it. He also mentioned that sometimes you might end up in situations in which you will have no choice but to fight no matter how well you might handle your fear or the circumstance you're in. I took all this to heart and, for better or worse, decided to put it into practice immediately. (And, yes, I eventually learned the error of my racial fears.)

After having a confrontation with a black boy in the hall between classes one day, my adrenalin was pumping as I entered the boys' restroom to tell Pete the story. I could not wait to let him know about my breakthrough in my struggle against my fears. As I related the story to Pete, I was overjoyed with excitement and conveyed to him the details of the scene. While describing to Pete the look on the boy's face when he saw I wasn't afraid of him, I let the "n" word slip.

The restroom went dead silent.

I froze in place for a moment then slowly began to look around. Terror gripped me as the largest of the six black boys in the restroom zipped up and addressed my comment. The boy stepped in front of me and asked, "What'd you say, nigga?"

As I stood there scared to death and speechless, Pete stepped in between us.

"Does it look like he was talking to you?" Pete said, to my surprise.

Pete was half the size of this boy. By the look on the boy's face, he was as surprised as I that Pete made such a bold remark in my defense. "What did you say, white boy?" he asked.

"Did I stutter? Or are you just stupid?" Pete replied.

The only thing going on in the room at that time was Pete interacting with his new friend. At first, I was sure the six would jump us, but to my great relief, the others were now only interested in watching this match.

Shortly after squaring off, Pete and the boy began slugging each other like clockwork. I am not kidding! This fight was just another walk in the park for these two. The black boy had to be twice as strong as my friend. Yet Pete was putting up a fight that could have gone either way at any time. Just when Pete would get pinned up against the wall or in a corner, he would somehow break loose and continue to throw blow after blow. At

The Depth of Grace

one point the boy had Pete's arms pinned to his chest while holding him up against the wall. Pete's response was several head butts to the boy's nose. Sure enough, the boy let go and they were at it again.

I knew Pete's childhood had hardened him, but for the first time I witnessed what the story of his life had created in him. This was no ordinary kid. He was tough as nails and wasn't intimidated by the boy and his five buddies in the least bit. Not that he could have handled them all, but I guess Pete figured, what was the worst thing that could happen? He'd told me before about how he had been jumped many times on the streets of his old neighborhood and he wasn't afraid.

The fight was pretty even as the school bell rang. When everyone finally split, Pete had been pinned against the wall in one of the stalls with a foot in the toilet. He wasn't winning at the time, but from what I had seen already, he would have soon struggled loose and continued the rumble.

What Pete did for me in the restroom that day affected me on the inside—something I have never forgotten. Pete fought my fight and was there when I needed him most. He knew I was afraid and took my burden upon himself. I was overwhelmed with a sense of love. I knew the kid loved me, and a bond was formed in the restroom that day that would not be broken.

Naturally, as I spent more time with Pete, I began to toughen up really fast. We had hard-core wrestling matches just about every day for extended periods of time. He showed me things he learned on the streets about fighting, and I paid close attention. Pete was the toughest kid I'd ever met and he proved it to me over and over again. It wasn't long before wrestling with the other kids became a joke and fighting became second nature.

Over the next several years we backed each other in every difficult situation that came our way. If it was a fight, it was a fight. Whatever we needed, we were there for each other. Our friendship became based on this concept.

Later Pete finally talked to me about his dad, or lack thereof. He informed me that his mom had been raped and that he didn't even have a dad. He discussed some of the many hardships he had experienced up to that point. Two of his uncles had died of AIDS, and these tragedies were just a handful of the many this kid had suffered. Pete was troubled and few understood him.

Of course, Pete didn't have a good reputation. Kids at school referred to him as "that bad-ghetto white boy." And he was! But there were things about Pete that people didn't understand. They didn't know or care about his past and the things he'd experienced that made him the way he was. Among other things, Pete didn't choose his childhood. He didn't choose the torment on his insides over the peace in the hearts of other kids. The challenges that Pete grew up with simply could not be understood by most.

I was certain the other kids couldn't see Pete's heart through his scars and bad attitude. People missed out on not getting the chance to know him. He was willing to do anything to help someone and was a loyal friend.

During one phase as eighth graders, our little group of friends thought it was cool to steal hood ornaments from cars. We roamed the streets in search of our next prize. The more expensive the car ornament, the greater the respect for the thief. We were all very brave; however, Pete always found a way to separate himself from the pack and win the greatest respect from our clique.

One time Pete, our other best friend Mike Mertle, a friend named Clark, and I were walking past El Chico's restaurant in our neighborhood in search of our next ornament. I took note of a Dodge Ram, parked just outside the restaurant, and tossed the challenge to Pete. The truck was facing a table of people eating, and the only thing between them and the truck was a sidewalk and a glass window.

Without hesitating, Pete walked over, jumped on the front bumper, and gave the little ram head a tug. After his first attempt failed, he jumped up on the bumper again and stripped the ornament from the vehicle. Pete had the ornament in his hand, but word quickly reached the manager, who soon burst out of the restaurant. He wore a button-up shirt and looked around thirty years old. He immediately set out in pursuit of my buddy. We all took off running, and once I was across the street, I glanced back to see if Pete was going to get away. The man was right on Pete's heels about to grab him when Pete stopped, dropped to a squatting position, and tripped the man into a front flip. I chuckled and continued my flight. The stop-drop-and-flip move was often used among ourselves. Now it had paid off. To see him pull off the stunt in that die-hard situation was honorable in my eyes. Pete was the coolest kid I knew and I loved him deeply.

We ended up passing middle school without mastery. Our bad behavior in middle school actually took us to the next level. We somehow passed eighth grade with straight F's and missed plenty more than the acceptable attendance rules would allow. Many times we skipped school until we got caught. We didn't care one way or the other.

Pete lasted a couple of months at Byrd High School before dropping out and going to work. It wasn't long after he began working that we began to grow apart as our lifestyles diverged. We began to hang with different people and do different things. I was living the high-school life. Pete lived and worked with a man named Pete Block, who owned an air-conditioner company.

Pete's new boss had money and drove a Ford F-350 extended-cab long bed with a Ferrari engine under the hood. I saw them driving all over town, and every time they passed by, "Big Pete" would blow the horn and "Little Pete" would hang out the window and wave, smiling from ear to ear. Knowing what I know now, I can see that the smile on his face wasn't conveying how he felt on the inside. His smile could only have meant he was happy to see his old buddy.

After about a year went by, I began to hear that Pete was getting heavy into drugs.

I can remember sitting around my home with a group of friends telling stories about him. We would share tales about some of the crazy things Pete did over the years. He fought anyone crazy enough to fight him, and alcohol caused him to get careless with his life. I can remember even in middle school, when some friends and I would hang out and tell stories about him. Many times after telling these stories, we would make bets on how old Pete would live to be. Some bet he wouldn't live past seventeen years of age. Some bet he wouldn't live past nineteen. No one ever bet that Pete would live to see twenty-one.

In many ways Pete was a legend. Everyone knew him as being the toughest kid they'd ever known—and a loyal friend. Pete knew a lot of people and many people knew him. He was often the favorite among the parents of our friends. He was my mom's favorite, for sure. It was hard to imagine how someone with such a rough childhood could be so loyal and giving. I feel like it was his appreciation of our love that captivated his heart. Pete didn't have anything to offer anyone. However, Pete did whatever he could for people. If it was fighting for them, then that's what he did. If it was staying up all night on the phone to hear a best friend pour out his emotions as he wept, he was there. Pete was a giver who didn't have anything to give, except himself.

As the end of my freshman year of high school approached, I lost contact with Pete. By that time I was having serious trouble myself. I drank heavily on the weekends and was a full-blown alcoholic by the age of fifteen. Alcohol was the substance that did the best job of drowning out the emptiness and pain on the inside. Violence moved my name through the local high schools and developed my reputation. If there was a fight at a party and I was there, I got involved.

Very few times did I fight someone because they had a problem with me. The time Pete fought for me in the restroom that day was the last fight I only watched. From then on out, I fought for all of my friends and they never asked questions. I often fought for people I didn't know. I would decide for myself who the aggressor was and then defend the weaker of the two. I was known for this kind of behavior. Many times I fought for someone who was being jumped by several others. Ironically enough, of the seventy-plus streets fights I endured over the first twenty-four years of my life, I only lost the last one. Most of the time, I did the right thing—in my eyes, anyway. A few times, though, I got drunk and got a little too loose with my dukes.

On the way to a party during my sophomore year of high school, the car I was riding in (full of people), and two other cars following (full of people), pulled up to a gas station to buy more beer. We had already been drinking, and I was pretty drunk by this time. Exiting the parking lot, we cut off a car and the girl in the passenger seat gave us the finger, no doubt echoing the sentiments of the guy who was driving the vehicle.

"Y'all want me to knock that dude out?" I asked my buddies in the car.

"You won't," they chorused.

"Oh, I won't? Turn around!"

After all three cars in our little caravan turned around and pulled back into the parking lot, I got out and walked toward the fellow as he headed for the front doors of the store. Noticing he was spooked, I asked him, "Where do I know you from? You look so familiar!"

Lightening up a bit, he began to walk my way. As soon as he was in reach, I decked him with a right, never missing a step. He dropped to the pavement like a dead horse. I chuckled as I walked back to the vehicle, amazed at my performance while receiving applause from my friends.

Every year, my hometown of Shreveport, Louisiana, holds a Red River Revel Festival. This event entails eating crawfish, listening to bands, looking at arts and crafts, and, of course, drinking beer. Back then, we were technically too young to drink, but we never left home without a fake ID and had no problem getting alcohol at the festival. My friends and I would often join a large group of other kids in the park section of the gathering. After drinking about twelve beers one particular night of the festival, my

The Depth of Grace

friend Mike Mertle walked up to me and told me how a guy we both knew had just pushed him into some bushes for no reason. This boy hung with a group of older kids that we didn't get along with at the time—and the boy was easily the toughest of the bunch. But none of that really mattered to me. Our own little group was just a bunch of hotheads who wanted the reputation of being the toughest in the area.

"Okay, Mike, where is he?" I asked.

"Follow me," he said.

When Mike pointed him out, I noticed that he stood in the middle of several of his friends, many of whom I was also familiar with. I immediately began to walk in their direction. As they acknowledged my sudden arrival, I took off my shirt, threw it at the guilty party's feet, and, never missing a step, caught him with that right I was famous for and knocked him to the ground. His friends backed off in disbelief as I jumped on top of him and delivered blow after blow after blow as if he had really caused my friend some kind of harm. After a couple of seconds, an officer pulled me off the boy, helped me find my shirt, and told me, "Get the heck out of here before I take you to jail!"

"Yes, sir!" I said, without argument.

This kind of unwarranted and senseless violence happened on occasion, but most of the time, I fought for someone who actually needed my help.

One of the editors who read an early draft of this book's manuscript brought it to my attention that I didn't mention what was going on inside of me that caused me to fight so much.

"What made you so angry?" she asked.

Really, it was never about anger, which I'll explain in a bit. I can honestly only remember one instance where I actually got angry during a fight.

I was twenty-four and he was a twenty-nine-year-old guy who I ended up finding out was no stranger to fighting himself. I had a severe drug addiction at the time, which probably only added to my frustrations. We fought outside of a bar after I broke up a fight between him and a good friend of mine. Once I broke it up, my friend walked off and this fellow ran around a Suburban to meet my friend on the other side. I met him at the other side and to his surprise threw him on the ground.

"Okay, it's you now, big boy," he snarled after picking himself up off the ground.

J. Bronson Haley

I was shocked at his comment. After all, most people in the bar scene knew me or my name well enough to know to avoid any confrontation with me.

"Look," I said. "There's no need for this. The cops are probably on the way and no one has been hurt. You go your own way, and I'll go in a different direction."

By this time about fifty people had gathered and were watching.

"No. We're about to fight," he said, again to my surprise.

A little frustrated, I took off my shirt and muttered, "If a fight is what you want, you got it!"

I threw the first punch and missed, but immediately grabbed him, hoisted him into the air, and dropped to the ground. By second nature I rolled over on top of him, put my left knee in his chest, and got a fistful of his shirt with my left hand. I went to work with my right while explaining the details of his mistake. Moments later I was pulled off by a local bouncer. As I stood up, I saw that the crowd had swelled in number to around a hundred people by this time.

My friends and I got ready to leave the scene as those in the crowd recounted the details of the fight. Also mingling about were the club owners, managers, and bouncers of these two particular bars that sat side by side. They were familiar with both of us and shocked that we had met up under the circumstances.

Feeling an incredible amount of adrenalin and excitement—combined with the fact that I was on OxyContin and out of shape—I scrambled to put my shirt back on, but then I heard my friend Art Colbert yell, "Bronson! Look behind you!"

I turned and saw this fellow approaching me from behind with several friends backing him. I still didn't have a clue who he was. At this point in my life, I wasn't going out much. By now the crowd of a hundred people was outside the back of the bars that opened up into a parking lot. I didn't realize everyone knew this guy. However, I knew enough to know that those watching knew me better than him and I knew where their loyalty stood. At various times in the past I had taken up for many of those who stood around. Most of them were my friends.

"What in the $%&@ are you doing?" I asked him.

"Let's go again!" he said.

"Listen, dumb-$@! The cops are surely on their way. Neither one of us is hurt. There is no sense in this. And trust me … you don't want me the second time around."

The Depth of Grace

"Actually, I do!" he said to my absolute astonishment.

"I am telling you in advance: you do not want to do this."

"Don't think I haven't done this before!" the man assured me.

"You haven't done this with me before!"

"Let's go again!" he demanded.

I made sure everyone who stood around saw clearly that I did my best to avoid this fight. I knew it was fixing to get nasty and wasn't sure what was going to happen. He was a little more confident than he should have been and I wasn't sure why at the time.

"Okay, but you're making a big mistake!" I told him as I tossed my shirt to a friend.

Upon squaring off, I stood with my hands at my hips. This stance was uncommon, but I knew what I was doing. My opponents always assumed they had more time to throw a punch with my hands at my hips, and they tended to hesitate because of this—and hesitation will get you knocked out on the streets.

I threw a quick right and missed by like three feet. Yes, I was a little embarrassed. A few moments later I threw another right and missed again by around three feet. I chuckled as I dropped back in embarrassment to debate the situation.

This guy knows what he's doing, I thought.

Before I threw another punch, I checked him with my right foot by slamming it down in front of me as though I was going to throw a punch. In response he moved to the side like Michael Jackson.

He definitely knows what he is doing, I thought, confirming my suspicions.

I was not going to beat this fellow on my feet. Little did I know, he was taking notes himself.

I threw another punch but wasn't trying to hit him. I needed to get close enough to grab him. In doing so, he clocked me with a right just before I grabbed him, picked him up high into the air, and slammed him on the ground with a hint of frustration. Just like before, I rolled over on top of him, put my knee in his chest, grabbed his shirt with my left hand, and went to work with my right. After four or five punches and an increase in frustration, I raised up with the intent to knock him out with the next right. I dropped a heavy punch and he moved his head. I broke my hand in three places as my hardest punch met the pavement.

Now I was upset.

21

J. Bronson Haley

As I felt something very powerful grip my soul in that instance, I gave him around ten right elbows, five knees, and even dropped a few head butts before his friend jumped on top of him to shield him from the blows. At the same time, my friend Art grabbed me while making sure I knew it was him: "Bronson! Bronson! It's Art!"

That really was the only time I ever actually got angry in a fight. Something came over me, and whatever it was, it was very strong. The man I fought went to ICU with a suppressed skull fracture, a broken nose, and a dislocated shoulder. All of those injuries took place in the last ten seconds of the second fight. Had our friends not intervened, he would be dead right now—no question about it.

It wasn't until after the second go-round with the guy that I finally found out who he was.

"Bronson, do you know who that was?" Art asked.

"I have no idea."

"Everyone in Shreveport/Bossier is scared to death of that guy. He's a professional kickboxer and the toughest dude on the streets," he said.

Right then, as we walked back into the bar, I saw the guy's poster up on the wall. He had a fight coming up in New Orleans. I soon discovered that he had previously been discharged from a local police department for roughing up a civilian. The night before we fought, he had kicked a man's teeth out at a local bar and put him in the hospital. Turns out this kickboxer had a reputation for using his training to rough up folks on the streets. Right after our fight I had felt bad for the dude because of the extent of the injuries I had inflicted on him. Now, though, I didn't feel so bad when I learned who he was. He didn't show up at the bars much after that night from what I heard. Around a year later he was arrested for murder.

So in all honesty I did not fight because of anger. I'm not sure if the violence brought back memories from my childhood or not, but I fought like a madman who always had something to prove. And while I took to fighting like a fish to water, mostly I was very protective by nature and couldn't stand to watch someone who was afraid get bullied around or forced to fight. That was my favorite scenario to run into. Very rarely did I fight because of me. I could count those instances on one hand. I mostly fought for my friends and innocent people—or at least people I could justify as innocent in my own mind. People who witnessed these encounters might differ with me when I say that I didn't get angry. But it was just a show I put on that would make them think that. Most of the

The Depth of Grace

time I was able to intimidate my opponents to the point of humiliation and never throw the first punch. Only my close friends knew about that side of me. Most people who did not know me would have said I was terribly mean.

Something else also happened that I don't quite understand. After a conflict reached a certain point, something would change in the atmosphere. Once I decided that someone had taken things too far and knew they would hurt me or someone else if they got a chance, I changed into a different person. I felt stronger, faster, and smarter—and fear was never an issue. I felt as though I had more time than they. It didn't make any difference how many there were, how big they were, or how bad they were. I felt in control and did whatever I had to do to stop the conflict. Sadly, most of the time, it meant hurting people.

Whatever the case, I experienced what it was to be afraid and weak with my buddy Pete that day in the bathroom. I have never been evaluated by a professional, but my best guess is that the memories of my mother being physically abused and my inability to help her, combined with my fearful restroom experience, triggered something inside that led to my violent behavior. My mother and my best friend Pete were always in my heart, and they motivated me to protect people. It gave me a hero complex, for better or worse.

1st REST STOP:
SIMON PETER

Since the stories I'm sharing with you are sort of like mileposts of my life's journey, I thought I should offer you a few rest areas along the way. So every couple of chapters or so, I'll get off the highway and share some stuff I've learned—the hard way, in too many instances. I trust you'll find some refreshment at each Rest Stop.
Enjoy ...

At one low point in my life, I fully understood that I couldn't beat my drug addiction on my own. After several attempts at trying—leading only to failure after failure—I shut myself away with God. Having eliminated all other options but not willing to give up, I opened my Bible and began to read. To be honest, it wasn't a good feeling coming to grips with the fact that my only hope was reading the Bible. That thought alone frustrated me and caused me to doubt. However, I sucked it up and cracked open the book. I skimmed small sections of the Old Testament, and I ran through the New Testament like a Navy SEAL. Of course, I didn't pay much attention because I knew what the Bible would say about me: I was a sinner! I was ashamed enough without reading about how bad I was.

I have to be real with you ... I didn't understand or believe much of anything I read. That was discouraging! For example: "The people walking in darkness have seen a great light; on those living in the land of the shadow of death a light has dawned" (Isaiah 9:2). What?

The Depth of Grace

And, "In the beginning was the Word, and the Word was with God, and the Word was God. He was with God in the beginning" (John 1:1-2). Huh?

And how about, "The Word became flesh and made his dwelling among us" (John 1:14). Are you serious?

To be 100 percent truthful, I had already experienced somewhat of a miracle by this time: I had read through part of the Old Testament and the entire New Testament in a month's time. The downside of this miracle was that I felt further discouraged because my only hope, the Bible, didn't seem to be helping in my struggle.

Still, a few things I picked up on along the way were interesting and a bit enlightening. During my first trip through the Gospels, I paid more attention to Simon Peter than any of the other disciples. I didn't have any real spiritual reason for this. I simply thought he was the most entertaining of the twelve. To be perfectly honest, it seemed to me that Simon Peter struggled with what we know today as ADHD (attention deficit hyperactivity disorder). I'm not joking! Don't believe me? Okay, I'll tell you why.

Did you ever hear about the time when Jesus first called Simon Peter to the ministry? Here's how the Bible tells it:

> As Jesus was walking beside the Sea of Galilee, he saw two brothers, Simon called Peter and his brother Andrew. They were casting a net into the lake, for they were fishermen. "Come, follow me," Jesus said, "and I will make you fishers of men." At once they left their nets and followed him. (Matthew 4:18-20 NIV 1984)

Simon was supposed to leave his nets, but did you notice that he ran off and left his boat right where it was, as well?

And what about the day that Jesus allowed Simon Peter, James, and John to go with Him up the mountain to meet with Moses and Elijah, both of whom reappeared from the ancient past? After a quick hike up the mountain, the four of them stopped: "There [Jesus] was transfigured before them. His face shone like the sun, and his clothes became as white as the light. Just then there appeared before them Moses and Elijah, talking with Jesus" (Matthew 17:2-3).

Try and picture this moment! The three disciples with Jesus knew very well that Moses and Elijah were famous for their prophetic ministry and service to the God of Israel. So pay close attention to how Peter responded

J. Bronson Haley

to the presence of these honorable prophets: "Peter said to Jesus, 'Lord, it is good for us to be here. If you wish, I will put up three shelters—one for you, one for Moses and one for Elijah'" (Matthew 17:4).

What? Do you see how Peter's mind began to race, and he couldn't keep his mouth shut? "Hey, Jesus! Now I know why you brought us with you. And I agree! This is a perfect campsite! I should build three huts so that you, Moses, and Elijah can worship God's creation together!" Now there's a thought. According to Mark's gospel, Simon Peter freaked out and started babbling like a baboon: "[Peter] did not know what to say, they were so frightened" (Mark 9:6).

But here comes my favorite part of this scene! "While he was still speaking, a bright cloud enveloped them, and a voice from the cloud said, 'This is my Son, whom I love; with him I am well pleased. Listen to him!'" (Matthew 17:5).

Can you believe this? God basically had to put a majestic covering over Jesus and the prophets to protect them from Peter. When God has to step in to shut you up, you are doing too much!

Okay, let's look at the day that Peter walked on water. Jesus had told the disciples to go ahead of Him to the other side of the lake while He prayed by Himself. When Jesus was ready to meet the disciples, they were still in the boat, fighting the waves and the wind. So ...

> *Jesus went out to them, walking on the lake. When the disciples saw him walking on the lake, they were terrified. "It's a ghost," they said, and cried out in fear.*
>
> *But Jesus immediately said to them: "Take courage! It is I. Don't be afraid."*
>
> *"Lord, if it's you," Peter replied, "tell me to come to you on the water." (Matthew 14:25-28)*

Did Peter want to walk on the water because he was a man of great faith? Of course not! Peter was simply bored to death in the boat and could not sit still any longer. Even better than that, look at what happens next!

"But when he saw the wind, he was afraid and, beginning to sink, cried out, 'Lord, save me!'" (Matthew 14:30). Now that's funny! A little wind blows in and Peter gets distracted. He couldn't even focus on Jesus while walking on water! Peter then forgot Jesus was God and freaked out like he was going to die when he began to sink. "Immediately Jesus reached out his hand and caught him. 'You of little faith,' he said, 'why

The Depth of Grace

did you doubt?'" (Matthew 14:31). Peter jumped the gun! That's why he doubted! He didn't yet have the faith to walk on water. Impulse is also a big indicator of ADHD.

Pay close attention to this next scene:

> *He then began to teach them that the Son of Man must suffer many things and be rejected by the elders, chief priests and teachers of the law, and that he must be killed and after three days rise again. He spoke plainly about this, and Peter took him aside and began to rebuke him. (Mark 8:31-32)*

What? Peter now has authority over Jesus? You know something was wrong when Simon Peter interrupted Jesus, pulled him to the side, and proceeded to tell Him what He was and was not going to do. This had gone way too far! Jesus finally had to put his foot down …

"But when Jesus turned and looked at his disciples, he rebuked Peter. 'Get behind me, Satan!' he said. 'You do not have in mind the things of God, but the things of men'" (Mark 8:33). LOL! When Jesus Himself calls you "Satan," something is bad wrong with you.

The next example is my favorite by far! Do you remember the movie *Forrest Gump* and the scene when Forrest leaps out of a boat to swim to shore so that he could see his old friend Lieutenant Dan? Watch this!

> *Early in the morning, Jesus stood on the shore, but the disciples did not realize that it was Jesus.*
>
> *He called out to them, "Friends, haven't you any fish?"*
>
> *"No," they answered.*
>
> *He said, "Throw your net on the right side of the boat and you will find some." When they did, they were unable to haul the net in because of the large number of fish.*
>
> *Then the disciple whom Jesus loved said to Peter, "It is the Lord!" As soon as Simon Peter heard him say, "It is the Lord," he wrapped his outer garment around him … and jumped into the water. (John 21:4-7)*

When Peter acknowledged that it was Jesus on the shore, his mind began to race, and he once again lost control. He simply could not wait the few extra minutes that it would have taken them to reach the shore that was

J. Bronson Haley

only a hundred yards away. So, in his best Forrest Gump impersonation, Peter grabbed his clothes, yelled "Lieutenant Jesus!" and dove into the water.

Now do you believe me when I say Simon Peter had ADHD? Yeah, maybe I'm pulling your leg a little bit in this Rest Stop, but at the very least, we can see that Simon Peter wasn't some perfect saint walking around with a halo over his head. And, hey, that means there is hope for the rest of us, too!

CHAPTER 3

—

Trips over the Tracks

Continuing along my wayward path in life, my first experience with LSD was at a good friend's house. We were freshmen in high school at the time. Kasey had some woods and pastureland behind his house, and we decided to camp out one night just on the other side of the fence of his backyard. So we put up tents and built a bonfire.

When the sun went down, the tents were up and the fire was blazing. We each took two hits of acid. We sat around the fire telling stories while waiting on the LSD to kick in. After around twenty minutes, all hell began to break loose in the woods around us—at least that's how it seemed to us. Every shadow was an open door to an additional intruder, and Kasey and I tensed up big-time. We were both pretty scared, not knowing what was going on, or to what level the visuals would take us. After around thirty minutes, we settled down a bit and relaxed around the fire. By this time, it was pitch-black outside. Kicked back in our folding chairs, we blocked out our unfamiliar surroundings and gazed into the flames. But the hallucinations began to intenslfy. The fire looked like the gateway to hell, and we discussed the different images we captured of Satan's angels.

Sure enough, Kasey's father walked through the back fence, looking like King Tut, and joined our little party. Pops was proud of us for not going out drinking and getting into trouble on this Friday night. His steps thundered as he walked toward us with a smile that seemed to us like something out of *Killer Klowns from Outer Space*.

29

J. Bronson Haley

"I have a great ghost story to tell you two," Pops said as he made himself at home.

I don't remember if we said anything or not. Kasey got a little nervous and climbed into his red tent. His dad didn't look how he normally looked. Kasey lay on his stomach and looked out the door at the fire as his dad began to tell the story. I desperately wanted to get in the tent with Kasey, but he looked like the Devil in his red tent that glowed as the light from the fire soaked into the fabric.

I could not listen to the ghost story because of all the "turmoil" going on in the woods behind Kasey's dad. It was as though the trees and their company danced to the details of the story. When I would attempt to focus on Pops, his face would turn inside out. This was the most graphic, horrific, action-packed ghost story I'd ever experienced. This was even scarier than the ghost girl I saw in Waskom.

When Pops went inside and we started breathing again, Kasey and I decided to go for a walk through the woods. As we got used to the "animals" that seemed to walk with us, we crossed the railroad tracks and entered some woods that led us into a cow pasture. This was an extraordinary sight! A full moon hung overhead, and many "deer" and "rabbits "ran around—who knows what they really were … that's just what we saw. We moseyed through the pasture in awe of our surroundings when suddenly I stopped. I took note of a huge mushroom around thirty feet away.

"Kasey! Watch this!" I said.

After making sure the mushroom and I had his attention, I bolted full speed ahead while envisioning the large mushroom exploding into a million pieces as I kicked it. This was one exciting sprint! The images flying past my head reminded me of the starship *Enterprise* when it reached warp speed—only there were birds in my scene instead of stars. When I kicked the giant mushroom, I screamed and fell to the ground. Hopelessly rocking back and forth while holding my foot, I struggled to get a grip on reality.

"What in the heck did you do, Bronson?" Kasey asked as he approached.

"I kicked a freaking salt rock!" I hollered in sheer pain.

I will never forgive Kasey for collapsing beside me and polluting my soul with earth-shattering laughter. We continued to roam the surrounding cow pastures and woods. Back and forth, across the railroad tracks, from the campsite to the unknown, we made "trips" throughout the night.

When the sun began to rise, we decided to cook breakfast for Kasey's parents. Still hallucinating at 6:00 a.m., we cooked the most extravagant breakfast. I was wearing a blue apron with a blue bandana on my head. Kasey had on a red apron with a red bandana on his head. We cooked biscuits, cinnamon rolls, bacon, sausage, eggs, pancakes, grits, the whole nine yards. We had water, milk, and orange juice to wash everything down. We set up the table with plates, forks, spoons, knives, napkins, and lit two candles for authenticity. I'm still not quite sure who we thought we were at the time. Chef Boys R Wee?

Stupidly enough, we woke up Mom and Pops, sat down, and had breakfast. They were blown away at our arrangement and could not get over our well-planned, early morning feast. We were famous for waking up in the middle of the afternoon on the weekends.

We sat at the table for I don't know how long talking about who knows what. The only thing I remember clearly was one of Pops' last statements. "You know, Bronson, you really bring out the best in Kasey," he said, staring off into the distance with a lingering smile. I'm certain I will be getting a call from Mom and Pops shortly after this book is published, now that the truth has been revealed!

The drugs and alcohol were all fun and games for my friends and me at this point. The alcohol kept the parties jumping. The drugs were entertaining when we got bored. My friends and I were all young and simply having a little fun. No worries. No danger.

In the beginning everything was good. But little did I know just how much life would soon change as a result of these "innocent" little experiments with drugs.

CHAPTER 4

Burglary

One year later, as a sixteen-year-old sophomore, I sat down at a table in my mother's home with one of my best childhood friends, Mike Mertle. Mike, Pete Holt, and I were extremely close. I lived with my grandparents at the time, but Mom was out of town so we took advantage of the situation. Mike and I decided to have a little fun, given we didn't have school the next day due to a severe ice storm. Many homes, schools, and businesses didn't have power, and ice covered the streets. We picked up a case of beer and entered into a drinking game called "quarters." I'm not kidding when I say we finished the entire case of beer in an hour's time. I also took three codeine pills and two muscle relaxers. This was my first experience with pills, and on this night I got the full experience of what drugs mixed with alcohol could do for a person.

After I "stole" my mother's car, we went for a little ride. This was an '88 Oldsmobile with a 454 V8 engine under the hood.

I don't remember much about the wild ride through the neighborhoods we chose to terrorize. We ran over many trashcans and bags of leaves piled up on the edge of the streets. I do remember driving through the front yard of a house into the backyard, through the back fence, into another backyard, into their front yard, and onto the neighboring street. I'm sure you get the idea.

At around 1:00 a.m., after a few hours of joyriding, we pulled up to our old middle school, Broadmoor. We noticed that one of the T-building doors was open, and of course, we figured, "This is wonderful! What should we do?" After secretly parking the car on the basketball courts behind the school, we walked toward the T-building, entered through the open door, and trashed the place. This was great! Time to do everything we dreamed of as the bad kids who sat in these very desks at one time. After spraying the fire extinguisher and peeing on the teacher's desk, among other things, we exited that building and climbed through a window of the next, repeating the activities that most satisfied our bass-akwards intuition.

On our walk back to the car, Mike got another great idea. "Do you want to break into the main building?" he asked me.

Without thinking twice, I grabbed a five-gallon bucket of hardened concrete used to stabilize volleyball nets during gym class and began to bang it against the doorknob of the cafeteria. When the knob broke loose, the hatch released, and we entered with pride as if we won some sort of contest.

We did everything that two stupid drunk kids could think of to entertain themselves. We played basketball in the gym after breaking into the coach's office and peeing in the desks. We broke into the main office and urinated in those desks as well. Remember, we drank a lot of beer, very fast. After feeling as though we had enough fun, we exited one of the back doors of the building to police officers with guns drawn. They hollered, "Get down on the ground now! Get on the ground!"

It took me a moment to fully understand what was happening. In my disillusioned state of mind, I had forgotten about the possibilities of getting caught and didn't understand what was happening. After I dropped the basketball in my hand, I got on the ground and we were placed under arrest.

Mike and I were put in separate cop cars while the officers searched my mother's car. After one officer looked into the backseat of the car, he walked over to my friend, pulled him out of the car, and walked him to my mother's car. The officer expressed his frustrations with Mike as he grabbed him by the back of the neck and shoved his head closer so that Mike could see into the back of the car. I couldn't hear what was said, but the officer was upset about something and Mike chuckled when he looked into the backseat.

Then the officer proceeded in my direction. "What is in the backseat of the car, son?" the officer asked plainly.

"Some beer, maybe?" I replied.

"Don't get smart with me, son!" the officer replied. "You might as well tell me the truth! You are going to jail anyway!"

The Depth of Grace

"Sir, I don't know," I assured the man.

He then walked back to my mother's car and pulled a television and an overhead projector out of the backseat while shaking his head. I laughed my rear end off at this sight. I could not believe how stupid we were. I had no memory of taking these items from the school.

We will never hear the end of this, I thought, feeling sure everyone at school would hear of our drunken adventure.

"Son, you are one lucky kid," said the officer who drove my car as he climbed behind the wheel. "We are trained to shoot in order to protect ourselves and our fellow officers anytime a suspect reaches into their pants in the dark. You are supposed to be dead right now," the officer assured me with all seriousness.

I didn't respond because I had forgotten that, just prior to my lying on the ground after coming out of the back door of the school, I grabbed a small UPS package that I had stuck under my belt and laid it on the ground.

On the way to the station, the officer began to describe the details of the event we were listening to over his radio. There was a high-speed car chase on I-49, which was still under construction. The incomplete interstate was also covered with ice.

"These guys are going to jail for one count of first-degree murder and three counts of attempted first-degree murder," the officer said. "You screwed up pretty bad, but these four will get the death penalty. Straighten up, kid. It only gets worse from here."

I was embarrassed walking into the city jail. The officer thought it was cute that I had a sock on one of my hands and wouldn't let me take it off before I entered the building.

Jerk! I thought.

I figured I was being such a smart criminal all night long. Too bad my drunken state made me completely forget about the school's silent alarm!

After being transferred from city jail to the juvenile detention center, I sat quietly while waiting to be booked into the population. Still in a delusional state of mind, but sobering up, I noticed I was covered in blood. After a few moments passed, I began to recall memories of punching out a U-Haul window, brass knuckles in hand, during the course of our night out on the town. It was funny to hear Mike recall a detail of this story I had forgotten about as I discussed this book with him …

"You were standing, facing the door of the U-Haul acting as though it were a person talking smack to you. Then you began to punch at the

35

J. Bronson Haley

window as though trying to intimidate it. Suddenly, a 'ding' sounds as you accidentally tapped the window with the brass knuckles. 'Oh, yeah?' you said as if it had challenged you by the ding. You then punched it out," he said.

But sitting in the detention center waiting area, I remembered none of this. A few seconds later one of the ladies working the desk looked at me and asked, "Where'd you get all this change, boy?"

"I'm a great poker player," I said, sarcastically.

After a moment I remembered stealing the change out of the coach's office in the school. They rented uniforms to students for gym class and I took advantage of the situation. Now I had the next four days to think about my future.

It was the little things that captured my attention on my first full day at the detention center. As I looked out the window of my six-foot-by-eight-foot two-man cell, it was hard for me to imagine that I could not walk outside if I wanted to. It was hard to accept the fact that not even my dad could come get me and take me home. It's hard to describe the feeling of having your freedom taken away. This is something most Americans never experience. We are born free and most of us live in freedom for our entire lives. Only slavery can take an American's freedom from him or her. I understand this now, but then I had no idea.

The juvenile detention center was a sad place to be. During the day many of the kids would go to court to face charges for whatever crime they committed. Some would come back saying that sentencing had been put off. Some would return saying that they would be staying for a few months. A couple guys came back telling me they would be locked up for the next three or four years. One was sentenced to fifty years for first-degree murder. He would be transferred to the big jail upon turning twenty-one. I saw all this from the perspective of a sixteen-year-old kid. Most of the kids imprisoned with me didn't have a chance in the world. On their faces I could read that most had accepted who they were and had already sucked into their guts the consequences of their actions as they moved forward with life.

Is there anything good in this world? I asked myself. If there were, I had not yet experienced it. *If there isn't, I don't want to be here.*

I knew I wouldn't be locked up for long. This was my first offense and I was in school with decent grades. However, the thought of losing just a couple of months of my life to this hellhole was beyond a horrible thought. I could see clearly that this was no life to live. Drugs, alcohol, and violence

The Depth of Grace

were the root of the problems with these kids—and me—and there was no question about it.

While locked up, I began to understand that a bad day in freedom is a dream to those who do not have it. Many will dream this dream for the rest of their lives. They will sit on their prison bunks at night and replay the day they forfeited the one life of freedom that they were given. They yearn to go back and change what they did. If only they could go back and think a little harder about the possible consequences of their actions. While free, we can think a little harder about the consequences of our actions and know that our bad day in freedom is a good day to the ones who did not think hard enough.

As I said, I was living with my grandparents at the time of my arrest. They always took me in when I needed them and never failed to assure me that I was going to be great one day. I hated that I had let them down.

After four days I was released to my grandfather. Expecting him to walk up to me shaking his head in disgust, I was surprised when he put his arms around me and gave me a big hug instead. I will never forget that hug. I didn't get from him what I deserved and it broke my heart. It was love that I needed most, and my grandmother and grandfather gave it to me for free. I felt horrible for what I'd done. However, this failure only added to the pain that had led me to drink the beer and take the pills the night of the burglary.

When I arrived home, my grandmother handed me a newspaper clipping from the morning of my arrest. I first noticed the mug shots of four of my friends. Then I read the headline: "Springhill's Slaying Leaves One Dead and Three Injured." Do you remember the high-speed car chase the officer and I listened to in the car on the night of my arrest? Those were friends of mine. The paper mentioned the district attorney—the dad of a friend—seeking the death penalty.

When I later talked to Mike, who was arrested with me, he described his experience in jail. Since he was seventeen years old at the time, he went to the big jail. A couple hours after he was booked in, one of our friends from the car chase was put into his holding cell. His head had already been stapled together after being beaten with flashlights by the officers. The two shooters had run from the car after the cops shot out the tires. K-9 units caught up with them and held them until the officers arrived. Mike mentioned our friend repeating to himself over and over again, "Oh my God, I'm going to jail for life. I'm going to jail for life!"

J. Bronson Haley

On the night of the murder, the four guys had gone to a drug dealer's apartment to score some pills. The dealer told them, "I ain't dealing with a ..." He referred to the black one of the four using his African-inherited name. They left, picked up two shotguns from a friend, and returned. Two of the four stayed in the car as the other two headed toward the apartment of the drug dealer. They broke out the living room windows with the shotguns and began shooting. The dealer was killed and his three friends were injured.

These were my friends. I knew them and they were not bad people. However, they got hooked on drugs. I watched as they changed over time. They were doing outrageous amounts of cocaine among other drugs. They were no different from me before the drugs got hold of them. And that scared me more than anything.

2ND REST STOP:
JACOB'S JOURNEY: PART 1

First, understand that the "Jacob" spoken of in this chapter is the Jacob from "Jacob's Ladder." He is Jacob, son of Isaac, grandson of Abraham—"Father Abraham" that is. Jacob is a man who will never be forgotten for his heroic service to God. But we'll also see in this Rest Stop and the next that Jacob was just like the rest of us in many ways. I am not intentionally dogging him or making fun. The purpose of this chapter is to give convincing proofs that Jacob was not perfect and instead very much human—just like you and me, no matter where we may be in our lives.

The battle between Jacob and his brother Esau began at a young age. Well, they didn't even have an age yet. Here's a message their mother, Rebekah, received from God before they were even born: "Two nations are in your womb, and two peoples from within you will be separated; one people will be stronger than the other, and the older will serve the younger" (Genesis 25:23-24).

So, at this point, Jacob and Esau were just a couple of little pieces of flesh. However, this wasn't a battle of flesh and blood. This was a battle over the fatherhood of God's chosen people, Israel. One was strong enough for the job; God chose the other. According to my New International Version Key Word Study Bible (which I'll refer to several more times throughout this book when digging deeper into Hebrew and Greek word meanings), *goy* is the Hebrew word for *nations* in the Scripture above. The word means "person, inhabitant, populace, people, tribe, nation." So the two boys were described as boys who would have many descendants (a large family).

Leom is the Hebrew word for *peoples* used in the Scripture. *Leom* means "people, nation, community." It signifies togetherness; that is, what a group of people share in common as a cohesive unit. The Scripture indicates that the families of these brothers would be separated. This Scripture also indicates that the older of the twin boys would end up serving the younger. This is ironic because by tradition the firstborn son received double the inheritance of the other and also received the blessing of his father before he died. Yet the Lord spoke to Rebekah and assured her that it would be the younger son who would get the blessing of God and that the older would indeed serve the younger.

> *When the time came for her to give birth, there were twin boys in her womb. The first to come out was red, and his whole body was like a hairy garment; so they named him Esau. After this, his brother came out, with his hand grasping Esau's heel; so he was named Jacob. (Genesis 25:24-26)*

What? Jacob came into this world taking advantage of his own twin brother? Why didn't he just wait his turn to exit the womb? Jacob was zero years old! Was it by nature that he grabbed his brother's heel, slowing Esau's progress to quicken his own? Instead of Esau getting out on time, Jacob got out ahead of time. Let the scandals begin ...

Rison is the Hebrew word for *first* used in this Scripture. The word means "first (as to place, time, or rank), foremost, chief." By tradition Esau was to be the chief of the two boys. Also, *aqeb* is the Hebrew word for *heel* used in this Scripture. It is derived from the word *aqub*, which means "to grasp the heel, to deceive." The name *Jacob* was derived from the word *aqub*. We know that all Scripture is God breathed. It turns out that God knew Jacob would be a deceiver—a liar. The Lord went ahead and gave him the name "Jacob," which actually would describe his character. It comforts me to see that God was not concerned with Jacob's weaknesses when He chose him. The Lord knew Jacob was going to make mistakes. But the Lord also chose him to father His own people, Israel.

> *The boys grew up, and Esau became a skillful hunter, a man of the open country, while Jacob was content to stay among the tents. Isaac, who had a taste for wild game, loved Esau, but Rebekah loved Jacob. (Genesis 25:27-28)*

The Depth of Grace

In this Scripture, *tam* is the Hebrew word for *content*. It means "to be blameless" and signifies "having integrity, complete, whole, and upright qualities." However, we know that Jacob only appeared this way. Of course, Jacob was a godly man. But we know he was also a deceiver as his own name implies, and he often lied to get what he wanted. *Sadeh* is the Hebrew word for *open country*. This word is used to signify "pastureland, unfrequented country," which is potentially dangerous because of its isolation or because of wild beasts.

Esau was his father Isaac's prize possession. He grew up to be strong, skillful, brave, and everything a father could want in a firstborn son. Esau was not afraid of the potential deadly animals that roamed the land, and he would have no problem carrying on his father's good name and taking care of the family when he passed away. This was the boy who would, by tradition, take charge and partake in the covenant of Abraham. By tradition Esau was going to father God's chosen people. However, the Lord intervened and saw Jacob as fit for the job even though he was not the firstborn and even though we see in Scripture that he was not qualified: "Jacob was content to stay among the tents." He turned out a "momma's boy." Some believe in the theory that he was sickly during his childhood and young adult life. Whatever the case, Jacob was weak, and he and his mom spent a lot of time together and were very close. Jacob didn't get the training he would need to father any nation, much less God's chosen people. However, Rebekah was determined to see to it that God would honor the promise He had made to her that concerned Jacob: "the older will serve the younger."

> Once when Jacob was cooking some stew, Esau came in from the open country, famished. He said to Jacob, "Quick, let me have some of that red stew! I'm famished!" …
>
> Jacob replied, "First sell me your birthright."
>
> "Look, I am about to die," Esau said. "What good is the birthright to me?"
>
> But Jacob said, "Swear to me first." So he swore an oath to him, selling his birthright to Jacob. (Genesis 25:29-33).

In my opinion that was downright wrong! Didn't Esau provide Jacob with the meat in the stew? Jacob wouldn't have eaten had it not been for Esau. Esau starved because of the hard work that accompanied him as he

J. Bronson Haley

made sure Jacob, Mom, and family had food to eat and were taken care of. However, Jacob was a deceiver, a twister, as we already know. Was his name not Jacob? He wanted Esau's birthright, so he deceived his brother in order to get it. But he didn't stop there. Read on as the tale of the "twister" gets even more twisted.

Esau worked hard his whole life to please his father and earn his blessing. He did a wonderful job too. Isaac was a proud father. When Isaac grew weak in his old age, it came time for Esau to receive the blessing of the Lord and take charge of the family. Esau invested much blood, sweat, and tears into the inheritance that was rightfully his, and he had no doubt looked forward to this day his entire life.

> *When Isaac was old and his eyes were so weak that he could no longer see, he called for Esau his older son and said to him, "My son."*
>
> *"Here I am," he answered.*
>
> *Isaac said, "I am now an old man and don't know the day of my death. Now then, get your weapons—your quiver and bow—and go out to the open country to hunt some wild game for me. Prepare me the kind of tasty food I like and bring it to me to eat, so that I may give you my blessing before I die."*
>
> *Now Rebekah was listening as Isaac spoke to his son Esau. When Esau left for the open country to hunt game and bring it back, Rebekah said to her son, Jacob, "Look, I overheard your father say to your brother Esau, 'Bring me some game and prepare me some tasty food to eat, so that I may give you my blessing in the presence of the Lord before I die.' Now, my son, listen carefully and do what I tell you: Go out to the flock and bring me two choice young goats, so I can prepare some tasty food for your father, just the way he likes it. Then take it to your father to eat, so that he may give you his blessing before he dies." (Genesis 27:1-10)*

What? You have got to be kidding me! The Lord already told Mom that Jacob would be blessed! And she goes off and pulls a stunt like that? "Hey, Jacob! I thought of a way to get the blessing early! We will deceive your father in the name of God!" What a scandalous wench (pardon my French)! How dare she deceive the Lord's chosen (her husband) to get the Lord's blessing

The Depth of Grace

for her favorite boy. And what kind of woman screws over her own son like that? What did Esau do to deserve this treatment? He worked like a slave every day of his life to feed her, her husband, and her little "girl" Jacob!

Have you ever noticed that children often end up acting like their parents? Sometimes, child and parent will share in the same struggle(s) and people who know the family will say, "He's just like his dad (or mom)!" Well, Jacob was just like his mother!

> *Jacob said to Rebekah his mother, "But my brother Esau is a hairy man while I have smooth skin. What if my father touches me? I would appear to be tricking him and would bring down a curse on myself rather than a blessing." (Genesis 27:11-12)*

What, Jacob? What do you mean you would "appear" to be tricking him? What was wrong with your brain that made you think you were not *really* tricking him? Jacob was a man of God who was chosen by Him to father the nation and people of Israel. But at this time he was more worried about the curse that might come on him if Isaac caught him in a lie than the curse of the great I AM! God chose Jacob, for sure! However, he had a lot to learn. The Lord would have no choice but to humble Jacob and teach him what it meant to trust in God. Jacob also needed to experience the fruit of his deceptive ways.

Jacob finally got the courage to deceive his dad at the instruction of his mother. He and his mother prepared for the event, and Jacob did as he was told. Isaac ate and Jacob was blessed.

> *"May God give you of heaven's dew and of earth's richness— an abundance of grain and new wine. May nations serve you and peoples bow down to you. Be lord over your brothers, and may the sons of your mother bow down to you. May those who curse you be cursed and those who bless you be blessed." (Genesis 27:28-29)*

Poor Esau! His own twin brother robbed him of the blessing of God. Jacob wasn't fit to take care of himself much less lead and support the family.

The next scene is a sad one, so get out the tissues.

When Esau came in from hunting, he cooked the wild game and brought it to his father, just as he had asked him to do ...

43

J. Bronson Haley

> *"My father, please sit up and eat some of my game, so that you may give me your blessing."*
>
> *His father Isaac asked him, "Who are you?"*
>
> *"I am your son," he answered, "your firstborn, Esau."*
>
> *Isaac trembled violently and said, "Who was it, then, that hunted game and brought it to me? I ate it just before you came and I blessed him—and indeed he will be blessed!"*
>
> *When Esau heard his father's words, he burst out with a loud and bitter cry and said to his father, "Bless me—me too, my father!"*
>
> *But he said, "Your brother came deceitfully and took your blessing."*
>
> *Esau said, "Isn't he rightly named Jacob? This is the second time he has taken advantage of me: He took my birthright, and now he's taken my blessing!" Then he asked, "Haven't you reserved any blessing for me?"*
>
> *Isaac answered Esau, "I have made him lord over you and have made all his relatives his servants, and I have sustained him with grain and new wine. So what can I possibly do for you, my son?"*
>
> *Esau said to his father, "Do you have only one blessing, my father? Bless me too, my father!" Then Esau wept aloud.*
>
> *His father Isaac answered him, "Your dwelling will be away from the earth's richness, away from the dew of heaven above. You will live by the sword and you will serve your brother. But when you grow restless, you will throw his yoke from off your neck." (Genesis 27:31-40)*

I don't know about you, but I would have been ready to kill Jacob for that stunt—and we soon find out that Esau felt exactly the same way.

> *Esau held a grudge against Jacob because of the blessing his father had given him. He said to himself, "The days of*

44

The Depth of Grace

mourning for my father are near; then I will kill my brother Jacob."

When Rebekah was told what her older son Esau had said, she sent for her younger son Jacob and said to him, "Your brother Esau is planning to avenge himself by killing you. Now then, my son, do what I say: Flee at once to my brother Laban in Harran. Stay with him for a while until your brother's fury subsides." (Genesis 27:41-44)

Jacob was no match for Esau. He had no choice but to flee his father's house if he wanted to live. And Rebekah could do nothing more for Jacob at that point. Esau did not fear God and would have had no problem dealing with his mother when his father was gone. Jacob got the blessing of the Lord early. He didn't trust his heavenly Father enough to trust that He would bless him like He promised Rebekah before the brothers were born. As a result, in order for Jacob to father Israel as he was called to do, God would have to earn Jacob's trust. Jacob was terrified at the consequences his actions dealt him. But the Lord saw Jacob's failure as an opportunity. He was either going to learn to trust God, or die. God keeps his promises!

Thus far Jacob had lived under the protection of his father his entire life, and he had been raised under his mother's wing. I am certain that Jacob was terrified when his mother and father prepared him for a journey that would take him far from home. He was weak, doubtful, and, ironically enough, Jacob was everything God needed from a person in order to adequately teach him to trust Him. God cannot use a man who can do everything himself. So, yes, Jacob was scared to death—and God was excited! Jacob could have been a nice boy and should have allowed God to prove Himself His way. Instead Jacob robbed his brother and had no choice but to pay the consequences.

"May God Almighty bless you and make you fruitful and increase your numbers until you become a community of peoples. May he give you and your descendants the blessing given to Abraham, so that you may take possession of the land where you now reside as a foreigner, the land God gave to Abraham." Then Isaac sent Jacob on his way....

Jacob left Beersheba and set out for Harran. When he reached a certain place, he stopped for the night because the sun had

45

J. Bronson Haley

> *set. Taking one of the stones there, he put it under his head*
> *and lay down to sleep. (Genesis 28:3-5, 10-11)*

Don't you know this was one lonely night for Jacob? For the first time in his life, he slept without the protection of his father and love of his mother. Jacob was left alone to sleep with his failure. Now he was in the open country where the wild beasts roamed—and how about another dose of irony, considering that the open country is where his brother Esau enjoyed spending so much time as a hunter of those same wild beasts? Jacob, though, was in this dangerous territory by himself and he was terrified. He wasn't sure if he would overcome the mess he had gotten himself into, and he could see no light at the end of this dark tunnel. Jacob wasn't sure if he would ever see his mother and father again. Jacob was lonely and afraid—just like you and I are sometimes in life.

> *He had a dream in which he saw a stairway resting on the*
> *earth, with its top reaching to heaven, and the angels of*
> *God were ascending and descending on it. There above it*
> *stood the LORD, and he said: "I am the LORD, the God of*
> *your father Abraham and the God of Isaac. I will give you*
> *and your descendants the land on which you are lying. Your*
> *descendants will be like the dust of the earth, and you will*
> *spread out to the west and to the east, to the north and to*
> *the south. All peoples on earth will be blessed through you*
> *and your offspring. I am with you and will watch over you*
> *wherever you go, and I will bring you back to this land. I*
> *will not leave you until I have done what I have promised*
> *you." (Genesis 28:12-15)*

Samar is the Hebrew word for *watch over* in this Scripture. The word means "to keep, guard; to preserve, protect; to watch (as a watchman of cattle or sheep)." The Lord assured Jacob on the first night of his journey that he would be okay. *Sub* is the Hebrew word for *bring back*. This word is often used in reference to the return from exile. In this promise God assured Jacob that He would be responsible for his protection and ability to return to his father's house.

When I first started studying this passage, I was comforted when I saw that God spoke to Jacob even in the midst of his sin. God spoke promises to Jacob in the prime of his failure, as a matter of fact. I felt like God spoke

The Depth of Grace

to me in my sin. At the same time, I doubted that He would have anything to do with me because of the magnitude of my failures.

> *When Jacob awoke from his sleep, he thought, "Surely the LORD is in this place, and I was not aware of it." He was afraid and said, "How awesome is this place! This is none other than the house of God; this is the gate of heaven." (Genesis 28:16-17)*

Wow! During the midst of the loneliest, most terrifying night of Jacob's life, God spoke to him. Not only did God speak to Jacob, but He also confirmed the blessing of his father. Jacob needed this word from the Lord. He was excited that he may not have messed up to the point of complete and total failure. This all sounded wonderful to Jacob—and to me, too! However, Jacob was still young in his faith and doubted—and so did I.

> *Early the next morning Jacob took the stone he had placed under his head and set it up as a pillar and poured oil on top of it. He called that place Bethel, though the city used to be called Luz.*
>
> *Then Jacob made a vow, saying, "If God will be with me and will watch over me on this journey I am taking and will give me food to eat and clothes to wear so that I return safely to my father's house, then the LORD will be my God and this stone that I have set up as a pillar will be God's house, and of all that you give me I will give you a tenth." (Genesis 28:18-22)*

In summary so far: God made a promise, Jacob set up a pillar in remembrance, Jacob made a promise contingent upon God's promise. This vow was nothing more than Jacob asking God to prove that it was indeed He who had spoken in the dream. Jacob made a deal with God. It was now up to the Lord to prove Himself. If God proved Himself, then Jacob would have the courage to return to his father's house and face his brother, Esau.

And with that, I'm going to have to leave you hanging until the next Rest Stop, when we'll finish up Jacob's incredible journey. Until then just think about the fact that God is never finished with us because of our failures—never!

CHAPTER 5

House Arrest

When I was arrested for burglary at my old middle school, I was given a court date to plead either guilty or not guilty to the charge. At the instructions of my new lawyer—Mr. Hester, Kasey's dad—I pled guilty and was placed on house arrest until my sentencing date, which was only a couple of months away. Mr. Hester was saddened that I had gotten myself into trouble. I felt like he was relieved that he sent Kasey off to school when he did. Sure, we had a good time camping out that night. However, I was dealing with the aftermath at this point. Drugs and alcohol are a dead-end road, and life is not some game. I was a full-blown alcoholic by this time and had already tried to quit drinking several times.

One Friday night, several months prior to my arrest, my closest friends and I searched for this group of hotheads who tried to jump another friend, one of the four arrested for murder the weekend before. With me were Parker Yalta, Sam Newton, Dave Horton, and Jim Carson—a few of our toughest friends. We searched all over town for this group of unfortunate people on this particular night, and from what we understood, they were looking for us at the same time. We didn't have any luck finding them the first night. The second night was long and slow as well. Around 10:00 p.m. that Saturday night, we decided to stop by my mom's house and hang out for a while until we caught wind of where our enemies were hanging out. We had people watching out all over town. I know this sounds ridiculous. However, to us, this was serious business! None of us played sports. The

49

only thing we took pride in was our ability to party our rear ends off and kick butt whenever necessary.

Several vehicles were parked outside of Mom's house when my friends and I pulled up. I recognized the vehicles and so did my friend Parker.

"What in the heck is going on?" I asked Parker.

"I don't know, Bronson."

"These are their vehicles for sure!" I said.

"Bronson, I know!" Parker said.

"Well, I'll be darned if they are going to pull a stunt like this and not learn from it," I said, making sure that everyone in our group got their minds prepared for what we were about to do.

When I opened the door and looked through the kitchen into the living room, I saw around eight older boys who fit the description. In the kitchen were my mother and her new boyfriend.

"Bronson! What's wrong?" my mother asked. I didn't respond. "Come in here and meet Josh and his friends. They've been wanting to meet you."

I thought I was going to stroke out! The boys we spent so long looking for—and who were looking for us—were my mother's new boyfriend's sons and their friends. They were a bunch of country boys from a small town north of Shreveport.

"Do y'all have any idea how close y'all came to getting your #@! kicked right here in this living room?" I asked as I walked in.

"You must not know about FSU!" one of them replied.

They all wore Florida State University hats and T-shirts. But for them, FSU stood for F#@$%&! S*!$ Up. They liked to fight as much as we did—and this would have been a great match. But it didn't play out that way, being in my mom's house and all. So we told war stories. We stood around and recounted our best fighting stories to each other for hours. It was almost like we were all long-time friends who hadn't seen each other since grade school. That was one interesting night. But it was just a lull in the kind of life I was living—too hard, too fast. I was used to excitement and action every day, all the time.

So, as you can imagine, after almost two months of house arrest for my burglary charge, I couldn't stand it any longer, so I called my new stepbrother, Jason, to ask him if he wanted to go to the lake. He had told me earlier that a bunch of our friends were going up there and that I was invited.

"You know I do!" he said.

The Depth of Grace

"Ask your dad if we can take Joe's truck," I told him. Joe was the oldest brother who was out of town.

"I'm trusting you, Bronson. Don't let me down," my new stepfather said as he dropped the keys into my hands.

"You have nothing to worry about! I promise!"

Right after leaving, we stopped and picked up my friend Sam Newton. "Hey, Sam, grab your ice chest and throw it in the back of the truck. And grab your fake ID!"

We then stopped at the store and filled the ice chest with two cases of bottled beer and ice.

"Okay, now we're ready for the lake," I said.

I was so happy to get out of the house, it wasn't even funny. I had never even been grounded before. House arrest was killing me! The thought of everyone else going out and having a good time, and me chillin' at home with my grandparents, really did do some psychological damage.

Sitting patiently at a busy intersection, I got a little antsy thinking about the sun, the girls, and, of course, the beer in the back of the truck.

"Hold on!" I said as I took a right on red and gave the truck a little extra gas so that the approaching car would not get pissed at me for pulling out in front of him or her.

"Bronson!" Sam said as if he didn't realize I saw the car. "It's too late now, you freaking idiot!"

I glanced in my rear-view. I had forgotten that Joe's truck didn't have a tailgate. I watched in dismay as the rest of the day crashed in the middle of the intersection, glass flying everywhere, and the tires of the oncoming car going flat as it ran over the mess I'd just left in the street. Let's just say we got out of the area—fast.

After buying a new ice chest, more beer and ice, and a bungee cord, we were back in business. When we arrived at the lake, I was relieved to see that the sun and girls were still to be seen, and I got right to drinking the overpriced beer out of the overpriced ice chest. I shouldn't have drunk so fast because I blacked out and didn't get to enjoy most of the remainder of the day. The three of us had already drunk around six beers apiece by the time we arrived at the lake. I didn't eat anything that day on purpose so that I would have no problem getting hammered. Whatever the case, the sun, the girls, and the beer were a blast, and after around four or five hours, we loaded up and headed back to town.

I started coming to my senses when I realized that, after pulling out of the park, I took a right instead of a left on this highway, which led to nowhere. We were all wondering why we hadn't made it to town yet. Sam and Joe were as drunk as I.

"Do either one of you two idiots know if there is a gas station anywhere near?" I asked.

We were about to run out of gas and I was certain we wouldn't have enough to make it into town if we turned around. This seemed very funny to me, but at the same time, I didn't want to have to walk to a gas station that might not even exist. We were out in the middle of nowhere by this time.

"Thank God!" we all said in unison as a gas station appeared in the distance.

I quickly jumped out and paid for the gas after pulling in and parking at the pump. Once on the road again, we were beginning to sober up a little. I began to fully comprehend how stupid I was acting on house arrest. About that time, I looked down at the dashboard and realized that neither Sam nor Joe had actually pumped the gas when I went in and paid for it. I quickly pulled over to prepare for a U-turn. I thought it would be cute if I pulled a *Dukes of Hazzard* and cut a fishtail in the midst of the U-turn. I was successful only in plowing into the side of a fifth wheel.

"Holy mother of @#$@##%#@$@#$@#$@#$@#$" we all said in unison upon crashing into the side of the mobile travel trailer being pulled by a dully truck.

I tried to get away but my front left tire was flat. This Nissan truck was sitting on 39-inch groundhog swampers.

"Okay, you two hide the beer in the woods and I'll go talk to these people," I said to Sam and Joe.

I was in a state of shock by this time. I was going to court in two days to be sentenced for breaking into the school. This accident was most likely going to get me booked into LTI (a local detention center for very bad kids), and that wasn't a comforting thought.

When I reached the people who were in the truck pulling the travel trailer, they looked at me like I was Bigfoot and watched me like *Lifetime*. It didn't dawn on me until later that they probably watched as my two buddies dragged the ice chest of beer off into the woods. Not to mention that the truck was parked around one hundred yards away from the point of impact. Whoops!

"Okay, where is the ice chest?" an officer said, as he and several others soon approached.

"What ice chest?" one of my idiot friends asked.

The Depth of Grace

"Just go get it!" I said with a frustration rooted in defeat.

I realized by this time that the people we hit definitely saw my friends drag the ice chest off. The officers would have only made things harder on us had we made them find it.

"Who was driving?" one of the officers asked.

"I was, sir," I said.

At his instruction I followed him to his car and got in on the passenger's side. I don't have much recollection of the conversation that the officer and I had in his car. I do remember his asking me if I had been drinking.

"No, sir," I replied.

"There is no sense in lying to me, son," he said.

"Okay, I drank some beer at the lake and probably shouldn't have been driving," I said.

That's all I remember about that conversation. After writing up the report, giving me a failure-to-yield ticket, and doing who remembers what else, the officer took Sam, Joe, and me to a gas station closer to town, dropped us off, and told us to find a ride home.

The idea of getting out of the house, going to the lake with friends, and drinking some beer sounded like fun. We went—and I guess you could say we had fun. Only, I was an alcoholic. This trip to the lake was actually launching me further into a life of trouble and suffering. It was the alcohol that had gotten me put on house arrest and a ticket to court in the first place. If I had gotten a DUI, I would have served time in prison. Plus, if I had made that U-turn a split second earlier, that dully truck would have slammed into my driver's side door and I would have been killed on impact. The truck was traveling at least sixty miles an hour. I could have killed my friend Sam and my stepbrother as well. For what reason? Because I wanted to go to the lake and have some fun due to the boring nature of house arrest? Why is it that fun like that is never really worth the risk?

3RD REST STOP:
JACOB'S JOURNEY: PART 2

Okay, back to Jacob and his life journey. Remember, Jacob's mother had instructed him to go to her brother's farm in Haran and stay with his family until Esau cooled his temper. Many days and nights into his journey through the dangerous open country, he noticed some shepherds who watered their sheep at a well.

> Jacob asked the shepherds, "My brothers, where are you from?"
>
> "We're from Harran," they replied.
>
> He said to them, "Do you know Laban, Nahor's grandson?"
>
> "Yes, we know him," they answered.
>
> Then Jacob asked them, "Is he well?"
>
> "Yes, he is," they said, "and here comes his daughter Rachel with the sheep." ...
>
> While he was still talking with them, Rachel came with her father's sheep, for she was a shepherd. When Jacob saw Rachel daughter of his uncle Laban, and Laban's sheep, he went over and rolled the stone away from the mouth of the well and watered his uncle's sheep. Then Jacob kissed Rachel and began to weep aloud. He had told Rachel that he was a

The Depth of Grace

> *relative of her father and a son of Rebekah. So she ran and told her father. (Genesis 29:4-6, 9-11)*

Why did Jacob weep aloud? I think he released the buildup of fear and fright that he had acquired along his journey. When Jacob saw that he reached his destination and sensed that he had finally arrived at a safe place, he broke down and wept like a little girl.

Jacob ended up falling head over heels for Rachel. It was love at first sight! Because incest was attractive at this time, Jacob decided to marry her. His uncle Laban had no problem with this. He saw this wedding vow as a good opportunity to screw over his nephew. "Sure, you can marry my daughter if you work seven years of hard labor. The wedding depends on how much you love her, Jacob." Jerk! You see, Laban was Rebekah's brother. Can you see how the sins just flow right through the family?

Jacob worked seven years so that he could marry Rachel. The Bible says that these seven years felt like only a few days to Jacob because he was so in love with her. Finally, when the time came, Jacob waited in bed in the dark to receive his beloved bride. Remember, this moment ran through Jacob's mind every second of every day for seven years. And guess what happened to Mr. Trickster Jacob? As a reward for Jacob's hard work, his uncle Laban sent in the ugly older daughter instead of Rachel. The trickster was tricked by a master manipulator.

Jacob wanted to marry Rachel, but was scammed into marrying her sister, Leah. He still got to marry Rachel, but he had to agree to *another* seven years of labor for Laban. So Laban and Jacob screwed each other over back and forth for more than twenty years. However, God's hand was with Jacob and he prospered greatly during this time. After twenty-one years passed, Jacob could look at his life and see that God was with him. He had children and the number of his clansmen and herds was great. Everything he touched prospered. God protected Jacob—God held up his end of the deal. Jacob knew that God would eventually tell him to return to his father's house as He originally told him at Bethel. And one day …

> *Jacob heard that Laban's sons were saying, "Jacob has taken everything our father owned and has gained all this wealth from what belonged to our father." And Jacob noticed that Laban's attitude toward him was not what it had been. Then the LORD said to Jacob, "Go back to the land of your fathers and to your relatives, and I will be with you." (Genesis 31:1-3)*

J. Bronson Haley

So where did Jacob find the courage to return to his father's house and face Esau? He was able to return because God proved the truth in the promise He had made to Jacob at Bethel. Jacob could look at his life and see that God did everything He said that He would do, and that He had not left him.

Jacob left because he knew God was with him. However, Jacob was still Jacob. He even deceived his way out of town.

> *When Laban had gone to shear his sheep, Rachel stole her father's household goods. [LOL ... the sins just plague the whole family, don't they?] Moreover, Jacob deceived Laban the Aramean by not telling him he was running away. (Genesis 31:19-20, my comment added)*

But Laban wouldn't let Jacob get away that easy! It didn't take Laban long to catch up. Laban and his men were stronger than Jacob's group, and he planned to hurt Jacob when he found him. This wasn't a big deal though: God saw it as an additional opportunity to prove Himself to Jacob and encourage him.

> *Jacob had pitched his tent in the hill country of Gilead when Laban overtook him, and Laban and his relatives camped there too. Then Laban said to Jacob, "What have you done? You've deceived me, and you've carried off my daughters like captives in war. Why did you run off secretly and deceive me? Why didn't you tell me, so I could send you away with joy and singing to the music of tambourines and harps? You didn't even let me kiss my grandchildren and my daughters goodbye. You have done a foolish thing. I have the power to harm you; but last night the God of your father said to me, 'Be careful not to say anything to Jacob, either good or bad.'" (Genesis 31:25-29)*

Yeah, right! Like Laban was going to send Jacob off with joy and singing to the music of tambourines and harps! Maybe after God scared the literal hell out of him that night, but no way was he going to send Jacob away to music of his own accord.

Keep in mind that this was an extremely difficult trip for Jacob. He was still worried about the wrath of Esau, even though he knew God was with him. In the next few days he would meet Esau for the first time since

The Depth of Grace

he robbed him over twenty years ago. When Laban left, God knew Jacob was terribly troubled.

> *Jacob also went on his way, and the angels of God met him. When Jacob saw them, he said, "This is the camp of God!" So he named that place Mahanaim. (Genesis 32:1-2)*

Jacob knew God was with him, but he still struggled with his ways. He was used to doing things his way and he trusted only in himself. Jacob began to think of ways to handle Esau. He pretty much knew he was in big trouble but still trusted himself more than God. Jacob decided to send messengers to deliver a message to his brother, which basically was this: "Tell Esau that I have been successful and worked all this time to impress him and win his favor." What? Come on, Jacob! That's ridiculous. Quit lying and simply trust God! You and I know that trusting God isn't always easy. Trusting the Lord wasn't easy for Jacob, either.

> *When the messengers returned to Jacob, they said, "We went to your brother Esau, and now he is coming to meet you, and four hundred men are with him." In great fear and distress Jacob divided the people who were with him into two groups, and the flocks and herds and camels as well. He thought, "If Esau comes and attacks one group, the group that is left may escape." (Genesis 32:6-8)*

What? Run that by me one more time! I don't think I heard you clearly, Jacob. You plan to sacrifice half of the family—and possibly the whole family—because you would rather trust yourself than Jehovah-Jireh, the God who provides? This is the man God chose to father Israel! The Israelites would be God's chosen people! Why in the heck is Jacob risking it all to do things his way? It's because Jacob was a lot like you and me.

Finally, Jacob started using his head …

> *"O God of my father Abraham, God of my father Isaac, Lord, you who said to me, 'Go back to your country and your relatives, and I will make you prosper,' I am unworthy of all the kindness and faithfulness you have shown your servant. I had only my staff when I crossed this Jordan, but now I have become two camps. Save me, I pray, from the hand of my brother Esau, for I am afraid he will come and attack me, and also the mothers with their children. But*

J. Bronson Haley

> *you have said, 'I will surely make you prosper and will make*
> *your descendants like the sand of the sea, which cannot be*
> *counted.'" (Genesis 32:9-12)*

Well, Jacob is getting better. At least he prayed to God as if his life depended on it. However, when he woke the next morning, he was at it again. Jacob immediately began to dream up ways to soften the blow he was destined to receive from Esau. Of course, the wrath of Esau was only Jacob's destiny for himself. But he could not see the Lord's destiny because he was a liar who depended only on himself.

"I'll give him gifts!" Now, there is an idea. "I will give Esau a small portion of what I received due to the blessing I stole from him." Do you see how he is not thinking clearly? Jacob divided up his herds and sent them as gifts for his brother. He told his servants exactly what to say. After he sent everyone ahead to meet Esau, Jacob stayed behind with his family. Jacob had been desperate up until this point, obviously. Here, the reality of possibly losing his family and his life became very real to him. With each second that passed came more distress and fear and doubt and worry and sorrow and guilt and the realization that it was his own fault that he and his family were in this situation.

> *That night Jacob got up and took his two wives, his two*
> *female servants and his eleven sons and crossed the ford of*
> *the Jabbok. After he had sent them across the stream, he sent*
> *over all his possessions. So Jacob was left alone, and a man*
> *wrestled with him until daybreak. When the man saw that*
> *he could not overpower him, he touched the socket of Jacob's*
> *hip so that his hip was wrenched as he wrestled with the man.*
> *(Genesis 32:22-25)*

This "man" he wrestled with was God. You see, Jacob reached a place in his life where he did not have the strength to move forward on his own. Jacob was terrified and very alone. He had no choice but to get alone and seek God. He had watched everything God ever promised him go before him and knew they would soon face his brother—who, in Jacob's mind, was no doubt planning to kill them. Jacob was afraid for his wives and his children. Jacob was afraid for his life. Now he was alone. Jacob was alone with God.

I'm sure he thought about the times he deceived his brother over and over again. Don't you know he wished he hadn't done that? Well, what's

The Depth of Grace

done is done, isn't it? Jacob got alone with God and wrestled all night. During that time he thought about the promises God made him over the years. He knew God had protected him for a reason. But he was afraid. All night he wrestled with this distress, fear, doubt, worry, sorrow, guilt, and the realization that he, his wives, and his children would soon die if God did not intervene. By morning his hip was dislocated from wrestling and Jacob was at rock bottom but not quite ready to give up: "Then the man said, 'Let me go, for it is daybreak.' But Jacob replied, 'I will not let you go unless you bless me'" (Genesis 32:26).

The Lord gave Jacob his free will to go ahead without Him. Jacob refused. In his last effort to save himself and his family, Jacob grabbed hold of the Lord and refused to let Him go. "The man asked him, 'What is your name?' 'Jacob,' he answered" (Genesis 32:27). In other words, "I am only Jacob. I am a deceiver who by himself can accomplish nothing. I am worthless without you, Father."

As it says in the New Testament: "God opposes the proud, but shows favor to the humble" (James 4:6).

So ... "Then the man said, 'Your name will no longer be Jacob, but Israel, because you have struggled with God and with men and have overcome'" (Genesis 32:28). Here, God reminds Jacob that he would have been dead by now had He not been with him. "You have wrestled with Me and man, yet you are not dead. Your uncle could not compare with My favor even with all his experience. You can see that everything you did prospered and you were not harmed, just as I said. Now trust Me and go face your brother. I held up My end of the deal; now you hold up yours!"

What would you do at this point? There is nothing you can do but obey. God has His way of keeping His chosen people.

The sun rose above him as he passed Peniel, and he was limping because of his hip,....

Jacob looked up and there was Esau, coming with his four hundred men; so he divided the children among Leah, Rachel and the two female servants. He put the female servants and their children in front, Leah and her children next, and Rachel and Joseph in the rear. He himself went on ahead and bowed down to the ground seven times as he approached his brother.

J. Bronson Haley

> *But Esau ran to meet Jacob and embraced him; he threw*
> *his arms around his neck and kissed him. And they wept.*
> *(Genesis 32:31, 33:1-4)*

God keeps His promises to us! The Lord allowed me to see the truth in this passage when I needed the courage to return to my heavenly Father's house. I began to think about the promises God made me when I had asked Him to come into my life. The Lord assured me that He had been there through all of my sufferings. He also assured me that, now that He had me, He would never leave me. When I fell into sin, I didn't have any intentions of returning to the Lord. But the more time I spent away from God, the worse off I became.

Four years later I had failed to the point that it seemed impossible to return even if I chose to. God used this message from Genesis to confirm to me that it was He who spared me over the years. Many say that God would never help people who are in sin. This message conveyed to me that it is the character of my Father, who saved me, to protect me even if I fail miserably, just as Jacob failed miserably. When God proved to me in the Scriptures that it was He who protected me over the years, I had hope that I would overcome and that He would somehow restore me. With this message, I turned and faced into the wind. Here I picked up my Bible and began to make my way back to the feet of my Savior. This message gave me hope that God was not finished with me!

At this point, I was in the same place in my own life as Jacob was when he fled his uncle Laban's house. I knew the outcome for Jacob, having read and understood the message. I understood that I was not going to be able to see how God was going to deliver me from my personal "Esau." Like Jacob, I was lonely and in fear. I had a drug addiction among other struggles. Like Jacob, I doubted. But, also like Jacob, I chose to turn and face into the wind.

God also revealed to me in this passage that it was okay that I had made a personal vow to Him to tell the world about Him (see the Introduction of this book, as well as Chapters 19 and 20 for more on this). We should make vows to the Lord just as Jacob made his vow at Bethel. We should give God a chance to prove Himself just as Jacob did so that our faith can grow. When God proves Himself, we must face into the wind just like Jacob. This is the character of God: when we are obedient, we put the ball in His court. And trust me, the ball is safe in the court of Almighty God.

CHAPTER 6

Not Dead Yet

It was November 26, 1996. As a junior in high school, I woke up in a dark room with strangers standing around me. Not knowing where I was or what was stuck down my throat, I began to panic. As I jerked the tubes out of my throat and the cord out of my arm, I was bombarded by angry people wearing white, green, and blue. As my lungs filled up with blood, I began to choke. The harder I fought, the worse it was, and eventually I lost consciousness.

My mother was standing at my side when I awoke twelve hours later. She kept repeating to me, "Everything is going to be okay, honey. Everything is going to be okay."

If everything is going to be okay, then why can't I move, and why am I hooked up to these machines? I wondered. I knew the machines were keeping me alive, and Mom didn't look very confident about what she was telling me.

Lying there in that bed, I began to think about the things my grandmother used to tell me about Jesus and God. It was clear to me that there was nothing good in the world I was living in. I could do nothing about my alcohol problem, and I was definitely going to die if something didn't change. I honestly wasn't sure if I would make it out of that hospital room. I decided at that moment that, if there was any good in this world, and if I got the chance, I was going to find it.

And if I find it, I'm going to tell people.

61

J. Bronson Haley

A little more than twelve hours before, I had been ejected through the front windshield of a vehicle traveling sixty-five miles per hour down Highway 80. My friend and I were on our way to his camp house to sleep for the night. We had been out drinking and partying with friends, and had big plans of going duck hunting the following morning.

In the hospital the nurses picked at me because my bangs, eyebrows, and eyelashes looked as though they had been singed by fire—which was pretty much right on the money. At a field party on the outskirts of town, I had been jumping through a bonfire that shot flames well above my head the night before. In this field was a crowd of high-school kids who hung out and drank large amounts of beer from a keg.

Weeks later my mother told me a story about the experience she had at the crash site the day after the wreck. She was standing over the section of road where I was found. A man pulled over and approached her as she gazed at the tape on the road that indicated where I was lying when the ambulance arrived.

"Did you know this boy?" the stranger asked.

"Yes, I'm his mother," she replied.

He then mentioned that he was the first person on the scene of the accident.

"He looked dead to me. His right eye was bulged out and his face was covered in blood. He didn't move," the man told my mother. "There was one thing that I couldn't figure out about this scene. His friend was running down the street and I am sure he was trying to find a phone to call an ambulance. The two people in the car they hit were still sitting in their car. Yet your boy was wrapped in a white sheet, as if someone laid him in the street."

My mother wrote a poem describing her emotions on that day.

The Day Before Thanksgiving 1996:
To God I Give the Glory

My heart is full of joy today
Because of two lives not taken away.
One was my son, the other his friend
God's light shined bright, this was not their end.

Sound asleep before he flew
Crashing through a windshield, he never even knew.

The Depth of Grace

Covered by a sheet before anyone found him
God was there with His arms all around him.

Not expected to live, his recovery was swift
Only from God, this miracle was a gift.
On Thanksgiving Day, I watched as he slept
Tears of joy, on and off I wept.

I love my son and in my heart I knew
God kept him alive for He has things for him to do.
His plan is unknown to Bronson right now
But His promise is joy when on knee we bow.

To Jesus I look and thank Him so
My son was a blessing from Him I know.
A promising young man with a smile I love
I pray he always looks to you, Lord, above.

What more can I say? It was a miracle. As screwed up as I was, God had preserved me for higher things that I knew nothing about at the time. But now I do—and I'm making the most of every second I have.

4TH REST STOP:
FOLLOW ME

Have you ever struggled with something that you just simply could not overcome? Have you tried over and over again to win a struggle only to experience defeat with every attempt? Glory to God! I've got good news to the world of struggling people: you can do absolutely *nothing* to free yourself! Isn't that comforting? It was comforting to me!

I tried and tried and tried again to simply overcome my failures—to pick myself up by my bootstraps, as they say, and just rely on my willpower. But it seemed impossible! I was discouraged when I could not gain victory in my life. Yet I was comforted when God's Word confirmed to me that I was fighting a losing battle. "So I was right all along!" I said to myself. "There is nothing I can do to overcome!" Glory to God! The first step to recovery is to accept the fact that you are defeated.

Have you ever told people to quit doing something that they were struggling with? "Quit doing drugs! Quit having sex before marriage! Quit walking in anger!" The list could go on and on. But none of us can just quit, so stop telling everyone they can!

Are these struggles not sin? Isn't sex before marriage sin? Do you know some people struggling with sex before marriage? Quit telling them to stop having sex before marriage! You are causing them to be discouraged!

Has anyone ever enjoyed being angry? You know how it is with some people: anger boils up inside of them and they throw a temper tantrum, acting like a lunatic. They don't enjoy it, though! Does anger management help control the outbursts? "Listen, Mr. Tantrum! Just clench your jaws and think about cute little kittens!" When you tell an angry guy that he

The Depth of Grace

is less than a man because he gets angry all the time, it discourages him. "I hate you!" is what these people say on the inside. Angry people can do nothing to avoid getting angry!

Okay, are you ready for the truth? Fine! "Jesus replied, 'Very truly I tell you, everyone who sins is a slave to sin'" (John 8:34).

"Oh, Bronson!" you might say to me. "Don't be ridiculous. I can quit this or that if I really want to." Excuse me? Make a list of the positive things that have come from your struggles. Why not do without the negative? Less negative is more positive in life as a whole, right? Oh, you don't want any more positive in your life? You have too much? Will you do me a favor? Get real!

There is nothing you or anyone on earth can do to help you get free of sin in the long run. In some ways sin itself makes us feel like we are experiencing short-term "relief" from the pain in our lives—but we're never actually set free. This short-term relief comes in many different forms: drugs, alcohol, sex, unhealthy emotions, and any other sinful indulgence you can think of. People might be able to resist sin as a relief valve for the short-term. However, in the long run, they settle for their "sin(s) of choice." The problem is that sin destroys us, and the curse of sin intensifies over time. As the curse grows stronger, the addiction grows stronger. In due time one becomes a slave to death. Anyone who fights this battle alone has lost the battle to begin with. The reality of slavery to sin and death becomes too much for some people to handle. Often times they commit suicide. That's right: this isn't a game.

Let's look at this from God's point of view, so say you are God. You have a little earth and you have created little people whom you love deeply. But all the people were cursed because God created that woman. Just kidding! We were all cursed because Adam sinned. Do you see it is not your fault that you are a sinner at heart? So relax and blame Adam! It's his fault!

However, it makes no difference who is at fault when it comes to the curse that comes with sin—and the curse is even more impossible to break on your own than the sin itself, because the curse of sin only leads to one thing: eternal death, as in forever and ever when we die. Back to you being God: what if you sent your one and only Son to earth to suffer the most horrific death imaginable so that these people you created and loved deeply could be free of the curse that comes with their sin? Would anyone get free of this curse without accepting what your Son did for him or her? Not on

65

J. Bronson Haley

my clock they wouldn't! Remember: "So if the Son sets you free, you will be free indeed" (John 8:36).

The day will never come when God allows someone to walk free from the curse of sin without accepting His Son as Lord and Savior. I realize that for some it seems more difficult than this, because many times we cannot understand how to get free. Consider, "The god of this age has blinded the minds of unbelievers, so that they cannot see the light of the gospel of the glory of Christ, who is the image of God" (2 Corinthians 4:4). The god of this age is Satan. Sin is the fuel for those who have been blinded, which is every person who has ever been born. Yes, including Mother Theresa. We were all cursed when Adam fell into sin. It's the sin that keeps us from receiving the truth. Until we receive the truth, we will not see or understand the things of God. Jesus is "the way and the truth and the life" (John 14:6).

I understand that, for some, repenting from sin is not as easy as people say it is: "Accept Jesus and you will be saved." But this is the truth! However, many times the lies we have bought into keep us from being able to accept Jesus or repent of our sin. Only one answer remains for these people! God must speak to the lies that keep them bound. If God speaks to the lies, the lies will surely listen, right? Isn't the Devil the father of lies (John 8:44)? Can the Devil talk back to God? Didn't God kick Satan out of heaven for his rebellion? Yes! That's why he's here harassing us! When God speaks to the lies that keep you from receiving Christ, or repenting of your sin, you will receive Christ and repent of your sin. "Then you will know the truth, and the truth will set you free" (John 8:32).

If you do not understand what truth is or have not received Jesus—relax. It's not up to your mind to convince itself to believe in Jesus. That's impossible! That's why so many people get discouraged. People say, "But I just don't have any faith." Understand something real quick: it's not up to you to give yourself faith or increase your faith. You cannot just say, "I am going to believe like Abraham," and then believe like Abraham. It was up to God to prove Himself to Abraham and it's up to the Lord to prove Himself to you. God has not changed. "God is not human, that he should lie, not a human being, that he should change his mind. Does he speak and then not act? Does he promise and not fulfill?" (Numbers 23:19). If God proves Himself to you, then you will have faith. It's only up to us to learn how to walk. It's up to God to prove Himself and allow us to hold to or increase our faith.

The Depth of Grace

One might say, "But so-and-so told me this and that was going to happen and nothing happened." Glory to God! Now we know the Lord didn't ask so-and-so to speak to you. "If what a prophet proclaims in the name of the LORD does not take place or come true, that is a message the LORD has not spoken" (Deuteronomy 18:22). The God of Abraham confirms His Word!

If you have not accepted Jesus as your Lord and Savior, you have lived with the curse of sin for your entire life and do not know what it feels like to be free. Throughout this book I am addressing the lies that keep people from receiving the truth—being "able" to believe. If you identify with the struggles I have addressed (or will address), and God speaks to these struggles, will you not be set free of these struggles?

"But I repented one time and nothing happened." Be sure of this: if you receive salvation, you will surely know it. A big misconception exists in the church today about this, even though the Bible is clear about it: "Everyone who calls on the name of the Lord will be saved" (Acts 2:21). This is the truth and this is the Word of God. "Declare with your mouth … and believe in your heart … [and] you will be saved" (Romans 10:9). This is the truth and the Word of God. However, the Word of God also says, "No one can come to me unless the Father who sent me draws them, and I will raise them up at the last day" (John 6:44). Jesus made this crystal clear during one of His first moments alone with the twelve disciples:

> *When Jesus came to the region of Caesarea Philippi, he asked his disciples, "Who do people say the Son of Man is?"*
>
> *They replied, "Some say John the Baptist; others say Elijah; and still others, Jeremiah or one of the prophets."*
>
> *"But what about you?" he asked. "Who do you say I am?"*
>
> *Simon Peter answered, "You are the Messiah, the Son of the living God."*
>
> *Jesus replied, "Blessed are you, Simon son of Jonah, for this was not revealed to you by man, but by my Father in heaven."* (Matthew 16:13-17)

It is clear in this Scripture that the decision to accept Jesus as the Son of God is not compelled by the mind or by the words of people alone. The Spirit of God must draw us to repentance so that the truth in the decision

J. Bronson Haley

we are making might be revealed in us. Yes, people can be used by God to lead the lost into His kingdom, but this must be done by His Spirit. No one can simply talk someone into accepting Jesus as Lord and Savior. It is even by His Spirit that we might experience a godly sorrow for our sins and desire to repent (2 Corinthians 7:10). And it is only by His Spirit that we are able confess with our mouths and believe in our hearts (Romas 10:9-10). Simply put, we can only come to Jesus and be saved by His Spirit.

The word of God also says that, "Opponents must be gently instructed, in the hope that God will grant them repentance leading them to a knowledge of the truth" (2 Timothy 2:25).

Paideuo is the Greek word for *instruct* used in this verse. It means "to train, educate, discipline, and punish." God didn't say this to scare anyone. However, He does say that some must be gently instructed in the right direction and they should look for Him to *grant* them repentance—give them the ability to believe and overcome. The Lord, though, says that He will lead you to "the truth [that] will set you free."

An additional comforting thought is that God had to gently lead me to the truth so that I was able to repent and be set free. In the Rest Stops that follow, I am going to take you on this journey. The cry of my own heart was, "Lord, I need proof that Your Word is alive." I didn't need far-fetched stories when I was on the brink of suicide. For those who do not identify, rejoice that you do not understand that. Those who do identify, you also rejoice, because in this book, through Jesus Christ, by the Word of God, you will be led to the truth that will set you free.

I learned through reading my Bible that God never had a problem with proving Himself to people. The heroes of faith in God's Word had great faith because God proved Himself to them over and over again. The Lord never asked anyone to just start believing in miracles. They believed because God spoke a word and then proved Himself faithful to His word. His people saw the word come to pass—and they experienced freedom when He spoke the word. Do you want proof in the things I am telling you? Yes, you do! For all you know, this could be a bright idea that I dreamed up. But ... "Then the disciples went out and preached everywhere, and the Lord worked with them and confirmed his word by the signs that accompanied it" (Mark 16:20).

I heard a lot of bright ideas spoken to me by others on my road to recovery. Many of these people were Christians. Lots of Christians have "scholarly" advice on what a struggling individual should do to overcome. Even nonbelievers who are bound themselves can come up with a "perfect"

The Depth of Grace

plan on how to overcome. I didn't overcome anything until God spoke to me through His Word. Thankfully the Lord will also use people to speak to us through His Word. That was the job of the apostles. The apostles used the Scriptures to back up what they said. We need to back up what we say with the truth so that the truth may set others free. After all, the Bible states, "Do not go beyond what is written" (1 Corinthians 4:6).

Without the truth about who God is and who we are in Him, we are subject to the lies of Satan. Isn't the Devil a fallen angel? That makes him wiser and stronger than we. Can we rebuke Satan without God's voice? The Devil tried to lead Jesus astray during His forty-day fast in the desert. Jesus spoke Scripture to His enemy who tempted Him. The Word of God gave the Son of God victory over Satan. Shouldn't the children of God speak His Word so that we might not be led astray? Before I fell hard in my faith (you'll soon read about my experience in coming to faith), my heart's desire was to preach the truth of God and serve Jesus Christ. I loved Him deeply. However, I missed the whole point. We can only battle Satan with the Word of God. What was I going to tell people that might help them? Without God's Word I would be ineffective and lead many astray. Guess what? I was ineffective and led many astray. That isn't the ministry of the church of Jesus Christ.

I took note that Peter sinned even after Jesus called him to the ministry, just like me. Most people recognize Peter as being one of the most prominent apostles. Many people understand that Peter struggled more than any of the others and we have an idea why. My big question was this: "How did Peter change into that great man of faith we read about in the book of Acts? Who was Simon (another name for Peter) that he ended up writing two books of the New Testament?" If there had been a way to change, I would have done it by that time. Desperately needing a breakthrough in my own life, I paid close attention to every aspect of Peter's walk during my second trip of reading through the gospels. We all need to know how Peter changed to understand true change.

Let's look again at the time when Jesus called Simon Peter to follow Him: "'Come, follow me,' Jesus said, 'and I will send you out to fish for people" (Matthew 4:19).

Why did Jesus want Simon? He was a dirty sinner who probably cussed like the sailor he was. And there wasn't anything Simon could do to change. No one likes the fact that they do wrong and do things that hurt themselves and other people. Simon Peter didn't understand himself and certainly didn't understand why the most righteous man he had ever seen

69

J. Bronson Haley

or heard about wanted him. On another occasion, possibly just after Jesus had called him to be a disciple, Peter was so overwhelmed by Jesus' love for him that he fell to his knees before Jesus and could only cry out: "Go away from me, Lord; I am a sinful man!" (Luke 5:8). Did Peter really want Jesus to go away? No. Peter didn't want Jesus to change His mind about calling him into His inner circle. However, Simon knew he didn't have what it would take to be a disciple of this righteous man who had called him. Maybe he briefly fantasized about the idea of being His disciple, but he feared the reality of who he was even more. "Then Jesus said to Simon, 'Don't be afraid; from now on you will fish for people'" (Luke 5:10).

It comforted me to understand that Jesus was not concerned about Simon's sin. As a matter of fact, Jesus never even mentioned his sin. He didn't ask this fisherman to change and get his life right *prior* to following Him, either. Jesus didn't ask Simon to overcome anything. Jesus didn't say, "Stop cussing, leave your pride in the boat, repent, buy some new clothes, learn the Scriptures, practice praying, learn how to preach, and then you can be my disciple." If Jesus had demanded that Simon Peter do these things, he would have been discouraged. Jesus knew better than Peter—and He knows better than you and me—that in our sin we are slaves to sin. If someone had walked up to me while I was a drug addict and told me to quit the drugs and do this and that, I would have been discouraged. The only demand Jesus made of Simon was that he follow Him. Jesus first called him: "Come." Second, He said, "Follow me." Jesus took the burden upon Himself to transform Simon, if he was willing to follow: "I will send you out to fish for people." Simon Peter decided to answer the call and follow. How many of us understand that we have a lot better chance at changing when it's up to Jesus to transform us?

A few days after Simon was called to follow, he received a whisper in his ear from Jesus: "'You will be called Cephas' (which, when translated, is Peter)" (John 1:42). Was Simon Peter already changed just after a few days? No. We know that he continued to screw up the whole time Jesus walked the earth. At this moment he hadn't even confessed Jesus as his Lord and Savior. So why did the Lord mention to Simon that He would be called "Peter," which means "Rock"? Jesus took note that Simon Peter was willing to follow him. Because he was willing to follow, Jesus went ahead and declared to him that he would one day be the rock He would use to establish His church. Simon Peter could not change into the "Rock." However, he could put one foot in front of the other. And sure enough, that is all Jesus asked of Him. Too often, we take the burden from Jesus

The Depth of Grace

and put it on our own shoulders. Then we complain because the burden is too heavy. Of course it is! So allow the Son of God to carry the burden of transforming your life into what He wants it to be!

Let's jump ahead to more than one and one half years later in Peter's life to take a look at a passage that we looked at in part earlier in this Rest Stop …

> *When Jesus came to the region of Caesarea Philippi, he asked his disciples, "Who do people say the Son of Man is?"*
>
> *They replied, "Some say John the Baptist; others say Elijah; and still others, Jeremiah or one of the prophets."*
>
> *"But what about you?" he asked. "Who do you say I am?"*
>
> *Simon Peter answered, "You are the Messiah, the Son of the living God."*
>
> *Jesus replied, "Blessed are you, Simon son of Jonah, for this was not revealed to you by man, but by my Father in heaven. And I tell you that you are Peter, and on this rock I will build my church, and the gate of Hades will not overcome it." (Matthew 16:13-18)*

At this point, are we all not proud of the man we now know as the apostle Peter? Because we understand that Simon might have been ADHD, we know that reaching this point was no easy task. He stuck his foot in his mouth over and over again during his walk with the Lord. Peter screwed up repeatedly, as we saw in the 1st Rest Stop. As a result Jesus had to humble him time and again. Remember, Peter could have gotten his feelings hurt when Jesus called him "Satan" and quit his walk with the Lord (see Matthew 16:23). But he didn't. He just kept following Jesus, which was all that the Lord required of him. Jesus took upon Himself the burden of transforming Peter, and in the Bible we see glimpses of how Peter's heart began to change thanks to the grace of God.

I've heard it said that mercy is not getting what we do deserve, and grace is getting what we don't deserve—as in God's unmerited favor. Grace is what we need to experience change. We receive grace (sometimes called "favor" in the Bible) in our humility: "God opposes the proud, but shows favor to the humble" (James 4:6). Jesus humbled Peter because He understood that His Father opposed him in his pride. When we start

71

J. Bronson Haley

thinking we have everything figured out and begin to determine what God is and isn't doing without referring to His Word, we will be humbled—trust me. If we rebuke the very Word of God as Peter did in Matthew 16:21-23, the Word of God will in turn humble us. Jesus was and is the Word of God in the flesh. It is His job to make sure the Father does not oppose us because of our pride. We can either humble ourselves or Jesus will humble us. I have found through personal experience that it's easier to humble myself.

So, as I said, I was comforted when God opened this truth to me through His Word. All Peter could do at the time Jesus called him was to walk with the Lord. Should we try to do more than Peter did? Can we get our hearts right with God on our own? Does Jesus expect us to? I couldn't do anything about my shame, guilt, doubt, unbelief, pain, suicidal tendencies, and downright hopelessness. I couldn't even pray. However, I could put one foot in front of the other and follow Jesus to the degree that I knew how at the time. Better than that, I could sit on my rear end and read my Bible. God will only ask us to do what we are able to do.

I was taking a huge risk by reading my Bible in my condition. I had heard many times that one should not read the Bible while drunk, high, or doing anything sinful. "That would be disrespectful to God!" Well, I was a drug addict. I didn't have any choice. God showed me the truth about the calling of Simon Peter while I was high on OxyContin. Don't get me wrong! I wasn't proud of this at that time and I'm not today. But my shame was the reason I didn't go to church. The shame kept me from praying. I could not beat the shame. I was just too fully aware that I wasn't worth the recliner I was sitting in when I got this revelation. Yet it was so comforting to see that Simon Peter wasn't worth the boat he was fishing out of when Jesus called him—and that the burden of transforming Peter's heart and life was taken on completely by Jesus. Now that's something to hang onto when it seems like there's no hope for positive, lasting change in our lives!

CHAPTER 7

———

Saved

A short time after I was released from the hospital following my nearly fatal car accident, I began to think of one of my old girlfriends who not long ago had suddenly disappeared from the crowd I ran with. Her name was Barbara Mason and she'd left Shreve High School to enroll in Evangel Christian Academy. I called her out of the blue one evening and asked how she liked her new school. At this point I desperately needed a change in my life and knew I needed to get away from my current group of friends. Barbara said that she loved the school and then invited me to church that night to witness a team of strong men break bricks and rip through entire phone books with their bare hands. I agreed to go, so Barbara picked me up from my home just a couple of hours later and we headed to church.

The strong men put on quite a show, and the church was packed with people screaming and hollering as these men tore thick phone books in half and bent steel bars as they braced them in their clenched teeth, just to mention a couple of their incredible displays of strength. I'll never forget the excitement at the end of the show as a man named Darwin was introduced to the crowd. He was one of the strong men, and as he walked toward the podium with tears streaming down his face, he grabbed all of my attention.

Darwin began to share about his old life on the streets—a life filled with violence and addiction, among other problems. He described the pain he had experienced and explained his hopeless life in great detail. It was evident that this man had been through much worse than I.

73

J. Bronson Haley

He then spoke about the day his twin girls were born, seven years earlier. He sobbed as he described his emotions upon first hearing that he would soon become a daddy. He was a drug-dealing drug addict at the time. The news crushed him because he knew that he didn't have the skills he needed to be a father. He didn't want to be alive much less raise a baby living the only lifestyle he knew.

Darwin said that he didn't talk to his girlfriend much during her pregnancy. He also decided that he wasn't going to be there when she gave birth. He hated who he was and hated that he was the father of these babies.

True to his word, he wasn't there when his babies were born, but Darwin did show up a few hours later. He wept as he described the feeling of walking into the hospital to see his twin girls while he was high on crank (methamphetamine) and carrying a pocket full of drugs. When he approached the nursery, he told the nurse his name and asked if he could see his girls. She gave him a funny look as she left him to notify the doctor of his arrival. The doctor shook his hand and then led him into the nursery. He was introduced to one of the girls, and Darwin gave us a vivid description of his emotions when he set his eyes on his daughter for the first time:

"She was the most beautiful thing I had ever seen," Darwin told the audience, sobbing the whole time. "I couldn't believe I helped create something that beautiful and innocent. I had never loved anything before, and the love I experienced for my baby girl was the best feeling I'd ever had."

Darwin continued his story, saying that after a few moments of gazing at his daughter, he looked around and asked the doctor about his other girl. He was then led down a long hallway into another room. He wept even more as he described his anticipation at meeting the twin of his baby girl.

"I knew she was going to be just as beautiful as her sister," he said to us.

When Darwin looked into the incubator, which was twice the size of the one he had just seen, his eyes rested on a baby girl whose head was as big as her body and whose insides were sitting on the outside.

"I could hear her screaming, 'Daddy! Daddy! Please make the pain go away! Daddy! Why did you do this to me?'" Darwin said.

When I heard him say this, I started crying.

The Depth of Grace

A couple of weeks after the birth of his girls, Darwin was at home by himself watching TV and flipping through the channels when he stopped on a Christian network. The pastor was in the middle of asking the viewers to pray the prayer of salvation. Darwin got down on his knees at the instructions of the pastor and received Jesus as his Lord and Savior. Seven years later he found himself married to the mother of the daughter who survived, and ministering the gospel of Jesus Christ to troubled kids like myself.

He told one last story that I'll never forget. One morning while getting ready for church, Darwin was standing in front of a mirror fixing his tie as his little girl, then around seven, walked up and stood beside him. Examining herself in the mirror, she asked, "Daddy, what did my sister look like?"

Still looking into the mirror, Darwin pointed at his baby girl standing next to him and said, "She looked just like that beautiful little girl right there."

Not long after Darwin finished on the stage, Pastor Donnie Moore gave an altar call and invited anyone to come forward to receive Christ as their Lord and Savior. I didn't hesitate in that instant. I got up out of my seat and walked down to the front. I had no doubt in my mind that, if God could heal Darwin's broken heart, he could heal mine. I knew that, if God still loved Darwin after the things he had done, he would love and forgive me as well. I was saved January 15, 1997, and to God I give the glory.

But the story certainly doesn't end there. In fact it's just starting in a lot of ways …

CHAPTER 8

—

Free Beer and Cigarettes

I wish I could say that I did a one-eighty after giving my life to God that January night in 1997. Sadly, though, I chose to ignore God for the most part and instead ran right back to my old way of life, and that only meant one thing in the end: more trouble. Sure, I was still saved. I was still forgiven, and God still loved me. But, faced with following the narrow path of true life and real love, or continuing back down the wide path of destruction and sin, I chose to go back to my old ways and resurrect my old sinful self—the very person I'd said good-bye to when I was saved.

So, one Saturday night during my 1997 "summer of sin," my friend, Joe, and I were at a pay phone seeking directions to a party south of town. At this point we had each consumed roughly a twelve-pack of beer, maybe more. While I was on the phone, I heard a window break nearby. I looked over at Joe and he just stared at me, apparently in eager anticipation of my response to the fact that he had just broken the window in the front door of this little neighborhood grocery store. I quickly hung up the phone and walked over to the broken window. Without saying a word, I climbed through the window and Josh followed. We each grabbed a twelve-pack of beer and a carton of cigarettes, then left.

Burglary didn't seem like a big deal, no doubt because our blood-alcohol level was through the roof. When we finally arrived at the party, we passed out cigarettes, hung out for a while, and then headed back to town. No one had asked about the cigarettes and we didn't say anything.

77

J. Bronson Haley

Being the complete idiots we were that night, we later stopped back at the grocery store, ready to take our stupidity to the next level. The store was located on a dark winding road that led from town to a couple of uptown neighborhoods and then to the middle of nowhere. It was no surprise to us that, at 2:00 a.m. on this Sunday morning, no one had noticed yet that the store had been broken into. On this visit we filled my 1986 CJ-7 full of beer, cigarettes, and cigars.

Our friend Turk had been hanging out with the two of us just about every night of this particular summer, so we went straight to his house after we left the store the second time. We woke him up and shared the goods we had acquired. We sat around for a while slamming some of the beer and then found ourselves on the road again to ... you guessed it ... the grocery store. By this trip I had it all figured out.

"Turk, you and Joe run the beer from the cooler to the door and place it outside through the window. I'll load the Jeep."

But one big thing slipped my mind. Because two of our crew were on the inside and only one on the outside (namely, me), the beer began to stack up in front of the store.

With beer in hand and even more of it stacked up behind me, I froze in my tracks as a vehicle pulled into the parking lot. When the beams of the headlights crossed my path, the vehicle stopped. As I stood there, confronted by the lights, I pondered my next move.

I can't run because we're in my vehicle. My Jeep is super slow. Think of something fast, Bronson!

Suddenly I heard girls laughing from inside the car. Not knowing what to do or what to think, I just stood there in all my thieving splendor.

"Bronson! What in the heck are you doing?" a girl asked as she got out of the vehicle, laughing in disbelief.

I had never been so relieved to be so humiliated in all the days of my life. The girl who exited the car was the best friend of one of my friend's older sister. When I realized who she was, I chuckled and assured her, "There's plenty of beer for everyone!"

She walked right by me on her way to the pay phone, shaking her head with a "You are a freaking nut" look on her face. When she walked back to the car, she stopped, looked at me with a smile, and said, "You are crazy!"

"Can I have a kiss with that compliment, sexy lady?" I asked before she left with her friends.

The Depth of Grace

As I continued with our mission to steal every beer and cigarette in the store, I became frustrated at having fallen even further behind due to the interruption. Finally, I decided to increase the workload and haul even more at one time to my Jeep. But then ... see if this sounds familiar:

With beer in hand and even more of it stacked up behind me, I froze in my tracks as a vehicle pulled into the parking lot. When the beams of the headlights crossed my path, the vehicle stopped. As I stood there, confronted by the lights, I pondered my next move.

The only thing different about this scenario from the last was that I had to turn sideways to get a good look at the vehicle because the beer stacked in my arms blocked my front view. After a few moments laughter filled the air. This time it was a guy and he fell out of the truck, laughing hysterically.

"Bronson! What in the heck are you doing?" asked one of my best friends, Max Rodkey, who is now a Shreveport fireman.

I dropped the beer and broke in laughter.

"Max, the beer is on me tonight!" I said, barely able to spit the words out of my mouth.

Unlike the girls, Max gladly accepted some free beer before he took off.

After the three of us completed our mission, we took everything we had to the house of another friend, Dan Galloway. We filled his refrigerator, kitchen cabinets, bathroom cabinets, and every other cabinet and countertop in the house. Beer even littered the floor of his home.

Dan's house was the perfect place for our stolen booty because Joe, Turk, and I spent a lot of time there during that summer—mainly because Dan threw parties about six times a week. So our evening of breaking and entering and reentering and reentering again ended with stashing our big haul at the site where we would likely get wasted the next evening. At that point I'd have to say my walk down the aisle to ask Jesus into my heart felt like a fuzzy blur in the rearview mirror of my life—a blur that I could conveniently ignore to keep living the fast life. Yeah, I'd been saved, but I hadn't allowed God to transform my heart or life one bit ... yet.

5TH REST STOP: LICENSE TO SIN?

Jesus had been invited to one of the Pharisees' houses for dinner. While He reclined at the table, a prostitute walked up behind Him, weeping. This woman had heard that Jesus was changing the lives of many sick people. She'd no doubt heard about Simon the Leper being healed of his leprosy and receiving a new life. This story caught the attention of everyone in town. Everyone who had ever been pronounced to have leprosy lived a life of shame and seclusion. Also, with leprosy often came a premature, lonely, smelly death. The shame that came with this disease was very similar to the shame that came with prostitution. This prostitute could do nothing about her past. She was a whore and she was going to die a whore.

When she approached Jesus, she was hoping in her heart that He would forgive her for her mistakes and give her a second chance. She was ashamed of her sin and not sure of the outcome of her approach to Jesus. But what difference did it make? She lived a life of shame equal to death. After this prostitute stood behind Jesus for a brief moment with tears rolling down her face, she knelt and wet His feet with her tears and washed them with her hair. Then she took an alabaster jar of expensive perfume and poured it on his head. Jesus then explained this scene to the Pharisee, who happened to be named Simon ...

> *"Two people owed money to a certain money lender. One owed him five hundred denarii, and the other fifty. Neither of them had the money to pay him back, so he forgave the debts of both. Now which of them will love him more?"*

The Depth of Grace

Simon replied, "I suppose the one who had the bigger debt forgiven."

"You have judged correctly," Jesus said. (Luke 7:41-43)

Many were ashamed to be in the same room with this woman. Some doubted Jesus because He allowed her to touch Him. Some rebuked the prostitute for the waste of perfume. But Jesus said, "I tell you, her many sins have been forgiven—as her great love has shown. But whoever has been forgiven little loves little" (Luke 7:47).

The idea that this prostitute may possibly be forgiven, set free from her shame, healed of her broken heart, and given a new life brought her to the feet of Jesus. When has Jesus ever turned someone away because of his or her sin? It never happened in God's Word: "But go and learn what this means: 'I desire mercy, not sacrifice.' For I have not come to call the righteous, but sinners" (Matthew 9:13). (Attention: The same perfume she used to seduce men, she used to anoint Jesus. It was the very fragrance of her sin.)

You know from earlier Rest Stops that I really identify with Simon Peter—and I think a lot of people in life do. He was an everyday guy and a dude who had more than his fair share of failures. But this story about the prostitute helped show me why Simon Peter loved Jesus more than any of the other disciples: it was because he was the biggest screw-up of the twelve! He was the greatest sinner in the group! Peter had the largest debt to God! That is why he loved Jesus more than the others. Every time Peter screwed up, Jesus forgave him. Every time Peter was forgiven, he fell more in love with Jesus. Simon Peter found himself caught in the grip of Christ's love.

What amount of sin can keep God's children from the love of Jesus? Check this out …

I give them eternal life, and they shall never perish; no one will snatch them out of my hand. My Father, who has given them to me, is greater than all; no one can snatch them out of my Father's hand. I and the Father are one. (John 10:28-30)

J. Bronson Haley

Understand something, though! This does **not** give us a license to sin. We shouldn't cheapen God's unending grace by sinning all we can simply because we know we'll be forgiven. Here's what the apostle Paul says …

> *What shall we say, then? Shall we go on sinning so that grace may increase? By no means! We are those who have died to sin; how can we live in it any longer? (Romans 6:1-2)*

Do we need a license to hurt ourselves? We will always have a free will and can hurt ourselves anytime we wish—and many times we will suffer the effects of our sins in the here and now (think of the physical and emotional effects that come with alcoholism, sexual sin, drug addiction, etc.), even though God's grace covers our sins through forgiveness. Beyond that, in heaven, our earthly sins may diminish our reward, as Paul wrote in 1 Corinthians 3:12-15. Yes, we'll be saved and make it to heaven, but we won't enjoy as many rich rewards. So how can sin ever be worth it once we're saved?

The good news, of course, is that, when we sin and are then forgiven, our faith will grow as a result of God confirming His Word yet again. We will love Jesus more than ever. Who or what is powerful enough to snatch us, children of God, out of the Father's hand? Our sin? Do you think God sees sin as greater than His Son? I seriously doubt God would say to Jesus, "Sorry, Son, but You didn't suffer enough when You were dying on the cross for the big sin that Bronson just committed." No way! The blood of Jesus is sufficient to cover our failures. The love of Christ is eternal and cannot be lost. Jesus takes us back every time we mess up, and when we return, we will love Him more than ever. That's the way it was written. And remember: "Do not go beyond what is written" (1 Corinthians 4:6). Love and forgiveness, forgiveness and love: that is the gospel of Jesus Christ.

CHAPTER 9

A Confused Alien

Keeping with my old wild and crazy lifestyle during my summer of sin, Turk and I met up with several friends at a local rave one Friday night. The building was fit for small concerts and events of that nature. There was a live band, but it was a rave, which drew a different crowd: mostly goth-type people dressed up in everything from Tinker Bell outfits to fireman suits. LSD was the drug of choice at raves at this time. So, to satisfy the demands of the consumer, light beams and various little light toys flashed throughout the crowd.

Our other friends were taking one hit of acid each at the direction of the dealer. So Turk and I took two apiece. When the LSD kicked in, we entered into another dimension. We should have realized what would have happened because the freaky people who took this drug often were only taking one hit each. I remember sitting in a chair in the back of the room with Turk trying to get a grip on what the heck was going on in the building. The room was dark and full of people trailing laser beams like they were Luke Skywalker.

As the hallucinations grew in intensity, the music came alive inside of me, and I began to move with the songs. After a few moments of this ridiculous behavior, I found myself up and dancing. *Wait a minute! What is going on?* I was dancing for sure, only I had lost my mind.

After I merged into the crowd and got acquainted with my new dancing talent, I took off my shirt and threw it across the room. I don't know why I did that. It seemed like a good idea at the time. So get the picture of the

J. Bronson Haley

moment here: all these people are decked out in rave attire, then there's me in my Dr. Martin boots, khaki pants, and no shirt right in the middle of everything. Obviously LSD was pretty new to me. I had only done it a couple of times. I was also on twice as much as most people at this party. I certainly had never taken this drug around people I did not know.

Many people were sitting around the dance floor in metal fold-up chairs. It seemed entertaining to me at the time to dance over to them, take their chairs out from under them, and dance away. After dancing around for a few minutes, chairs in hand, I returned and placed them where they belonged. The people sat back down like nothing happened. Maybe it wasn't that big of a deal, but I thought it was fantastic!

After dancing for two or three hours, Turk and I found ourselves in the restroom drinking water from the sink like a couple of thirsty dogs. We were both dehydrated from sweating. When I say we did not stop dancing the entire time we were there, I mean we did not stop dancing. I danced with myself in the mirror as Turk took his turn drinking from the sink. "Turk, look … you can see through my skin," I told him, as I observed myself in the mirror.

Most people who walked in the restroom while we were in there left quickly. I'm sure we were a bit scary to others who were hallucinating themselves. We were actually more of the wild field-party type.

During my turn to sink-drink, a dude—with thick black mascara around his eyes and spiked dog collars around his neck and wrists, and dressed in black—walked up and said to me, "It's my turn," as if he were going to strong-arm me or something.

"It sure is!" I said, grabbing him by the back of the neck, slamming his face into the sink, and encouraging him, "Get you some water, you @$#!ing freak!"

When I thought he'd had enough, I threw him out of the restroom. Even in our tripped-out state of mind, Turk and I quickly came to the conclusion that it was time for us to leave.

The ride to our friend Dan's house was nothing to be taken lightly. With the night air blowing in our hair, we were amazed that the cops we passed didn't pull us over. At one point we were stopped at a traffic light and a cop pulled up beside us on our right. Looking up at the light, it seemed to us that two beams stretched from the two red lights directly to our front tires, as if they were lanes that might lead us to the moon. When the traffic light changed, the beams turned green, and when we hit the accelerator, we went airborne. I couldn't believe that the cop did not

The Depth of Grace

arrest us, given that we had just launched into outer space right in front of him. It wasn't until a few moments later that I realized we were only hallucinating.

When we arrived at Dan's house, we relaxed a bit. While Turk did who knows what in the bathroom, I sat in the recliner and took note of the waves that seemed to whitecap in the blue carpet. I then caught a glimpse of motion in my peripheral vision. Quickly I stood up and peeked out the front door into the yard while standing in the middle of the living room. I was too spooked to get any closer to the door.

"Turk! Get in here quick! There's something standing in the yard!" I yelled.

"Bronson! You're just tripping," he assured me from the bathroom.

"Whatever the case may be, you don't want to miss this!"

A little alien stood in the yard looking into the house.

"Do you see what I see?" I asked Turk, as he stood beside me and looked.

"Oh my gosh, Bronson … it's a little alien," he said.

"I told you!"

He wasn't a scary-looking alien. We certainly were not afraid. As we walked together closer to the door, amazed at the sight, the little fellow took a few steps back like he was afraid of us. We then stepped back a few feet and Turk began to motion him in with his hands.

"We come in peace," Turk said. "Come on in. We won't hurt you."

We stood there for who knows how long trying to talk this alien into coming inside. It was probably only a few minutes, but it seemed like a long time. The little guy would walk closer, only to back off again. Back and forth. Back and forth. Finally, Turk got frustrated and charged the door with a howling grunt. That was the last time we saw our friend from outer space.

As I look back, I can't help but wonder if the little alien was a neighbor or one of Dan's friends who came to visit but was timid because two lunatics started to call him inside the house like he was from another planet—and then charged at him. Dan never mentioned this incident. As for me, all I can say is … oh the places that drugs will take you.

CHAPTER 10

Telephone Pole

Turk and I had a female friend who worked at a local daiquiri shop/bar. During the daytime she was the only one who worked there, and she always allowed Turk and me to drink. One afternoon during my summer of sin, we sat down at the bar and ordered two flaming Doctor Peppers each, back-to-back. The bartender poured beer into a glass and then set a shot of Bacardi 151 on fire just prior to dropping it into the glass of beer. The idea was to slam the drink as fast as you could just after the bartender dropped the flaming liquor into beer. I know. It seems ridiculous: "Whoever can poison his brain the fastest wins!"

After we danced on the bar with our friend, we ordered a gallon of daiquiris with extra shots of Everclear and left. This liquor is twice the strength of vodka. As soon as we got to Dan's house, I had Turk hide my keys so that I couldn't do anything stupid in my Jeep. That's the last thing I remember about that day.

I awoke in a cold room with a severe headache at around midnight. I took note that I was wearing a pair of shorts and one sandal. After I looked around the room, my heart got a serious injection of fear.

"Oh my gosh! What did I do?" I asked myself in a panic.

I demanded answers from the five or six men in the holding cell with me.

"Somebody tell me what is going on!" I yelled.

In a panic I banged on the glass window separating us from our freedom.

87

J. Bronson Haley

"Somebody talk to me!" I screamed to the officers at the desk just outside of the cell.

I guess they were used to this kind of behavior. They didn't even flinch at my efforts to get their attention.

For several hours I pondered the severity of my situation. I had no idea why I had been arrested. I settled down a bit when I put two and two together and realized I wasn't injured. This fact gave me hope that I didn't hurt anyone. I knew for sure that, whatever happened, I had messed up my chances to return to Evangel Christian Academy for my senior year, which had been a hope of mine—because I knew that, even though I had asked Jesus into my life, I was still heading down a path that would only lead to a lot of pain and problems.

Finally, an officer led me down a long hall with three people standing at the end. My mother, stepfather, and an unfamiliar individual watched as I approached them wearing my unusual getup of a pair of shorts and one sandal.

"Where are your clothes, honey?" my mom asked. "Where is your other sandal?"

"Mom, I don't know. I don't even know why I'm here."

Turns out my Jeep and I met a telephone pole on a neighborhood street as I rounded a corner (I still don't know how I got my keys to even be driving my Jeep). An officer had been standing at the door of a home a couple houses down when I crashed. He then walked over and addressed me as I sat quietly in my Jeep. When I didn't respond, he reached over to take the keys out of my ignition, and I shoved him away and fled the scene of the accident in my vehicle. The officer mentioned to my mother that I only drove five miles per hour for around one mile. I then pulled over and he arrested me for DUI. He later stated that it was obvious that I didn't have any idea where I was or what I was doing. The officer was just glad I didn't kill myself or someone else. He could have charged me with felony evasion.

Looking back, I have to ask myself: did God intervene that night, not only to save my life and maybe the lives of others, but also to keep me out of even deeper trouble with the law—trouble that would have definitely kept me out of the Christian school (though I knew my chances were slim enough after my DUI)? That night had been no different than many other nights—only I got caught, which wasn't really a good sign that God had been intervening. I mean, He could have had me not get arrested at all, right? Then again, at the time, I had already asked Jesus in my heart

The Depth of Grace

and been saved, but I sure didn't know God or follow His ways—and the thought that He might have intervened did not even cross my mind.

But I know one thing about that night: after leaving the holding cell with my family, I knew that I missed Jesus deeply and I wished I hadn't messed up ... again.

6TH REST STOP:
DARKEST HOUR

On the first day of the Festival of Unleavened Bread, when it was customary to sacrifice the Passover lamb, Jesus' disciples asked him, "Where do you want us to go and make preparations for you to eat the Passover?" (Mark 14:12)

By the time that Jesus and His disciples gathered around the table for the Lord's Supper, Simon Peter was overflowing with glorious love for Jesus. He had screwed up so many times by this point that the love was just bubbling over. After supper Peter and the other disciples boasted about who would be the greatest among them. I can hear Peter now, "Guys, be real before the Lord! Don't you remember? I am the 'Rock!' The gates of Hades shall not overcome me! Talk to Jesus about my high calling if you have a problem with it. He chose me!"

In response Jesus said, "Simon, Simon, Satan has asked to sift all of you as wheat. But I have prayed for you, Simon, that your faith may not fail. And when you have turned back, strengthen your brothers'" (Luke 22:31-32). When Jesus referred to Peter as "Simon," I think He was reminding him of his past sins and how worthless he was before Jesus came into his life. Jesus also predicted in this Scripture that Peter would soon fail and return to his past life. Ouch! Simon was hurt that Jesus would bring up his past and doubt him, given that he thought he had become the super-disciple of the twelve.

The Depth of Grace

> *But [Peter] replied, "Lord, I am ready to go with you to prison and to death."*
>
> *Jesus answered, "I tell you, Peter, before the rooster crows today, you will deny three times that you know me." (Luke 22:33-34)*

Whoa! This comment hurt Peter. He was deeply in love with the Lord. He knew Jesus was troubled, given that His time of suffering was nearing. Peter was hurt because Jesus doubted his love and faithfulness at a time like that.

A bit later, when Jesus sensed that His time of suffering was at hand, he took Simon Peter, John, and James with him to Gethsemane so that He could pray in peace. "'My soul is overwhelmed with sorrow to the point of death,' he said to them. 'Stay here and keep watch'" (Mark 14:34). This was a perfect opportunity for Peter to prove to Jesus how much he loved Him and that he would not disown Him, no matter what.

Keep in mind: Jesus had never been this troubled before. The disciples never saw Jesus worried about anything. Jesus was the Son of the living God! All the angels in heaven were at His disposal. He was (and is) the great I AM! But in this particular moment, His soul was "overwhelmed with sorrow to the point of death"? Really? Wow. Just think about how the disciples must have been feeling when they saw Jesus like that. Jesus was their only source of strength, and I'll bet the thought of sharing the Good News without Him terrified them.

The disciples were also deeply sorrowful because Jesus had already told them that he would soon face one of the most horrible kinds of death in history: death by crucifixion. Peter might have loved Jesus the most, but the others loved Him as well. The disciples were very aware of the severity of the torture Jesus would soon face. They feared for Jesus and were troubled because He was troubled. They also feared for themselves. "If they are able to capture Jesus and crucify Him, what will happen to us?" Jesus called them to preach the gospel to God's chosen people—the very people who would support Jesus being nailed to the cross in just a few hours. These people who would soon crucify Jesus were the whole reason He came to earth in the first place. He loved His people so much that He was willing to suffer the most horrible death imaginable so that they could be set free from the grip of Satan, and spend eternity with Him. Jesus was depending on His disciples to reach His people.

J. Bronson Haley

By this time these apostles of God fully understood their purpose in life. However, they came to understand that they did not have the strength and courage it would take to fulfill their calling. The disciples were a nervous wreck and they could do nothing about the fear inside of them. Failure seemed certain and this truth no doubt tormented these men to the point of near insanity.

> *He withdrew about a stone's throw beyond them, knelt down and prayed, "Father, if you are willing, take this cup from me; yet not my will, but yours be done." An angel from heaven appeared to him and strengthened him. And being in anguish, he prayed more earnestly, and his sweat was like drops of blood falling to the ground.*
>
> *When he rose from prayer and went back to the disciples, he found them asleep, exhausted from sorrow....*
>
> *"Simon," he said to Peter, "are you asleep? Couldn't you keep watch for one hour?" (Luke 22:41-44 and Mark 14:37)*

Ouch! This is the second instance Jesus referred to Peter as "Simon." Again Jesus reminded him of his failure. Not only did Simon screw up again while Jesus prayed, but Jesus rebuked him specifically when He found them sleeping. Peter was failing his Lord during their last moments together. He was failing Jesus when the Lord needed him the most. At the same time, Peter was no doubt giving Jesus his best effort. And then Jesus rebuked *him* and not the others.

> *Returning the third time, he said to them, "Are you still sleeping and resting? Enough! The hour has come. Look, the Son of Man is betrayed into the hands of sinners. Rise! Let us go! Here comes my betrayer!" (Mark 14:41-42)*

Peter was at loss for words by this point. And you can bet that James and John paid close attention, as they so desperately needed Peter to survive. Jesus, their leader, was overwhelmed with sorrow and fear to the point of death. In a state of bewildered delusional shock, with his eyes half closed, Peter watched as ...

The Depth of Grace

... Judas, one of the Twelve, appeared. With him was a crowd armed with swords and clubs, sent from the chief priests, the teachers of the law, and the elders.

Now the betrayer had arranged a signal with them: "The one I kiss is the man; arrest him and lead him away under guard." Going at once to Jesus, Judas said, "Rabbi!" and kissed him. (Mark 14:43-45)

In a desperate attempt to protect his Lord and prove his faithfulness, Peter called forth every ounce of strength and courage at his disposal ...

Then Simon Peter, who had a sword, drew it and struck the high priest's servant, cutting off his right ear. (The servant's name was Malchus.)

Jesus commanded Peter, "Put your sword away! Shall I not drink the cup the Father has given me?" (John 18:10-11)

Peter's best was simply not enough. He was rebuked for his absolute best effort to win back the Lord's trust and prove his love for Him. On top of that, Jesus then basically said that He didn't even need Peter in the first place: "'Put your sword back in its place,' Jesus said to him, 'for all who draw the sword will die by the sword. Do you think I cannot call on my father, and he will at once put at my disposal more than twelve legions of angels?'" (Matthew 26:52-53). Ouch!

This was a bad day in the life of Simon Peter. Jesus had told Peter that he'd disown him, even though Peter swore his allegiance, even to death. Then he'd fallen asleep when Jesus wanted him to keep watch, and he was rebuked by the Lord whom he loved so much. Finally, a friend and a fellow disciple betrayed the love of his life with a kiss—and Peter was again rebuked when he tried to do something to stop the betrayal. Jesus was then led off to be tortured at the hands of cruel men—whom Jesus loved.

The Lord was depending on Peter to complete His mission by establishing the church. Yet Peter failed over and over again at the most crucial time in his walk with the Lord. Can we even begin to fathom the emotions running through this man whom Jesus once referred to as the "Rock"?

When the guards seized Jesus, His disciples deserted Him just as He had formerly predicted. One was so frightened that he ran off naked: "When they seized him, he fled naked, leaving his garment behind"

J. Bronson Haley

(Mark 14:51-52). Whoops! I guess that Peter wasn't the only one being humbled.

> *Simon Peter and another disciple were following Jesus. Because this disciple was known to the high priest, he went with Jesus into the high priest's courtyard, but Peter had to wait outside at the door. The other disciple, who was known to the high priest, came back, spoke to the girl on duty there and brought Peter in. (John 18:15-16)*

We are not sure exactly what was going through Peter's mind during this walk and upon entering into the priest's courtyard. We know he was overwhelmed with sorrow, failure, and fear to say the least. I'm sure he wanted Jesus to know for sure how much he loved Him. Jesus had previously mentioned being overwhelmed with sorrow to the point of death. Now, in the courtyard of the high priest, Jesus was being mocked, spit on, and beaten after being betrayed by one of His own and deserted by the rest. Peter knew Jesus was human like him and that He was hurting deeply. He probably felt that Jesus still thought he would deny him three times. Peter wanted Him to know for sure how much he loved Him and didn't want Jesus to feel as though he would deny Him during His darkest, most lonely hour on earth. So he followed along to watch, but, as he encountered a girl at the door, that's when it happened …

> *"You aren't one of his disciples too, are you?" she asked Peter.*
>
> *He replied, "I am not."*
>
> *It was cold, and the servants and officials stood around a fire they had made to keep warm. Peter also was standing with them, warming himself.…*
>
> *Meanwhile, Simon Peter was still standing there warming himself, so they asked him, "You aren't one of his disciples too, are you?"*
>
> *He denied it, saying, "I am not."*
>
> *One of the high priest's servants, a relative of the man whose ear Peter had cut off, challenged him, "Didn't I see you with him in the garden?"*

The Depth of Grace

Again Peter denied it…. (John 18:17-18, 25-27)

Now if that wasn't bad luck, I don't know what is! Was there a worse person to run into at this forsaken time in history? We know that the man whose ear Peter cut off was now out preaching the gospel after Jesus put his ear put back on in seconds without a needle and thread. And now the man's relative confronts Peter at this time? Overwhelmed with confusion, shock, fear, doubt, love, and many other emotions mixed together, Peter seems to have temporarily lost his mind …

> *Then [Peter] began to call down curses, and he swore to them, "I don't know the man!" Immediately a rooster crowed…. The Lord turned and looked straight at Peter. Then Peter remembered the word the Lord had spoken to him: "Before the rooster crows today, you will disown me three times." And he went outside and wept bitterly. (Matthew 26:75 and Luke 22:61-62)*

Not only did Peter end up denying Jesus three times, but he did it in the presence of the Lord being mocked, spit on, and beaten. To top it all off, immediately after Peter called down curses on himself, Jesus turned and made eye contact with him. I'm sure he did run off and weep bitterly.

As Jesus predicted, Peter returned to His old life a complete and utter failure. I'm not certain, but I feel that, during the next few days of his life, Simon often referred to many of the things Jesus taught him over the past three years …

> *"I am the vine; you are the branches. If you remain in me and I in you, you will bear much fruit; apart from me you can do nothing. If you do not remain in me, you are like a branch that is thrown away and withers; such branches are picked up, thrown into the fire and burned." (John 15:5-6)*

We do not know everything Peter did while Jesus hung on the cross and lay in the tomb. He certainly wasn't there to support Him while He was on the cross. The only disciple at the crucifixion was John: "the disciple whom Jesus loved" (John 13:23). We do know that Peter and the other disciples spent much of their time hiding behind locked doors in those days following Jesus' death. They were afraid of the Jews, the very people to whom Jesus wanted them to preach the gospel. As I talked about earlier,

J. Bronson Haley

Jesus longed to have fellowship with His people. That's why He suffered in the first place. The heart of the Father so burned for His people that He sent His Son to suffer the curse of their sin in full so that they would not have to. The disciples had failed Jesus and now fully understood that they would not be able to fulfill the call on their lives. Peter was the biggest failure of them all. And he was the one whom Jesus trusted the most.

During these three long days when the Lord was in the tomb, I am certain Peter recalled the times he and Jesus had together. He probably chuckled when he remembered the stupid things he said in front of Moses and Elijah during Jesus' transfiguration on the mountain. Peter surely thought about the time he walked out onto the water on impulse and began to sink when the wind blew and he lost his focus. He probably wept when he recalled Jesus holding out His hand and grinning at Peter's childlike faith. But now Peter had blown it big time and there was no second chance. Where would Peter find the courage to preach Jesus to God's people when he wouldn't even confess that he knew Jesus, or wouldn't even be caught dead in public during the crucifixion? We know that Jesus rose from the dead, but at the time, Peter and the other disciples did not yet understand this principle: "They still did not understand from Scripture that Jesus had to rise from the dead" (John 20:9).

I'm sure Peter cried aloud when he pictured Jesus hanging on the cross, battered and broken, and being mocked by the very people He was sent to earth to suffer for. Certainly Peter cried tears upon recalling the fact that Jesus, His Lord, suffered for nothing because of his own failures. And yet we know that Jesus wasn't finished with Peter—despite all of his failures. As dark as this hour was for Peter, a new day would soon dawn for him, one that was bright and shining with Jesus' love and forgiveness. And that's reason enough for any of us to have hope.

CHAPTER 11

Bricktown

With the end of the 1997 summer approaching, Dan threw a keg party at his house with plans to go downtown afterward with his friends. Along with a good friend named Johnny Calvert, Turk and I joined the party—to no one's surprise. By this time Dan often invited people over just to watch us. We always added a unique twist to the party. We were seventeen-year-old psychopaths who knew how to keep the party jumping. We immediately took some pills strong enough to kill a horse and proceeded with keg pushups. By the time the party was ready to relocate, the three of us were ready as well.

After being carded by the bouncer who worked the door of Bricktown— the largest club in downtown Shreveport—we walked about a hundred feet down past the front door and hung out. I have very little memory of anything that took place up until this point. I remember my legs feeling a little wobbly shortly after I took the pills and did keg pushups. Two or three hours later, as we hung out downtown, I began to actually be cognizant of my surroundings. I can't remember what Turk and Johnny said to the random people who walked by that night, but I do remember a man who crowded Johnny with an evident attitude. It looked to me as if he were trying to intimidate my friend.

"Hold on just a dadgum minute!" I said, interrupting him. "Why in the heck do you want to fight him? Why don't you pick on someone your own size? As a matter of fact, why don't you follow me?"

J. Bronson Haley

Stop and realize something: this was my rear end talking. The man was around six-two and 200 pounds. I was six foot and 170 pounds. I was also seventeen years old. We found out later that he was twenty-three. A sober battle with this fellow would have been very risky. I was in no condition to fight anyone at this time.

Anyway, we were about two hundred yards from Red River. A bridge began to slope upward at the entrance of the club. I encouraged him to follow me under the bridge because it was dark, and people couldn't see us fight from the club.

As I walked under the bridge, I was making my third mistake. The first mistake was deciding to fight in my condition. The second mistake was fighting a grown man who outweighed me by around thirty pounds. My third mistake was turning my back on this person, given my first and second mistake. (The fact that I was a drunken kid downtown was a different kind of mistake.) When I turned to square off with the man, I was blindsided and fell to the concrete. I had taken some serious punches in my day. However, a shot to the temple from this large guy with a build was rough. Shortly after I hit the ground, I propped myself up on one elbow. It took me a few seconds to gather my thoughts.

Dadgum, that hurt!

After I shook my head a bit, I looked up at this jerk-off who stood around ten feet away observing the fruit of his knockout punch with a smirk. This would have been a proper time to get angry; however, this was no time to lose my temper. Propped up on my elbow with a poo-poo-eating grin on my face, I said to the man, "You done #@%$ed up now!"

I wasn't as crazy as that last statement made me out to be. Fighting was the only thing at which I was well accomplished. My pride was hurt, and I was also very competitive. Intimidation was the only thing I could get going for me at this point. I know, I know … it sounds ridiculous to try and intimidate someone from the ground. But I had to think of something. Intimidation is the only way to go when in trouble. When outnumbered or fighting over one's head, like fighting this older stronger man, it's important to make him think you know something he doesn't. If it appears that someone on the streets is more confident than he should be, then he probably has a reason. Either he has a weapon, more people on his side, or he is very, very tough. Intimidation also causes people to question themselves and they hesitate as a result. Hesitation is a big no-no in a street fight.

The Depth of Grace

I realize the situation with this man was extreme. (And, yes, I no longer support violence!) The more trouble one is in, the more extreme he needs to be to overcome. When I made that comment and jumped to my feet, it scared the heck out of this fellow.

"Dude, get your boy! Get your boy!" he said as he grabbed Turk and used him as a shield.

"Dude, you're the one that $%&*ed up!" Turk said, as he pulled away from the man.

I threw the first punch and followed with several others before I backed out of his reach. At this time he took off his shirt and intimidated me a bit—this dude was ripped!

I knew by this time that I was not going to win a slugfest. When I came in the second time, he expected me to do the same thing as before. He expected an exchange of punches—most guys do in a fight like this. So I threw a right as I came in, but halfway into the punch, I ducked my head and tackled him. I did this because I knew that, the second time in, an opponent usually throws a punch too, and the dude I was fighting did just that, so I actually ducked under his punch. Plus it's easier to tackle someone when his weight has shifted into my direction.

We fought for around five or six minutes. An average street fight is around thirty seconds. Yeah—this was the real deal. Back and forth, we threw blow after blow. I used everything I'd ever learned and could not get an advantage. I was outweighed, outlived, and out of my element, but experienced enough only to keep him guessing. If he were going to knock me out, it would have happened on that first punch. And he knew that. Finally the man quit.

"I'm finished," he said and retrieved his shirt.

"Wait just a minute! I assumed that because you blindsided me in the %$@#ing temple that you wanted to fight. What the %$#@ is the problem? What in the $%&# do you mean you're finished?" I asked.

"You're bleeding. You probably have a concussion. Enough is enough. I'm done," he said.

"There is nothing wrong with me, you dumb-a## who decided to take a cheap shot on a teenager! I feel good enough to eventually kick your $%#@!" I said.

"No. I'm done," he said as he and his friend walked toward the club.

Don't let my talk fool you. I only said all that because I didn't have any sense. In reality I was finished when I propped myself up on my elbow after his first punch. I wasn't winning at the time he quit and seriously doubt I would have won had we continued to fight. I had a cracked nose and a severely swollen temple. I was hurt—and fortunate that the man quit when he did.

I used the white T-shirt I was wearing to try and stop my nose from bleeding. After five minutes of standing under the bridge, an officer walked up and escorted the three of us to the nearest bench at the door of the club. By this time, I was covered in blood, and my nose continued to bleed. After a few moments of speaking with the man I fought, his friend, and a couple of witnesses, the officer returned and said, "All three of you are going to jail!"

Turk didn't like the idea of going to jail, considering he wasn't the one fighting.

"I ain't going to jail!" he said, as he stood up. "He was the one fighting, not me!"

"Well, guess what? You have the right to remain silent." And the officer read Turk his rights. "You two can go," he said to Johnny and me.

Turk was arrested for public intoxication. Johnny and I headed back to Dan's house to sleep for the night.

These stories from that summer of sin are a bit funny at times and certainly extreme. However, there was nothing actually fun about that summer. Living in sin after being saved is nothing like living in sin and not ever having known freedom. Nothing compares to the love of God, and I honestly missed Him every day. Before being saved, this kind of partying and foolishness was all I knew. I didn't know any other way to live back then. When I was saved and met Jesus, something real happened in my heart. I had peace in my life and was happy. When I fell back into sin, I experienced the very thing that someone told me would happen: I was worse off than before. I cussed more, I drank more, and I did more drugs than ever. My behavior when I propped up on my elbow in this fight was no doubt a result of this increase in wickedness. If I hit a kid dead in the temple with a right and he hit the ground, propped up on his elbow, shook his head, looked up at me with a smile, and said, "You done %$#*ed up now!"—I would have been scared. But nothing scared me anymore—except a mad woman, maybe.

That summer was the fastest and most dangerous time of my life. I was a loose cannon capable of anything at any moment. I spent a lot of time wishing I had not messed up. I spent hours trying to figure out how to make up for my mistakes. I wished I could go back to Evangel, forget my failures, and start over in my walk with God. However, I realized how

The Depth of Grace

bad I had messed up and knew I had ruined my chances at Evangel. So I sucked it up and moved forward—resigning myself to the fact that I had pretty much thrown away my new life in Christ.

7TH REST STOP:
THE SACRIFICE

It was obvious when I read the book of Acts that Simon Peter eventually took on a leadership role and served the Lord with great power and authority. However, I didn't understand exactly what happened that transformed him from a scared, broken-down disciple to this mighty man of God. I certainly could identify with Peter's failures. I understood what it felt like to be defeated, feeling like I had done the best I could for Jesus, but still failing miserably. I understood what it was like to be in love with Him and continue to hurt Him over and over again. I know that Peter felt the same way. Did either of us need a man of God to comfort us, or to tell us to buck up and look forward to better days ahead? We wouldn't have listened. We did the best we could and our best was not enough.

So I was extremely curious to know how Peter was able to forgive himself and move on. How did Simon Peter receive forgiveness, knowing he would most likely screw up again? I didn't understand until I received insight into the depths of the sacrifice.

High on OxyContin, I noticed in the Old Testament that, during the Jewish Passover celebration, God's people would choose their best lamb for a sin offering so that their sins could be forgiven. The priest would then examine the sacrifice to make sure it was worthy to cover their sins. If the sacrifice was without defect, the priest would offer forgiveness for their sins. I took note that the priest never examined the person. He always examined the sacrifice. If the priest found the sacrifice worthy, their sins were forgiven.

The Depth of Grace

I wept as I recalled Jesus being referred to as the Lamb of God in the book of John: "John saw Jesus coming toward him and said, 'Look, the Lamb of God, who takes away the sin of the world!'" (John 1:29). I already knew that Jesus died so that our sins could be forgiven. I understood that He had purchased our sins with His blood and that, upon accepting Him as Lord and Savior, we would be set free from the curse of sin and receive eternal life. However, I didn't understand the truth hidden in the depths of His blood regarding repentance.

Most of us already know that we no longer have to bring sin offerings to be forgiven of our sins ⊠. God has provided us with a perfect sacrifice. Jesus is our sacrifice without defect. When He died at Calvary and three days later rose from the dead, Jesus made available to us forgiveness and eternal life—free of charge! What an incredible gift! Today He sits on His throne at the right hand of the Father in all of His glory. When we repent, we kneel before the throne of grace and ask God for forgiveness. So where is the extraordinary good news? Consider this …

My shame would not allow me to receive forgiveness or to forgive myself, and you know why. I simply could not return to God a complete and total failure and force the sin-infested aroma of my addiction and failures into the nostrils of the Almighty. I was too ashamed to come into His presence, much less ask for anything. So here's the good news: the Lord does not examine us when we come into His presence to repent! It makes perfect sense if you think about it: God the Father understands better than we do that we cannot fight the demons in our lives without His Son. The Lord understands that demons are stronger than us! And why would God allow us to return to His presence in good shape after rejecting His Son and His sufferings in the first place? When we return to God, why would the Lord examine us? Not going to happen, people! He examines Jesus who sits at his right hand!

"But, Bronson! One more thing! What about the ridiculous weight of my dinosaur-sized sin?" Tell me this: because of which of your sins will the Father say to His Son, "Jesus, My plan was not perfect after all … I'm terribly sorry, but You did not suffer enough for this person"? Not going to happen! The truth is that He did suffer enough, so His blood covers the darkest of our sins. Let's face it: we feel better when we pay the price for what we do wrong, whether we admit it or not. Would death by crucifixion be sufficient punishment for your horrible sin? Well, good for you! Jesus already paid the price! How many of us understand that the Lamb of God

J. Bronson Haley

is found worthy every time He is examined? No amount of sin can rob Him of this glory!

One other principle concerning repentance is very important to understand when you struggle to find the strength to forgive yourself or accept forgiveness. This next concept will give you the strength to repent under any circumstance, no matter how severe the shame may be: should we be too ashamed to go to the Father and accept the sufferings of His Son as sufficient to cover our failures? Or should we be more ashamed to tell Jesus, "I appreciate that You suffered horribly on the cross at the hands of the most skilled professional torture man in history—the Roman-era Hannibal Lecter, so to speak. However, You did not suffer enough for me!"

I may mess up tomorrow. You may mess up tomorrow. However, we will never be able to justifiably tell Jesus that He didn't suffer enough for us to be able to offer forgiveness to us.

CHAPTER 12

—

Transcripts

I pondered the magnitude of my summer of sin as I lay in bed with the phone in my hand. I was still enrolled at Evangel and didn't want to leave the teachers, the people, this place. However, I didn't have any choice because of my many failures. After a couple of hours of wrestling with fear and sorrow, I dialed the number.

"Evangel Christian Academy," the lady said.

"Hi, this is Bronson. Will you please transfer my transcripts to Byrd High School for me?" I asked.

The lady paused for a moment. "Bronson, let me have you talk to Mrs. Ellis, okay?" she said.

Mrs. Ellis was one of the ladies I loved most at Evangel. She taught English and worked as a counselor in the office. Every time she spoke to me, I felt like she loved me, and I knew she believed in me. I never understood why, but I knew she did. I was going to miss this wonderful lady. By the time she answered the phone, tears rolled down my face. I didn't let her know I was upset.

"Mrs. Ellis, I have decided to go back to Byrd and need you to send my transcripts," I said.

"Bronson, I will give you your transcripts. But you are going to have to come and get them."

"Okay, I'll be there shortly."

My salvation was a big deal at Evangel. Many of the students knew who I was before I arrived the previous semester. My name stood out in the

105

crowd, and because of my behavior many of the students knew the kind of person I was. They knew I used to fight, party, and get into trouble. The teachers embraced me and loved my story. God did something real in me when I was saved, and the change was obvious to everyone. During my first semester many teachers mentioned to me over and over again that God was going to use me one day to minister the gospel. *These people are crazy!* I thought every time they said something like that. Even the kids would tell me these things at random. I didn't understand why they were saying this, but it made me feel good. I didn't know why, but the people at this school loved me and believed in me.

It took every ounce of strength I had to get out of my Jeep and walk into the office. I had a black eye that was bleeding into my other eye thanks to the brutal fight I'd had with the older guy near the Bricktown club. My nose was fractured and my temple was still a bit swollen. The people at Evangel were the only ones who had ever believed in me, so I was extremely ashamed. However, I needed my transcripts.

When I walked into the office, the staff was busy with paperwork in preparation for the start of school. As I entered, though, everyone stopped what he or she was doing and acknowledged me. I received a hug from everyone in the office. I felt like the most important person in the room and struggled to keep from crying. After I requested my transcripts, Mrs. Ellis sat me down in the conference room, so it was just the two of us.

"Bronson, please don't leave us," she said.

"Mrs. Ellis, you don't understand. I've been in sin all summer. I have failed miserably. It will be better if you just give me my transcripts and let me go."

Please understand: this wasn't what I wanted. This school was the best thing that ever happened to me. I think Mrs. Ellis knew this, which is why she wasn't going to accept my leaving without saying something to me.

"Bronson, we are all sinners," she said. "Everyone in this building has messed up. If you leave us, it will be because you choose to leave. It will not be because we don't love you and don't want you to stay."

We talked some more and after a hug she gave me my transcripts—and I left. When I climbed into my Jeep, I broke down and began to cry.

"Who loves people this way?" I asked myself.

I didn't deserve to be allowed back into that private school. I was not strong enough to forgive myself for screwing up like I did. I didn't have the strength to return to that place. However, the love I received on that day was stronger than I. Mrs. Ellis loved me when I didn't deserve her love.

The Depth of Grace

This love pierced my heart and gave me the strength to forgive myself and receive forgiveness.

A few days later I met with my youth pastor and rededicated my life to the Lord. I ended up returning to Evangel for my senior year, and God completely restored me. I got involved in the local church and began to share my testimony. When I talked, people listened. I didn't understand why, but they did, and many appreciated the things I said. God also gave me a new home and a family who welcomed me as their own. I woke up to my childhood dreams every morning. God gave me more than I needed and continued to blow my mind every day. I received the James Landers Award at graduation for being the most turned-around student in my class. At the end of the ceremony, I gave a short word from the Lord and closed with the benediction. No doubt remained in my mind that Jesus was the only good in the world that I lived in.

CHAPTER 13

SOS
(Sold-Out Saturday)

One evening a man from Australia arrived at the home of the family I was living with. He was an evangelist and traveled the globe spreading the Word of God. The oldest daughter of the household met him online, and a few weeks later I gave up my bed so he had a place to sleep. Ouch!

I'd never met a man of God quite like this one before and was suspicious of his every move. He was sold out for Christ, for sure, or so it seemed! The guy wouldn't even wear a T-shirt without the name of Jesus written on it somewhere. Of course, this was all fine and dandy. But something was up with this fellow brother in Christ and I watched him like a hawk.

The man's name was Denny. He stayed for a week, and I noticed that every night he would go upstairs by himself into the exercise room for about an hour. In this room was a treadmill and a StairMaster. The room also had a couch and a television set.

What is this guy doing? I asked myself each night.

He carried a bag with him upstairs and he went by himself.

Ah-hah ... he is looking at pornography.

The last night of his visit, he asked me if I'd like to come upstairs with him.

"Nah, I'm going to stay down here and read my Bible," I said, trying to subtly convict him.

"Brother, the Lord has asked me to pray for you," he said.

109

After I followed him up the stairs and into the room, I found a safe place to stand two feet from the foot of the door. He looked at me a little funny when I opened the door right after he shut it.

I don't know you, sir, I thought.

When he turned off the lights, I was certain something was up with this man. I was familiar with séances from my past experience with Stepmother and had learned about all I needed to escort this stranger out of the house and into the street. I was relieved a bit when he turned on the lamp. He then went for his bag and I stood at attention. I relaxed a little when he pulled out a CD and asked me, "Do you like *Winds of Worship?*"

After he put a CD into the stereo and turned up the volume, he told me to shut myself away with the Lord and worship His Son. When I began to worship Jesus, the presence of the Lord filled the room. I didn't know what it was about the dim lighting, but it had an effect on me. I think it was because I felt more alone with God. I felt very close to the Lord, and my faith increased as a result. A few moments later Denny walked over and prayed with me. It was a powerful prayer, and I recognized him as a man of God for the first time. We were upstairs for around two hours praying and seeking the Lord. The only other place I had experienced the presence of God like this was during worship at church.

The next day Denny caught a plane and headed north to preach the gospel. I headed to the Christian bookstore and purchased some worship music. I bought the two CDs we listened to the night before and found myself worshiping the Lord every day, sometimes for hours at a time. This time with God changed my life. If I became discouraged throughout the day, I was encouraged when I shut myself away with God and worshiped Him. When I became overwhelmed with doubt and confusion during the day, my faith was increased and my mind was renewed when I lifted my hands and sang to the Lord. I didn't know what was happening at the time, but something was happening and it was wonderful.

One evening while in prayer upstairs, I imagined kids in the balcony of the youth sanctuary at our church. They walked around with their hands lifted high and worshiped the Lord. I wasn't sure if this was a vision or my imagination. I didn't give it much thought, either.

Two weeks later my youth pastor asked me if I'd lead a Bible study for the youth on Saturday nights.

"Let me think it over, and I'll get back with you," I told him.

The following week I began to think about the night I envisioned the kids in the balcony of the youth sanctuary as I prayed. I wasn't sure what

The Depth of Grace

this "vision" meant or if it meant anything at all. The sanctuary could hold a thousand people. Our youth meeting on Wednesday nights brought around two hundred fifty kids to the service. A prayer meeting on Saturday nights for the youth? Kids in the balcony?

The next time I saw my youth pastor, I told him that I'd be glad to do something for the kids on Saturday nights.

"Can we start out by praying?" I asked him.

"Bronson, you do whatever you want. I trust you," he said.

I bought ten colored poster boards and wrote something different on each one. One read, "Pastoral Staff," another "Sunday Morning Service," and one even read, "Sink the Boats" (we have river boat casinos in our town). I made stands for the signs so I could set them up on stage for the meeting.

This will help keep the focus of the kids, I thought.

After dimming the lights very low, I turned on the four spotlights in the balcony and beamed them down at four of the signs. The spotlights had several alternative colors to use. I was trying to somewhat appeal to the kids. I would not have argued if a pastor had walked in and, after he looked around, said to me, "You're crazy."

"Thank you for confirming my suspicions, sir," would have been the nature of my response.

The first night four kids showed up. I briefly discussed with them the vision I had for this Saturday night.

"We are going to pray for a miracle. When we get our miracle, we will do something else. Stay here while I turn on some music."

We then all joined hands in a circle and opened in prayer. When we began to pray, the glory of God filled the room. We all roamed the sanctuary, hands lifted high, and prayed for two and a half hours.

The next Saturday was even more powerful than the first. We only had three kids, other than myself, but the power of God was so strong that at times I had to sit down because my legs felt weak. While observing the other kids, I noticed they seemed a little weak themselves. I didn't know exactly what was going on, but whatever it was, it was good and we didn't want to leave. Again, we worshiped and prayed for around two and a half hours.

Within two months forty-plus kids were showing up on Saturday nights to pray and worship the Lord. The kids ranged from ages ten to eighteen. A couple of adults even came regularly. Sure enough, kids began

111

J. Bronson Haley

to roam up to the balcony with their hands lifted high. Sometimes as many as fifteen to twenty were in the balcony at a time.

Was it a vision that I had? Was it my imagination? I don't know nor do I care. God did something amazing for the youth on Saturday nights at our church and they fell in love with Jesus. Christ was honored on this often lonely night and that's what matters.

8TH REST STOP:
BREATH OF GOD

Then he said to me, "Prophesy to the breath; prophesy, son of man, and say to it, 'This is what the Sovereign LORD says: Come, breath, from the four winds and breathe into these slain, that they may live.'" (Ezekiel 37:9)

During my second trip through the New Testament, I read a story that I'd read several times before about a certain man, but strangely enough it seemed like we had some things in common during this particular reading. This fellow was well known in his hometown. His life was dramatic and caught the attention of many throughout the years. His name stood out among the crowd just as my name stood out. There was a day when this man walked with his head high and made a difference in the lives of many people. However, he became very sick. Due to his sickness, he entered into a life of shame and seclusion—away from his past life—away from his family—and there was no going back.

I imagined that this man sometimes caught himself daydreaming about the hugs and kisses he had once received from his family. He'd smile as he rolled back time and pondered the treasured moments of his past life. He often wept when he thought about the pain he caused those who once believed in him. The man often wept aloud when he was reminded that his condition carried with it a death sentence and that he would never again return to the life he once lived to be embraced by those who loved him and those whom he loved. This person was trapped in a life of shame and

113

J. Bronson Haley

seclusion and was sentenced to death. His name was Simon (not Simon Peter, mind you), and he had leprosy.

Simon spent his time with a group of people who shared his illness. He and his new friends had everything in common. Those he hung out with were also consumed with shame and failure. They didn't feel so shameful when they were in seclusion. It was when they entered into the public that they covered their faces. When they came into the presence of "normal" people, the law demanded that they cry out, "Unclean! Unclean!" This group of lonely people embraced each other in their sickness and died one by one.

One day Simon was in the streets, warning the public to clear a path, when he caught a glimpse of an energetic bunch huddled together exchanging stories. These people were excited about something. Simon crept closer in an attempt to hear what they talked about. He didn't get too close because he didn't want to alarm them.

Simon listened as these people talked about an unusual man in town. It seemed that when this particular man spoke, people listened—and there was something unique about his words. All who received these words changed on the inside. Some He spoke to were healed of various diseases. Simon overheard one of the men mention a sickly man being healed when this extraordinary man touched him. So Simon crept even closer in an attempt to catch the name of this miracle worker.

"What is his name?" one man asked another.

"Some say John the Baptist, others say Elijah; and still others, Jeremiah or one of the prophets" (Matthew 16:14).

Someone else told how others confessed him as "the Messiah, the Son of the living God" (Matthew 16:16).

Simon had once read of a man who would one day come and be similarly described. He had read about this person in the book of Isaiah: "The people walking in darkness have seen a great light; on those living in the land of deep darkness a light has dawned" (9:2). Simon the Leper also read in Isaiah that the man would perform similar miracles as well: "Surely he took up our pain and bore our suffering" (53:4). Simon wondered if this man could be whom the Lord spoke of in the book of Psalms: "He sent out his word and healed them; he rescued them from the grave" (107:20). Surely "this was to fulfill what was spoken through the prophet Isaiah: 'He took up our infirmities and bore our diseases'" (Matthew 8:17).

Simply hearing these people talk about Jesus gave Simon the Leper a glimpse of hope for the first time since he was pronounced a leper. This

The Depth of Grace

was only a glimmer of hope. He wasn't sure if he even believed the things he had once read in the Scriptures. The stories he had read back then were far-fetched. The idea of him being healed was extremely far-fetched. The truth in the things he heard about this man named Jesus were far-fetched as well.

Many people did not know what to think about Jesus exactly. Some loved Him. Some hated Him. He was received by some and rejected by others. Some went back and forth in their beliefs. People would accept Him to reject Him and vice-versa. Some things everyone agreed on: He was a righteous man. He spoke with authority. People were healed and delivered of evil spirits everywhere He went. The people had a common knowledge of the man spoken of by the prophets whose description was dangerously similar. Whatever the case, Jesus was extraordinary, and He carried with him a sense of freedom.

Simon decided to risk it all and seek out this man called Jesus. One obstacle for him was the shame in coming into the presence of such a righteous man. Also, thousands sometimes gathered around Him to hear Him teach and witness the miracles. If Simon were to approach Jesus, he would have no choice but to cry out, "Unclean! Unclean!" and scatter the crowd. It was time for this leper to take a deep breath and walk.

> *When [Jesus] came down from the mountainside, large crowds followed him. A man with leprosy came and knelt before him and said, "Lord, if you are willing, you can make me clean."*
>
> *Jesus reached out his hand and touched the man. "I am willing," he said. "Be clean!" Immediately he was cured of his leprosy. (Matthew 8:2-3)*

I wept as I read this passage, considering what I'd read about the man known as Simon the Leper.

The Word of God says, "And let us consider how we may spur one another on toward love and good deeds, not giving up meeting together, as some are in the habit of doing, but encouraging one another—and all the more as you see the Day approaching" (Hebrews 10:24-25). At the time I was reading this passage, my shame would not allow me to go anywhere near others who followed Jesus. But when I read this story about the man with leprosy, I knew what I needed to do.

115

When I finally walked through the doors of my church, I recognized many people. Familiar ushers greeted me. The kids in my former youth group were now young adults, and I saw many of them as I found a seat in the back. I was very aware that I was not alone in this experience. Simon the Leper experienced the same doubt, fear, and just about every other emotion, I'd say. I am certain he covered his face on his journey to meet with Jesus. I am sure Simon's nerves were shot when he alarmed the crowd with his presence. Surely he, too, feared that he might not be healed of his sickness. He, too, knew that the truth in what he heard about Jesus was his only hope. If Simon had not approached the King, he would not have been healed.

In church that day, I sat paralyzed with the doubt, fear, and crippling emotion of a leper as our pastor alluded to an approaching altar call. When the call was given later, the extent of my fear and all the other horrible feelings increased. What do you do? You suck it up, get out of your seat, and walk. The doubt, fear, and every other emotion stood up and walked with me, but began to lose strength the closer I got to my destination. Hope began to come alive on this journey to meet with Jesus. Finally, I reached the feet of Christ. I did my best to hold back the tears as I stood there, but it seemed impossible. I then broke down and began to cry. I experienced a sense of relief upon exhaling the breath I had previously held in. I'm not sure what that breath was about, but it felt wonderful to let it go.

John Bosman, the minister, then began to call people up onto the stage one by one for prayer. After looking into my eyes, he called me up to join several others who stood on the stage and faced toward the crowd. Several others joined us, and the pastor began to pray over us one by one. When Pastor Bosman prayed over me, he assured me that God had plans to use me. I wept and I wept and I wept some more. In full view of my church family that I had missed deeply, I wept.

This day has been marked as a pillar in my life as the day God confirmed His Word to me: "I am with you and will watch over you wherever you go, and I will bring you back to this land. I will not leave you until I have done what I have promised you" (Genesis 28:15).

I was set free of my shame and my drug addiction on that Sunday morning. John Bosman is an incredible man of God who is used all over the world to lead the lost into the kingdom. We all need men (and women) of God in our lives! However, it was the Word of God that gave me the

The Depth of Grace

strength to join the assembly at this gathering, to take courage, and to finally split the crowd.

One way we follow Jesus is by reading about Him. When we read about Jesus, we can come across promises concerning us and cling to them. One promise that I held on to was from the verse I just shared: "I will not leave you until I have done what I promised you." When we are drawn by the Spirit and bring a promise from God to the feet of Christ, we receive the fruit of God's Word in full. I was healed of my own "leprosy" and addiction. The promises are in His Word. The fruit of the Word of God is what I received on that Sunday morning. Because of this fruit I received, I was able to write this chapter and make it come alive to you as it came alive in me at church that morning. Consider what is said of the life contained in God's Word …

> *All Scripture is God-breathed and is useful for teaching, rebuking, correcting and training in righteousness, so that the servant of God may be thoroughly equipped for every good work. (2 Timothy 3:16-17)*

> *By his breath the skies became fair; his hand pierced the gliding serpent. (Job 26:13)*

> *This is what the Sovereign LORD says to these bones: I will make breath enter you, and you will come to life. (Ezekiel 37:5)*

With that breath, I wrote this chapter, and by that breath you were able to receive "because we know that just as you share in [my] sufferings so also you share in [my] comfort" (2 Corinthians 1:7).

> *Then he said to me, "Prophesy to the breath; prophesy, son of man, and say to it, 'This is what the Sovereign LORD says: Come, breath, from the four winds and breathe into these slain, that they may live.'"*

> *So I prophesied as he commanded me, and breath entered them; they came to life and stood up on their feet—a vast army. (Ezekiel 37:9-10)*

J. Bronson Haley

I pray with everything in me that His breath of life will give you new hope for a life full of purpose and God's love—just as I pray it for myself every day.

CHAPTER 14

—

Streets of Gold

Once while praying at our Saturday night meeting, I began to think about my old buddy, Pete Holt. The prayer meeting had been going on for about a year at this time. I hadn't talked to him in a couple of years, but he was surely on my mind this particular night. After shutting down the youth sanctuary, I left the church and drove to his house. When I arrived, I was shocked to find his home dark and empty. Someone had been always home on a Saturday night at Pete's house in the old days. I felt sure that God had put him on my heart, so I said a little prayer as I backed out of his driveway.

I walked into church late the next morning as our senior pastor, Denny Duron, read prayer requests. No sooner than I had found a seat did he mention that Pete Holt was in Highland Hospital and needed prayer. As Denny read this request, I felt what seemed like electricity run through my body. I sprang out of my seat, left church, and headed to the hospital.

When I walked into his room, Pete at first looked ashamed because I was seeing him in this condition. But as I got closer, his face lit up and I gave him a big hug. We talked for a while and I assured him that we were going to hang out as soon as he was released.

He stayed in the hospital for a couple of days and then called me when he got out. After I picked him up from his home, we went to the mall and I bought him some clothes. Pete was very skinny by this time and looked rough.

119

J. Bronson Haley

We hung out for a couple hours talking about old times and got some good laughs. I reminded him of the times we used to skip school at Broadmoor. We had an operation we called "skip day" that was untouchable. I typically gave my mother heck every morning and begged her to let me stay home from school, but I didn't put up any fuss on a planned skip day ...

"Bronson, wake up, son," Mom commanded, as she rightfully anticipated a struggle.

"Yes, Mother," I said on these mornings. (One a side note, I'm certain Mom really worried about me some days, given my erratic behavior from one morning to another.)

After I got dressed, ate breakfast, and made sure I had my homework, I told Mom I loved her, and out the door I went. The walk to school was a little less than a mile every morning. When I left the house on a normal day, I would take a left once I reached the sidewalk out front. On skip day I took a right after exiting the house and would sneak around the house to our twenty-one-foot Hydro Sport bass boat that was covered by a tarp. After I walked to the back of the boat, I would lift the tarp and climb into the boat. I would then snuggle into Pete's extra sleeping bag and wait on him.

It was the perfect plan. It didn't matter if Mom came home for lunch or not. By that time the answering machine had been erased and there was nothing to worry about. Soon enough I'd hear Pete's footsteps and he would join me. His situation was a little riskier than mine. His grandmother was home most mornings. He had to turn the ringers off on the phones and unplug the answering machine.

In our never-used boat, we had food, Monopoly, and everything else we needed to enjoy ourselves for the day. It brings a smile to my face just writing about it. These were the kinds of good memories we relived with each other that day I took Pete home from the hospital.

"Hey, Pete," I continued, "do you remember the time we broke into my neighbor's guesthouse when we skipped school that day?"

My neighbor had a guesthouse that butted up to the fence in my backyard. We got bored one day and broke in.

"Do you remember when the owner walked over to the window we entered through, as we sat on the back porch?" I asked.

We began to laugh, recalling the details of the story.

"Yeah, I remember," he said.

The Depth of Grace

My neighbor looked over the fence at us after he noticed that the paint had been cracked on the windowsill, and he commanded me to come over and talk to him. I assumed the neighbor observed us climb over the fence and called him.

"Son, come over here right now!" he said.

Pete and I laughed even harder at the memory.

"Do you remember me standing there swearing to him I didn't break into his house while wearing *his* collared T-shirt?" I said.

By this time both of us were laughing so hard that we found ourselves crouched down and leaning up against the wall in the mall, with people walking by looking at us like we were crazy. We were crazy! But they hadn't ever heard the story.

"Do you remember the time my mom walked into the house after she cleaned out the boat when we moved the summer of our eighth-grade year?" I asked.

Pete couldn't respond because he laughed so hard.

"Bronson, Pete," my mom had said to us that day. "You guys will never believe this. A homeless person has been living in the boat!"

Pete and I had rolled on the floor laughing as Mom assured us that she was telling the truth.

"I'm not joking! There was more than one of them, too. Look, two sleeping bags and two pillows. They even played Monopoly!"

This was one hilarious meeting with my buddy Pete. After we left the mall, we went to the house I was living in. I then began to share my testimony with Pete.

"Since the day I gave my life to Jesus, God has continued to change me and bless me. He even uses me to help other people. Sometimes I share my testimony and people appreciate it. Pete, you know as well as I that being able to do that is a miracle in itself."

Pete came to church with me that night and gave his life to Jesus. He stayed over, and I told him about all the wonderful things Jesus was going to do for him.

"Look around," I said. "God gave me this family to live with and I have everything I need. I feel like I wake up every morning to a dream, only it's not a dream. I get to live it out every day. The Word of God says, 'No eye has seen, no ear has heard, no mind has conceived what God has for those who love him.' I could have never imagined being blessed this much. God is going to do the same for you."

J. Bronson Haley

For the first time during the course of our eight-year friendship, I saw a sense of hope in Pete's eyes. Pete believed everything I said to him. We talked a lot about heaven that night. We tried to imagine the angels and streets of gold. It was hard for Pete to imagine a place without suffering. I took Pete home the next day.

A couple of months later I got a phone call from Pete's girlfriend. She told me that Pete's mom had received a call the night before around 9:00 p.m. from Pete and he said that his roommate—Big Pete Block, whom you may remember from an earlier chapter—was acting crazy after Pete told him he was ready to move back in with his family. His girlfriend told me that Pete had finally decided to get back with her, the mother of his baby girl. Their child was around three years old at the time. At 2:00 a.m. the same night, Big Pete had called Pete's mom and told her, "You need to come get your son." When his mom pulled into the drive, Big Pete walked out of the front door with Pete—Little Pete—in his arms. After Big Pete placed Pete in the passenger's seat of the car, Pete's mother began to scream, "He's dead! He's dead!" as she placed her hands on his cold, unmoving body.

Big Pete replied, "He ain't dead yet, but it won't be long. You need to get him to the hospital."

Pete's death was ruled a drug overdose after the autopsy found Freon in his lungs, but I think that was impossible. His face had been covered in bruises and his hands were severely swollen. Plus Pete had been in the process of finally getting his family back after losing them to his drug and alcohol abuse. His grandmother mentioned that he had come to the house every day just prior to his death, overjoyed at the thought of his big breakthrough in getting his life back together.

Pete was murdered at twenty years old, plain and simple. He never lived to see twenty-one, just as his other friends and I predicted as kids.

His girlfriend asked me to speak at his funeral and I refused her request—I just couldn't do it. I sat on the front row with Pete's other best friend, Mike Mertle. Mike's father, Reverend Hank Mertle, led the ceremony and it was certainly the saddest funeral I had ever been to. Pete's family was sitting off to the right in a section reserved for the family of the deceased. When the time approached to view the body, we were directed to start from the back of the building. With my head down, I heard Pete's mom begin to cry aloud, along with others in the family. When I looked up, I saw Big Pete Block in line as the first person to view the body. He showed up to the funeral in a stretch limo with a police escort. A face-to-

The Depth of Grace

face encounter with the Devil is what the people in the room experienced on that day. Three weeks later Big Pete Block committed suicide.

As a friend, Pete had always made available to me everything he had to offer. It wasn't much in a worldly sense, but he gave all he had. He was there for me in the restroom when I got myself into trouble. Years later I was thankful that I'd had the opportunity to be there for him. Pete needed me after his drug overdose, and I made available to him all that I had. Our friendship was based on this concept. When Pete heard his best friend talk about Jesus, he believed. He knew me and knew I would never lead him astray. There is no doubt in my mind that our friendship was a miracle from God. Even as young hotheads, God was watching over us and had a plan for our friendship.

One might ask, "How can you mention God's plan after your friend had his life taken from him? He was murdered within a few of months of being saved."

In return I would say, "When Pete was born again, he became an heir to the throne of Jesus Christ. When he died, he went on to be with the Father. Today he walks the streets of gold with the angels we talked about the day that he was saved. Pete will never again feel any pain. He won the battle that day—a battle few understand."

CHAPTER 15

Silent Struggle

I had actually been struggling myself for months prior to Pete's death. I had spent about six months praying and seeking the Lord for strength, but just couldn't seem to break through the constant tug at my soul to return to my old way of life. During this time I continued to travel to different places and share my testimony with kids. I was still quite involved with the youth at my church. But I didn't let anyone know I was struggling because of everything God had done in my life. I didn't want people to think I was unappreciative. I didn't want to let anyone down, either, because I knew many people watched me. What kind of person goes around looking downcast after Jesus Christ has swept into his life and given him everything he had always dreamed of?

During this period I was invited to Grace Methodist Church to share with its youth group. From the time I woke up that morning to the time I walked into the church that evening, I was sickened with fear. The service started at 7:00 p.m. When I got home from school that day, I crashed into my bed a total wreck. I was sick to my stomach and ached all over.

Can I speak to these kids under this condition? I asked myself.

I stayed in bed for about three hours that afternoon. During those long hours I tossed and turned and had nightmares about my future. I loved Jesus deeply and dreamed of preaching the gospel one day. Adults and even children from church confirmed my calling to me on a daily basis. However, I was certain I would not be able to continue to serve God in my present condition.

125

J. Bronson Haley

While I tossed and turned, I thought about everything God had done for me since I was saved two years earlier. I was richly blessed and God continued to bless me every day. I woke up to my childhood dreams every morning, and God continued to be faithful in doing everything He had promised me. The Lord assured me when He called me to the ministry that he would be with me everywhere I'd go and would never leave me. God held up his end of the deal on a daily basis. I was the one having trouble with my end.

At around 6:00 p.m., I took a deep breath, got dressed, and headed to Grace Methodist Church. After I entered the youth sanctuary, I quickly found a seat. I felt as though I were a touch out of reality. God was with me, for sure. When I looked across the room, I could see that God was ready to do some amazing things in the lives of these kids. I was confident in Jesus, given that He had never once let me down. Me? I was a wreck on the inside and couldn't imagine a life of ministry in my present condition, much less a worse condition. I understood that pastors, evangelists, and great men of faith fought bigger demons that the ones I was battling with. "The Devil seeks to take off the head so that he can reach the body." I heard that from somewhere.

When I grabbed the microphone and began to speak, the glory of God filled the room. God gave me the words to say and many kids answered the altar call. Just prior to the altar call, the youth pastor dimmed the lights and turned up the music. All of the kids began to worship Jesus and pray with one another. God showed up just as He promised. I showed up by the grace of God.

Shortly after, I began to turn down my youth pastor when he asked me to help him with different activities. I also turned down Grace Methodist Church when staff members there asked me to come back and speak to their kids. I turned down Fellowship of Christian Athletes meetings at local high schools. I quit going to church and later completely isolated myself from everyone.

My friend Pete's death came when I was going through this difficult time in my life. The death of my grandmother was also thrown in during this time of isolation. Her prayers receive much of the credit for everything God did in my life. I know that God spared me because of the prayers and obedience of my grandmother. She was always there for me through my childhood struggles and never failed to harass me with mini-sermons about Jesus and how much He loved me. In fact, about one year after my car wreck, my grandmother told me about a prayer she prayed for me

The Depth of Grace

three weeks prior to the accident: "Father, whatever you have to do to get his attention, please do it," she asked. She was afraid that I would not recover if I continued down the path I was headed during that time. My grandmother had even once witnessed me come into her home after a night of drinking, with blood all over my clothes from fighting. At that point she honestly had no idea the extent of my careless and reckless life, but she knew it was getting worse at a rapid pace. She assured me she would never again pray that prayer over anyone: "Father, whatever you have to do to get his attention, please do it." So I know that I would not have made it without my grandmother, and I had more love for her than she could have possibly known. During this time of isolation, though, I didn't go to see her much. So I took her death very hard.

I remember being online one evening and receiving a random instant message from an unknown America Online member. I will never forget the words I read on the screen: "Are you the same Bronson that came to my church and changed our youth?" She was a leader in the youth at Grace. As tears rolled down my face, I assured the girl, "Only God could have changed your youth." I then signed off.

I had previously fallen back into sin because I started hanging out with the wrong people. I had disobeyed God. The Word of God says to stay clear of the enemy's campground. I had set up my campsite instead. This time, though, I was doing everything right and gave God my all. I didn't want to go down without a fight, either. I begged the Lord for strength and spent a lot of time with Him during this time of struggle. But I finally gave up. I just couldn't do it. So, when I eventually fell into sin again, I didn't have any intentions of ever returning to church. I guess you could say I signed off on God also.

9TH REST STOP:
MOST GLORIOUS HOUR

We know that Simon Peter returned to his former life when he accepted that he wasn't strong enough to be the "Rock" that Jesus needed to establish His church. After Jesus' death the disciples were defeated, and I cannot imagine what it must have felt like feeling as though the God of Israel stood idly by and watched His Son betrayed and murdered like that. You see, at that time, they did not yet understand the big picture: Jesus was crucified so that His people could come back into spiritual fellowship with the Father, and He trusted the disciples to reach them. Because they were not able to stay strong, did that mean that Jesus had been crucified for nothing? Who was going to establish the church? We know that the disciples did not yet understand from the Scriptures that Jesus had to rise from the dead. As a matter of fact, there was a lot they didn't understand about Jesus. No wonder Peter jumped out of the boat like Forrest Gump when the resurrected Christ appeared to them, as we saw earlier. He didn't think he would ever see Him again.

> *Early in the morning, Jesus stood on the shore, but the disciples did not realize that it was Jesus.*
>
> *He called out to them, "Friends, haven't you any fish?"*
>
> *"No," they answered.*
>
> *He said, "Throw your net on the right side of the boat and you will find some." When they did, they were unable to haul the net in because of the large number of fish.*

The Depth of Grace

Then the disciple whom Jesus loved said to Peter, "It is the Lord!" As soon as Simon Peter heard him say, "It is the Lord," he wrapped his outer garment around him (for he had taken it off) and jumped into the water. (John 21:4-7)

I don't know about you, but that is hilarious to me.

Jesus met up with the disciples several other times after He rose from the dead. Jesus initiated one of the most significant of these visits while two of His disciples were on the road to Emmaus, about seven miles from Jerusalem. They held their faces downcast as they discussed the details of everything that had happened: the life of Jesus, the crucifixion, their failures. Though they did not recognize Him, Jesus walked up beside them and joined in the conversation: "And beginning with Moses and all the Prophets, he explained to them what was said in all the Scriptures concerning himself" (Luke 24:27). Their hearts burned inside of them as He spoke. They had heard Jesus speak of these matters concerning Himself prior to the crucifixion, but they had not understood.

As they approached the village to which they were going, Jesus continued on as if he were going farther. But they urged him strongly, "Stay with us, for it is nearly evening; the day is almost over." So he went in to stay with them.

When he was at the table with them, he took bread, gave thanks, broke it and began to give it to them. Then their eyes were opened and they recognized him, and he disappeared from their sight. (Luke 24:28-31)

Remember: "In the beginning was the Word, and the Word was with God, and the Word was God" (John 1:1). And because Jesus' heart burned for His chosen, He suffered for their sins …

The Word became flesh and made his dwelling among us. (John 1:14)

For the bread of God is the bread that comes down from heaven and gives life to the world. (John 6:33)

Then Jesus declared, "I am the bread of life. Whoever comes to me will never go hungry, and whoever believes in me will never be thirsty." (John 6:35)

J. Bronson Haley

Jesus was and is the bread of life. He was also the Word of God in the flesh. Jesus was a walking Bible! When He walked beside those two disciples on that road, everything He said sounded wonderful, but they did not recognize Him. Their hearts burned inside of them and they were given some hope. However, they did not recognize that it was Jesus who talked with them. The truth is that we all have great ideas about how to help people. We have wonderful ideas about what God will and will not do in someone's life. We may speak the truth to people and their hearts may burn inside of them as a result. It all seems wonderful! However, according to the Word of God, they will not recognize that what we say is 100 percent from the Lord until we show them the Scriptures that back up what we speak to them. It was not until Jesus broke the bread that those two men recognized him: "He took bread, gave thanks, broke it and began to give it to them. Then their eyes were opened and they recognized him" (Luke 24:30-31). We break the "bread" by opening our Bibles or speaking the Scriptures. Jesus Christ was and is the bread of life!

You see, before this, the disciples did not understand why people would believe them if they were to tell others about Jesus. They began to understand when Jesus broke the bread and they recognized Him. When Jesus opens our minds to the Scriptures, we are no longer reading far-fetched stories. When we speak this same truth to those who suffer, they are no longer listening to far-fetched stories. At this time, these two disciples on the road to Emmaus began to understand why people would listen to them. These men who walked with Jesus quickly met up with the other nine disciples to discuss this glorious meeting with the Lord: "Then the two told what had happened on the way, and how Jesus was recognized by them when he broke the bread" (Luke 24:35).

The two disciples shared these new hidden truths they heard and understood about Jesus. They explained how Jesus allowed them to receive the truth in the Scriptures by opening their minds. However, the human mind cannot understand the things of God. The other nine disciples doubted because their minds had not yet been opened. So Jesus showed up during this meeting unannounced. His disciples were huddled together behind locked doors talking about this last encounter with the risen Lord.

> *They were startled and frightened, thinking they saw a ghost.*
> *He said to them, "Why are you troubled, and why do doubts*
> *rise in your minds? Look at my hands and my feet. It is I*

The Depth of Grace

myself! Touch me and see; a ghost does not have flesh and bones, as you see I have."

When he had said this, he showed them his hands and feet. And while they still did not believe it because of joy and amazement, he asked them, "Do you have anything here to eat?" They gave him a piece of broiled fish, and he took it and ate it in their presence.

He said to them, "This is what I told you while I was still with you: Everything must be fulfilled that is written about me in the Law of Moses, the Prophets and the Psalms."

Then he opened their minds so they could understand the Scriptures. He told them, "This is what is written: The Messiah will suffer and rise from the dead on the third day, and repentance for the forgiveness of sins will be preached in his name to all nations, beginning at Jerusalem. You are witnesses of these things. I am going to send you what my Father has promised; but stay in the city until you have been clothed with power from on high." (Luke 24:37-49, my emphasis)

Dunamis is the Greek word for "power" used in the last verse (this is the same word from which we get our word "dynamite"). *Dunamis* is from the Greek word *dunamai*, which means "to be able to." These two words were derived from the stem *duna,* which has the meaning of "being able, capable, and, sometimes, volitional ability." Simon Peter and the others began to understand that not only was Jesus going to restore them but also that He did not expect anything other than failure from them in the first place. According to the Word of God, the disciples were not yet capable of fulfilling the call on their lives. Jesus practically told them, "Of course you are afraid and in doubt and incapable of fulfilling the call on your lives. I have not yet given you the 'ability.' Relax! You have not received the 'power' from on high, which will make you 'capable' of serving me."

I wish I knew seven years ago what I know now. I would have asked God to open my mind to the Scriptures and prove the truth in His Word to me. If I had known then what I know now, I would have planted my face in the Word of God instead of in the carpet. I would have asked for new spiritual wine instead of drinking-age wine. I would have asked the

J. Bronson Haley

Lord to renew my mind. I instead clouded it with smoke. If I had known then what I know now, I would have built my house on the rock. Instead I smoked one. No, I actually never smoked a rock, but people do and many suffer greatly because of it.

Jesus has not simply walked up to me and opened my mind to the Scriptures, either. It doesn't work that way. How many of us understand that we must *ask* in order to receive? "For everyone who asks receives; the one who seeks finds; and to the one who knocks, the door will be opened" (Matthew 7:8). We must ask-ask-ask and then get in the Word of God—and ask more—so that we can receive-receive-receive. I made many mistakes in the beginning. I so believed in what God was doing inside of me that I would tell people that He was going to do the same thing inside of them. However, Jesus has never forced Himself upon anyone. God can speak and speak and speak to people until they are blue in the face. However, these people still have the free choice to reject and reject and reject Him. Jesus will seek us out. He will send people our way and they may speak wonderful things into our lives. But He will not force us to do anything. Instead of tying our own hands as before, we can tie His hands by being disobedient. But when we have the Word of God, the Devil loses his right into our lives and God is able to bring forth the miraculous. We need to ask God to open our minds to the depths of the Scriptures so that we are able understand. We will begin to see that it works! And we will continue to see that it works!

This last meeting the disciples had with Jesus had nothing in common with the Lord's Supper. Back then they had made boasts in their ignorance about how great they were, yet actually knew little about Jesus. During this last meeting, in their humility, Jesus shared the bread of life with His disciples and they drank new wine. They did not boast about how great they were. They knew, based on real-life experience, that they were capable of only failure without the "ability." These men of God clearly understood what it meant to be opposed by God and to try to answer His call at the same time. This was a glorious day for the kingdom of God. The disciples were no longer trying to believe far-fetched stories and no longer needed to worry about convincing the Jews to believe the same far-fetched stories. Because Jesus opened their minds to the Scriptures, the Word of God came alive inside of them.

We also have the prophetic message as something completely reliable, and you will do well to pay attention to it, as to a

The Depth of Grace

light shining in a dark place, until the day dawns and the morning star rises in your hearts. (2 Peter 1:19)

A good man brings good things out of the good stored up in his heart, and an evil man brings evil things out of the evil stored up in his heart. For the mouth speaks what the heart is full of. (Luke 6:45)

And our hope for you is firm, because we know that just as you share in our sufferings, so also you share in our comfort. (2 Corinthians 1:7)

For just as we share abundantly in the sufferings of Christ, so also our comfort abounds through Christ. (2 Corinthians 1:5)

The disciples began to depend on every word spoken by the Lord. It would only be through the truth hidden in the Scriptures that people would recognize Jesus in their words. They finally understood that their lives and the life of their ministry depended upon every word spoken by God. The more truth they were able to speak, the more powerful their ministry, and, for the first time, they understood this vital fact. It is the truth that sets the captives free.

"Again Jesus said, 'Peace be with you! As the Father has sent me, I am sending you'" (John 20:21). *Eirene* is the Greek word for "peace be with." The word means "peace, tranquility, repose, calm; harmony, accord; well-being, prosperity." Imagine receiving those words from Jesus after failing as they had failed! "Everyone calm down. Now that you have the truth hidden in the depths of the Scriptures, you are no longer failures. We are now in harmony! Today we are in one 'accord!' Finally, for the first time, you are 'capable,' so relax. Today I am sending you out with the 'ability' to fulfill the call on your lives."

And with that he breathed on them and said, "Receive the Holy Spirit. If you forgive anyone's sins, their sins are forgiven; if you do not forgive them, they are not forgiven." (John 20:22-23)

When Jesus breathed on them in this verse, they were saved and the Spirit of God birthed a new spirit in them. Man was in spiritual fellowship with God for the first time since Adam fell into sin. Also, they fully

J. Bronson Haley

understood the importance of being clothed with this "power" from on high. The disciples fully understood that, in order to establish the church of Jesus Christ without defect, they could not afford to miss or reject a single word spoken by the Lord.

On the shore that day when he leaped out of the boat to run to Jesus, Peter sat quietly as He pondered the fact that Jesus was not finished with him after all. It seemed too good to be true. Not only was Jesus not finished, but He was just getting started! If Peter was anything like me, tears welled up in his eyes when the Lord spoke to him about his redemption.

> *When they had finished eating, Jesus said to Simon Peter, "Simon son of John, do you love me more than these?"*
>
> *"Yes, Lord," he said, "you know that I love you."*
>
> *Jesus said, "Feed my lambs."*
>
> *Again Jesus said, "Simon son of John, do you love me?"*
>
> *He answered, "Yes, Lord, you know that I love you."*
>
> *Jesus said, "Take care of my sheep."*
>
> *The third time he said to him, "Simon son of John, do you love me?"*
>
> *Peter was hurt because Jesus asked him the third time, "Do you love me?" He said, "Lord, you know all things; you know that I love you."*
>
> *Jesus said, "Feed my sheep. Very truly I tell you, when you were younger you dressed yourself and went where you wanted; but when you are old you will stretch out your hands, and someone else will dress you and lead you where you do not want to go." Jesus said this to indicate the kind of death by which Peter would glorify God. Then he said to him, "Follow me!" (John 21:15-19)*

Isn't it something how we believe the lies that tell us we have to do this and that before we can return to Jesus and serve Him? I wasted a lot of time struggling to clean myself up so that I could return to Christ. We already know Jesus did not demand Peter to change when He first called him three years prior to this day. It was only necessary that Peter follow.

The Depth of Grace

We can see in this last verse that Jesus did not ask any more of Peter when He reinstated him. Peter simply picked up where he left off.

Then he said to him, "Follow me!"

Peter turned and saw that the disciple whom Jesus loved was following them.... When Peter saw him, he asked, "Lord, what about him?"

Jesus answered, "If I want him to remain alive until I return, what is that to you? You must follow me." (John 21:19-22)

Doesn't your heart just go out to this man we know as Peter? Immediately after the most glorious reinstatement in history, Peter got jealous of the disciple Jesus loved more. Men of God get jealous of other men of God just as a young child with one lollipop gets jealous of a kid with two lollipops. It's funny to me that Jesus put Peter and John together in ministry. Can you hear their arguments as they traveled the long roads from town to town?

"I love Jesus more and He knows it!" says Peter.

"Jesus loves me more and you know it!" John replies.

I love God's Word!

In the upper room 120 were present when God made the gift of the Holy Spirit available to His children. Upon receiving the Spirit, the disciples and their followers flooded out into the streets. Thousands of Jews, whom they had been hiding from, crowded around and began to mock them. These people who mocked them also mocked Jesus when He walked the earth. Many of the same people mocked the Lord as He hung on the cross, paying the price for their own sin. No doubt many of the thousands who gathered around were trying to intimidate those whom Jesus fully equipped with the Word of God. The disciples who were the strongest during the crucifixion and during the time Jesus was in the tomb now huddled together, pondering their next move. It was the "Rock" who stood up with the eleven, raised his voice, and addressed the crowd.

"Fellow Jews and all of you who live in Jerusalem, let me explain this to you; listen carefully to what I say. These men are not drunk, as you suppose. It's only nine in the morning! No, this is what was spoken by the prophet Joel:

J. Bronson Haley

'In the last days, God says,
I will pour out my Spirit on all people.
Your sons and daughters will prophesy,
your young men will see visions,
your old men will dream dreams.
Even on my servants, both men and women,
I will pour out my Spirit in those days,
and they will prophesy.
I will show wonders in the heaven above
and signs on the earth below,
blood and fire and billows of smoke.
The sun will be turned to darkness
and the moon to blood
before the coming of the great and glorious day of the Lord.
And everyone who calls
on the name of the Lord will be saved.'

"Fellow Israelites, listen to this: Jesus of Nazareth was a man accredited by God to you by miracles, wonders and signs, which God did among you through him, as you yourselves know. This man was handed over to you by God's deliberate plan and foreknowledge; and you, with the help of wicked men, put him to death by nailing him to the cross. But God raised him from the dead, freeing him from the agony of death, because it was impossible for death to keep its hold on him....

"Therefore let all Israel be assured of this: God has made this Jesus, whom you crucified, both Lord and Messiah." When the people heard this, they were cut to the heart and said to Peter and the other apostles, "Brothers, what shall we do?" (Acts 2:14-24, 36-37)

That was a powerful sermon preached by Simon Peter. There was something different about his words. When he spoke, it was as though God spoke through him. It was as though Jesus Himself spoke through Peter in an effort to reach His people. They knew it was Jesus speaking because Peter spoke the Word of God. They accepted Jesus Christ as their Lord and Savior. The truth set them free. The church grew from 120 to over three thousand at that moment. And that was just the beginning.

The Depth of Grace

One day Peter and John were going up to the temple at the time of prayer—at three in the afternoon. Now a man who was lame from birth was being carried to the temple gate called Beautiful, where he was put every day to beg from those going into the temple courts. When he saw Peter and John about to enter, he asked them for money. Peter looked straight at him, as did John. Then Peter said, "Look at us!" So the man gave them his attention, expecting to get something from them.

Then Peter said, "Silver or gold I do not have, but what I do have I give you. In the name of Jesus Christ of Nazareth, walk." Taking him by the right hand, he helped him up, and instantly the man's feet and ankles became strong. He jumped to his feet and began to walk....

The priests and the captain of the temple guard and the Sadducees came up to Peter and John while they were speaking to the people. They were greatly disturbed because the apostles were teaching the people, proclaiming in Jesus the resurrection of the dead. They seized Peter and John, and because it was evening, they put them in jail until the next day. But many who heard the message believed; so the number of men who believed grew to about five thousand.

The next day the rulers, elders and teachers of the law met in Jerusalem. Annas the high priest was there, and so were Caiaphas, John, Alexander and others of the high priest's family. They had Peter and John brought before them and began to question them: "By what power or what name did you do this?" (Acts 3:1-8, 4:1-7)

As these men attempted to intimidate Simon Peter, he no doubt began to think about the times they did the same thing to Jesus Christ when He walked the earth. Peter thought about the times he denied Jesus in His presence as He was being mocked, spit on, and beaten at the hands of these men who now questioned him. It was these men who had the Lord—Peter's Lord—flogged and nailed to the cross as an innocent man. These men who questioned Peter also mocked Jesus as He hung on the tree with nails driven in His hands and feet. Blood dripped from the open wounds Jesus received as payment for His love for Israel. Jesus had a crown

J. Bronson Haley

of thorns on His head as a sarcastic gesture and a sign above Him that read, "King of the Jews." These same men now questioned Simon Peter with the abusive and intimidating power of a more than corrupt government. On this day, though, the "Rock" was equipped to address the problem.

> *Then Peter, filled with the Holy Spirit, said to them: "Rulers and elders of the people! If we are being called to account today for an act of kindness shown to a man who was lame and are asked how he was healed, then know this, you and all the people of Israel: It is by the name of Jesus Christ of Nazareth, whom you crucified but whom God raised from the dead, that this man stands before you healed. Jesus is 'the stone you builders rejected, which has become the cornerstone.'" (Acts 4:8-11)*

Now that is how you address the men who crucified the Son of the Living God! "To all the people responsible for the sufferings of Jesus Christ: praise be to the Lamb of God! He has risen! He sits at the right hand of the Almighty! And you have been placed under His feet! Confess with your mouth and believe in your heart that Jesus Christ is Lord, or be thrown into the lake of fire for what you have done!"

> *When they saw the courage of Peter and John and realized that they were unschooled, ordinary men, they were astonished and they took note that these men had been with Jesus. But since they could see the man who had been healed standing there with them, there was nothing they could say. So they ordered them to withdraw from the Sanhedrin and then conferred together. "What are we going to do with these men?" they asked. "Everybody living in Jerusalem knows they have performed a notable sign, and we cannot deny it. But to stop this thing from spreading any further among the people, we must warn them to speak no longer to anyone in this name."*

> *Then they called them in again and commanded them not to speak or teach at all in the name of Jesus. But Peter and John replied, "Which is right in God's eyes: to listen to you, or to him? You be the judges! As for us, we cannot help speaking about what we have seen and heard."*

The Depth of Grace

After further threats they let them go. They could not decide how to punish them, because all the people were praising God for what had happened. For the man who was miraculously healed was over forty years old....

> *The apostles performed many signs and wonders among the people. And all the believers used to meet together in Solomon's Colonnade. No one else dared join them, even though they were highly regarded by the people. Nevertheless, more and more men and women believed in the Lord and were added to their number. As a result, people brought the sick into the streets and laid them on beds and mats so that at least Peter's shadow might fall on some of them as he passed by. Crowds gathered also from the towns around Jerusalem, bringing their sick and those tormented by evil spirits, and all of them were healed. (Acts 4:13-22, 5:12-16)*

Who was Simon Peter that the angels called upon him in Acts 10? Who was this scared fisherman that King Herod put into prison and posted four squads of four soldiers each to guard him for fear that Simon may escape, only to find Simon the next morning proclaiming the glory of Jesus Christ in the courtyard of the chief priest? His name was Peter. The "Rock" received the Word of God and was clothed with power from on high. He was a man of God who learned what it meant to follow Jesus Christ. He was a man who was not able to tell Jesus that He didn't suffer enough to cover his failures. Peter was a man of God who learned firsthand what Jesus meant when He explained the following Scripture while on the earth:

> *I give them eternal life, and they shall never perish; no one will snatch them out of my hand. My Father, who has given them to me, is greater than all; no one can snatch them out of my Father's hand. I and the Father are one. (John 10:28-30)*

Peter gave Jesus time to prove Himself. This truth came alive inside of this man called Peter, who was willing to get up when he fell and to follow the Son of God.

Simon Peter mentioned to Jesus before his final failures that he was willing to die for Him. Peter got his chance to prove His love for the Lord. He served Jesus with boldness. The "Rock" established the church

139

J. Bronson Haley

of Jesus Christ. Church history tells us that Peter was then crucified upside down because he didn't want the honor to die as Jesus had died. Because he shared in the sufferings of Jesus, he is now also sharing in His eternal glory.

And so it was with the remaining apostles of Jesus. They all died as martyrs, except for John, who died as an old man after suffering exile for his faith many years on the island of Patmos. That's the power of the Word of God: it can turn the most fearful, failing people into powerful witnesses of the Lord's love and grace!

CHAPTER 16

Sniper

I sat in the passenger seat of my truck as my peripheral vision captured a glimpse of motion from the shadow of death. Twenty feet to my right, out of this tall bush, walked what looked like a man toward the truck. Adrenalin that I was not yet familiar with charged my instincts, and I jumped out of the truck. Twigs on the man's head reached for the stars. He wore no shirt, but was clothed in mud. Twigs also stretched upward from his waist and feet. With my hands on my hips, I awaited the words that may save his life, because I was just about ready to tear into this guy.

But let's back up a bit …

About two years after I fell into sin again, I decided to become a commercial diver and headed to Jacksonville, Florida. There I met a man whom I became close to in an extremely ironic way. His name was Jared Volp. The morning we met, we were in the living room of the crack house we called home, receiving instructions from the CEO of our diving school on what to do in order to begin class the following day. Jared was wearing a green hoodie with "Marine Sniper" written on the back. He had a horrible scar that led from behind his left ear, down across his neck, and to the other side of his throat. He also had some fresh abrasions on his face. It looked to me like he'd been in a fight recently, but I wasn't sure. Captain Redd, the CEO, gave us strict orders not to drink alcohol on campus. The campus consisted of a marina on Trout River in the middle of the ghetto. The dorm was just across the street. It was a run-down who-knows-what.

141

J. Bronson Haley

Captain Redd seemed pretty serious: "I don't care what you do outside the gate. Just don't bring it to the dorm. (It was funny to me that he referred to this ghetto crack house as a dorm.) What goes on outside the gate stays outside the gate." He then addressed Jared and asked, "Boy, what happened to your face?"

"What goes on outside the gate stays outside the gate, sir," Jared said.

I knew right then that Jared and I would become friends.

When the meeting ended, I introduced myself to Jared and offered him a ride to the clinic to get the physical required by school. I wasn't quite sure what to think about him on the ride to the clinic. He talked in a low voice and seemed very mischievous. By the time we arrived, I realized what I was picking up on. Jared was at rock bottom, very alone, and didn't want me to know. He was a tough guy. My heart began to soften toward him.

"Why are you drinking so much water?" Jared asked, breaking the silence as we sat in the clinic.

"Because I don't want anything but water in my urine when I pee in the cup," I explained.

I had smoked some weed before I left home and didn't want to get kicked out of the school because of it.

He laughed and said, "That's what I thought. Don't worry, they're not testing for drugs."

"Are you sure? The handbook said we would be tested."

"We will … if we get hurt on campus. Trust me … if we were getting tested right now, I'd be drinking water with you."

Jared and I were both at odd times in our lives. A few years back he had received a dishonorable discharge from the Marine Corps for a crime he didn't commit. In the Marines he had been a scout sniper—and had been hardened by it. On the flip side I had given myself a dishonorable discharge from the ministry of Jesus Christ a couple years back. I hated myself and had great plans of becoming a deep-sea diver. Working at the bottom of the ocean seemed like a great idea at the time.

A few days later Jared mentioned landing a job at Applebee's. I encouraged him to quit. I wasn't sure why exactly, but Jared continued to grow heavy on my heart and I wanted to spend time with him.

"I need the money," he said.

"Don't worry about the money. I just sold my boat. I've got you."

When I made the offer, he paused for a moment, and then said, "I can't let you do that, Bronson."

The Depth of Grace

A couple days later I asked him again to quit his job. "Jared, I'm more interested in building a friendship with you than the money I have in the bank. It's not a big deal, seriously. Quit your job and let's hang out."

From that moment on, Jared and I were tied at the hip. We were nicknamed the "dynamic duo" by the staff, and built a strong friendship. We also got into a lot of trouble.

A couple of weeks later I mentioned to the captain that I wanted to talk business.

"Let's talk tonight over some drinks," he said.

By midnight Jared and I had gotten kicked out of the bar we chose to terrorize. When the captain exited the building, he popped off at three men standing next to their truck. I have never heard someone degrade men in this manner for absolutely no reason at all. However, Jared and I were boys with the captain by this time. He was like us and we had his back.

A quick side note before I continue with the story: Mark (aka "Junior") was the youngest of the five students at the school. He was an eighteen-year-old with an attitude. He was famous for saying, "Oh hell no!" when he would screw up at school. Jared and I often said the same thing when we would screw up, just to acknowledge him.

Back to the story from that night with the captain: just when the men had heard enough from Captain Redd, one of them grabbed a crowbar out of the toolbox of the truck. We were in north Jacksonville at the time. The difference between the character of those from the north side of town and those from the south was the difference between the greasers and the socialites from the book, *The Outsiders*. However, I was a mixed breed from Louisiana.

"Oh hell no!" I said and immediately walked toward the fellow with the iron tool in his hand. When I arrived just outside of his reach, I asked, "Do you have another one of those?"

He hesitated and I knocked him out. You see, I'm not like the people in the movies. I jumped on top of him and continued to beat him even though he was unconscious. Jared fought one of the other men to my right. He was on top of the man, working him over good, as three cop cars pulled in the parking lot. By this time I had already left the man I'd fought and headed toward Jared. Jared tried to get up because of the cops, but the man grabbed him and wouldn't let him go. He let go after I put the toe of my boot in his face a couple of times. The first kick did the trick and the second was due to adrenalin. I wasn't worried about the officers.

J. Bronson Haley

"You two stand over there with your hands out of your pockets until we figure out what is going on," one officer said to Jared and me. A few minutes went by before the officer returned and explained, "We have two men going to the hospital to get stitched up. We still are not sure what we are going to do with you two."

I didn't feel the need to say anything, yet.

As I suspected, the officer returned and said, "We have declared it a fair fight. The man pulled out a crowbar and you two fought with your hands. It was your fault the fight broke out. However, one of the gentleman is guilty of assault with a deadly weapon. You two are free to go."

It was on this night that I cut a business deal with the captain. From what I understood, commercial divers made their money offshore. However, they had to work as a diver tender for around two years before they broke out as a diver. A diver tender takes care of the divers while they work. I was certainly going offshore, but was not interested in being a diver tender. I had caught wind that the captain had a dive company in South America. After a brief conversation about this company and Captain Redd's saturation system, Jared and I were scheduled to head to South America in a few weeks. We would skip the dive tending part of the job and immediately start making good money—$400 to $600 a day.

"Just don't mention anything to Danny," the captain told us.

Danny was part owner, but a silent owner who didn't make the decisions. Captain Redd was the CEO of the school and a big-shot saturation diver who retired under the largest company in the world. He had made more than five million dollars during his ten-year career.

"If you serve a hard ten years, you can retire a rich man," he explained.

"I'll never be able to repay you for what you have done for me, Bronson," Jared said to me later as he pondered the reality of our breakthrough in the business.

Three weeks later Jared and I got bored after school let out for the day and convinced two of the other students to play a drinking game with us. One of the students, Mark, whom I mentioned above, was only eighteen years old, so we gave him the nickname "Junior" because he was the youngest at the school. The other student's name was Billy. Jared and I referred to him as "the preacher" because he used to be a Baptist pastor. After picking up a fifth of Bacardi, Jared, Junior, the backslidden preacher, and I sat at the table in the dining room and began a game of quarters.

144

The Depth of Grace

Quarters is a game in which a community shot glass is set up in front of the players. Usually all players have their own glass to drink from. This night, though, we passed the bottle of liquor instead. Holding a quarter with the thumb and index finger, we slammed it on the table, hoping to bounce it off the table into the shot glass. If we missed the glass, we drank the shot, refilled it, and passed the glass and the quarter to the next person. If we landed the quarter in the glass, we passed the full shot of alcohol and did not have to drink.

Quarters is a fast game and most people play drinking beer. We were playing with straight Bacardi. After taking a gulp, we chased it with Coke to kill the pain of the furious liquid draining into our stomachs. When the preacher began to get a buzz after the first couple of rounds, I heard him say under his breath, "This isn't good." I marveled at his wisdom.

After returning from the store with a second bottle of Bacardi, we continued our game. We chased this bottle with Sprite, having run out of Coke. As we approached the end of the second bottle, we were all pretty drunk. I chuckled as I heard the preacher say again under his breath, "This isn't good." Things then began to happen dangerously fast. I could sense the preacher getting nervous and feeling guilty.

We ran out of Sprite just after cracking the seal of our third Bacardi. To solve our problem, I walked into the kitchen and returned with a bottle of ranch-style salad dressing. By this time, we were so drunk, we didn't care. After we finished the third bottle of liquor (all but a couple of shots), Jared and I played a game of "whoever can make the biggest splatter of salad dressing on the wall wins." Back to back, we hurled the plastic bottle of ranch dressing from across the room into the surrounding cinder-block construction. We were very competitive by nature.

"The show must go on," Jared hollered, insinuating our need for more alcohol.

As Junior climbed into my truck, the preacher pulled me to the side and lectured me. "Bronson, listen to me. You are too drunk to drive," he said with deep concern.

"Listen up, preacher-boy! No need to worry! I am a professional drunk driver!" I explained clearly.

"Bronson, trust me. You are too drunk to drive," he said, determined to guide me down the straight and narrow.

"Billy! Why do you doubt?" I asked, even more concerned about his own faith.

J. Bronson Haley

I encouraged him to maintain his trust in God with a nudge toward the truck. I chuckled as he climbed in and shook his head. I heard him say again under his breath, "This isn't good." Billy really was a wonderful man. It was obvious that he loved God as much as each one of us. He, too, was at a crossroads in life.

With Junior in the passenger's seat, Billy in the middle, and me behind the wheel, my frustrations grew as Jared took his sweet time in the restroom. When Jared walked out the front door of the dorm toward the truck, Junior got a brilliant idea. "Let's pretend we're leaving without him," he said.

Jared took off running as I pulled out of the drive onto the road. Halfway down the block he dove into the passenger's window and grabbed the little handle attached to the roof on the inside of the truck while throwing his right leg around the door mirror. He held on for dear life as I continued to pick up speed. It would have made perfect sense for Jared to climb into the truck. However, by the time we pulled onto Main Street, Jared was on the hood with his chest up against the windshield and his face mashed up against the glass. With his mouth against the glass, he made faces at us as he exhaled.

Billy then preached another mini-sermon: "Bronson, seriously, this isn't good!"

"Relax, Billy-boy! I've got this under control!" I replied.

As Junior and I proceeded to give Jared the thumbs-up for his bravery and Billy continued to prophesy, I glanced into the parking lot of the grocery store to our right and took note of an officer who sat in his car as though watching for traffic violations. Through the expressions on our faces, Billy, Junior, and I conveyed to Jared that we had a serious problem. Jared then glanced in the direction of our attention and acknowledged our new friend.

"I knew it! I knew it!" Billy said to confirm the validity of his prophetic ministry.

As the officer turned on his flashing lights, I quickly pulled into a gas station to our left to ponder the situation. I had always been an expert at avoiding big tickets. The only time I had ever been convicted of DUI was the time I blacked out the summer of my junior year of high school. I knew all the tricks and had an incredible record of escaping impossible situations one way or the other. However, I had never been this caught a day in my life. (Please note: I am not proud of this. I put at risk the life of everyone

146

The Depth of Grace

on the road that night, which was not fair to anyone. I was a selfish fool and am extremely grateful that I didn't hurt anyone.)

When I stopped the truck, Main Street was to our right. There was a road about a hundred feet in front of us across the parking lot. The gas station was to our left. As the officer approached in his car from behind, Jared quickly slid to his right off the hood and onto his feet. After a quick word of encouragement to us, he ran diagonally toward the street in front and to the left. We watched as Jared disappeared around the corner of the store with a "Good luck!" yelled in our direction.

"Good luck? Is that all you have to say, you frickin' jerk?" I said.

The officer passed us by and hung a left onto the street in front in an attempt to catch Jared. He quickly turned around and stopped in front of my truck with his headlights beaming straight at us, which would provide plenty of light to capture the moment.

Jared had just been arrested for DUI the week before. On that particular night we had left a nightclub and he drove my truck because I was too drunk to drive. I gave him the same spiel I gave Billy when we left the dorm moments before: "Relax! I'm a professional drunk driver." But Jared ended up driving. After getting stopped by a cop, Jared was asked to step out of the car and participate in the standard field sobriety test. In doing so, Jared hosted the most entertaining performance I'd ever witnessed. Pound for pound, that is. I'd seen longer shows in my day, but Jared added the "Volp Twist" he became famous for.

He stood in the middle of several officers with his hands stretched from east to west. With his right foot six inches off the ground and head tilted back, Jared proceeded to poke himself in the eye with his index finger in an attempt to touch his nose. With a heartless motive an officer asked Jared a trivial question to add to the drama: "Why are your pants wet, son?" He had previously spilled the drink he had between his legs when we were pulled over. I anticipated his response as he stood there with his head tilted back, eyes closed, hands stretched out, and mouth quiet. This was very funny in a twisted kind of way. However, I did feel bad for him for a split second. He sure looked pathetic from where I was sitting. There were around five police cars on site by this time and around seven or eight officers standing around staring at Jared, and they, too, anticipated his response. There he stood, in all humility, hands from east to west and one foot still off the ground with his face toward space. Jared looked as though he begged the stars for a worthy explanation. Suddenly all the officers focused intensely on him and silence was all that could be heard.

147

J. Bronson Haley

It seemed as if Jared, the officers, and I were sealed off and from the rest of the world. It was as if the cop cars listened in and waited for my poor friend's response to the officer's question. This was the chief of all Kodak moments. The gap of silence between the officer's question and Jared's answer grew dangerously in width. The suspense reached its peak among all who watched as Jared received from the heavenly black hole the answer he so desperately needed. With all due respect and sincerity, he said to the officer, "I peed in my pants, sir."

When those words left Jared's mouth, hysterical laughter filled the air. I felt for Jared, but that was hands down one of the funniest things I'd witnessed in all my life. The officers literally leaned up against their cars and laughed to the point of tears. Even the cars danced to the music. One officer had previously given me strict orders to stay in the truck. But he didn't say anything when I rolled out of my truck onto the concrete and laughed my rear end off.

Cops see and hear many things in their line of work. This wasn't anything out of the ordinary. However, at this moment, they were all caught off guard. Jared wasn't just a drunk shooting off at the mouth with careless words. He was passionately searching for the words that might set him free.

After a few seconds Jared let his hands down and looked over at me with a grin rooted in humility and defeat. He was then read his rights and placed under arrest. The officers searched my truck and found a marijuana pipe. They explained that they didn't care who claimed the pipe. Jared was going to jail anyways and the charge wasn't a big deal. However, I had drunk around a fifth of Bacardi and I couldn't let Jared go down like that by himself. I claimed the pipe and climbed in the car with my buddy.

During the ride downtown the officer played back the video he captured of Jared running off the road twice prior to being pulled over. Tough night, for sure.

Okay, back to Main Street and the story at hand! We had pulled over and Jared jumped off the hood and ran. The officer passed us by and hung a left onto the street in front in an attempt to catch Jared. He quickly turned around and stopped in front of my truck with his headlights beaming straight at us. By the time the cop had turned around and parked in front of me, I had come up with a plan. As the beams of his car invaded my space, I stood at attention—fully aware of the camera. When the officer previously passed by to block off Jared, I jumped out and threw the keys across the parking lot. The officer now exited his car with confidence to address the situation.

As he approached me, he asked, "Are you the driver?"

"Noooo, siiir! I am entirely too drunk to drive," I said with a lazy slur.

"Well, where is the driver?" the officer asked with an awkward shift in body language.

"Officer, you will never believe this! My buddies and me (pointing to Billy and Junior) were at Jackie's bar drinking when we met two guys we didn't know. They wanted to go to Diamonds strip club. We three were too drunk to drive and assured the other two fellows that we should all stay at Jackie's to ensure the safety of the public as well as our own. They convinced me they hadn't been drinking so I agreed to allow one of the two to drive. After the three of us loaded up, one of the guys jumped behind the wheel and the other jumped onto the hood and off we went. When we pulled over and parked here, the guy who rode on the hood took off that way. When you passed by in an attempt to stop him, the driver jumped out and ran this way," I said, pointing toward the left corner of the store. "Now I'm ticked because this is my truck and I'm going to get the DUI! The a-hole even stole my keys!"

The officer and I had a little stare down for a brief moment. It looked to me like he was trying to keep from laughing. I was definitely trying to keep from laughing. We both held it together, and the cop said to Junior and Billy, "You two step out of the vehicle."

As Billy slid across the front seat, he accidentally kicked our third bottle of Bacardi. Junior and Billy both froze in place in the truck as the bottle broke at the policeman's feet. I quickly turned my attention to the officer. His facial expression resembled that of a sinner who held back tears at church. I broke into laughter to break the silence, and the poor officer couldn't hold it together any longer. He broke down and laughed with me. Junior and the preacher allowed a slight chuckle to seep through the cracks of, "What in the heck is going on?"

Finally, Billy and Junior slowly exited the truck.

"Son, what's your name?" the officer asked the youngest of our trio.

"Mark," he said.

I then retrieved the keys when I "noticed" them near the left corner of the store. They waited patiently for me to retrieve them. The officer gave clear instructions when I explained that I had found the keys.

J. Bronson Haley

"You two get in the truck. Mark, you drive. Now get the heck out of here before I take all three of you to jail!"

He wasn't mad by any means. He was bewildered and obviously entertained at our stupidity.

As we pulled out onto Main Street, I explained to the preacher, "Now, Billy … you know it's a sin to worry."

"Bronson, I was a cop for thirteen years. That was nothing short of an absolute miracle," he said in all seriousness.

I didn't respond to his comment. It sure seemed like a miracle. I didn't think the Lord would help me because of my failures, but deep down inside I wanted it to be Him.

After one trip through the neighborhood, Junior and I sat in my truck in the driveway of our crack house dorm wondering what to do about Jared.

"Do you think he knows how to get back to the dorm in his condition?" I asked.

"I don't know," Junior said.

We had been pulled over only around two miles from the crack house. Jared had already had plenty of time to show up, but he was nowhere to be seen.

I sat in the passenger seat of my truck as my peripheral vision captured a glimpse of motion from the shadow of death. That's when a man came out of a bush, shirtless, clothed in mud, and covered in twigs.

After I jumped out of the truck, I stood there with hands on my hips, waiting for the words that may save his life. After a brief moment of confusion, I realized that it was Jared.

"I killed a man," he said.

At the time, I had no idea what Jared was talking about. Only later did I realize that Jared—while drunk and in a major state of mental chaos—had reverted back to his training as a Marine sniper. When he came out of those bushes, he looked like he was headed to war. And his head must have been back in some fight he'd been in, because he hadn't killed anyone that night, so he must have said, "I killed a man," due to some dormant memory that resurfaced right then.

I immediately began to try and snap him back into reality. In an effort to do so, I pushed him a few times, which wasn't a good idea. Jared was one tough dude, and he wasn't having any of it. So we went at it, wrestling and cussing and screaming at each other. Neither of us really tried to seriously hurt the other, but we were putting on an amazing display of strength

150

The Depth of Grace

and fighting skill. At one point the preacher tried to get between us, and I grabbed him by the back of the neck and threw him forward so hard that he ended up rolling into a front flip. Jared and I scrapped like two bull elephants. The violent struggle woke the neighbors, and they called the cops. When the officers arrived, the instructor of the school pulled into the drive. Jason, the instructor, immediately went inside and noticed the dorm was a wreck. He also noticed that the door to his room had been kicked in. (Jared and I persuaded Junior to kick in the door just before our last trip to the liquor store. However, Jared took the rap.) Rightfully upset, Jason conveyed to the cops the devastation inside.

"&%$# you, Jason!" Jared added to the details of the instructor.

Jared couldn't stand Jason, and everything Jared had held inside up until that point came out in the presence of the men in black.

"Officers, I am the only one who knows how to deal with Jared. I promise that when you leave, he will calm down and go to sleep," I explained.

After around ten minutes of pleading with the cops, they left with the words, "Just make sure we don't have to return."

"I've talked with Danny (the part-owner and administrator of education of the school) and we'll have a meeting at 8:00 a.m. to discuss everything that has happened," Jason explained before he slammed the door to his room.

Jared and I had already caused enough trouble at the school to have Prince Edward kicked out. Nothing major other than the DUI that Jared received. On occasion we got the other students too drunk to show up for class. It was the combination of a lot of little things that boiled the blood of the staff. For instance, Jared and I would often steal the dive station and take it for rides up and down Trout River in the middle of the night. No one ever found out about that (until now), but every now and then, I parked the sixty-foot barge backward into its place. Every morning the students set up the dive station on this barge to prepare for the day. I did this to exercise the power I had over Captain Redd due to the deal we made and rub this un-understood favor into the face of Jason the instructor and the other students. Danny (the very silent co-owner of the school) was a stand-up man and would not have approved of Jared and me going to work without the proper training. Danny was not in on the business side of the deal, either. He was a silent owner who would have been furious to the point of hiring lawyers had he found out what I knew. This was the reason Captain Redd went to bat for Jared and me on every occasion. "You

J. Bronson Haley

keep your mouth shut and I'll do the same," he'd say. This was the nature of our relationship. However, the dynamic duo had taken things a little far with this last ordeal.

Within fifteen minutes we had everything we owned in the back of my truck and were headed to Louisiana. Thus ended my dreams of plumbing the depths of the ocean blue as a deep-sea diver.

CHAPTER 17

Mexico

Having left my truck in town, I walked across the Mexican border from Laredo, Texas, and the poverty-stricken environment and sickness in the air overwhelmed me. Within minutes I was approached by one of the hustlers of the underworld. A white American male in his early twenties, walking alone, must have sent up flags for these Mexican street boys. They knew I was in Mexico to see the doctor.

"You need to see docta? I know good docta. Come with me. I know best docta," the boy said.

We walked about ten minutes into Mexico. Once we reached the right building, I was led through a door into a room. Three cots sat in this room. Each cot was up against a wall and had sheets and pillows. The fourth wall had another door that led into another room. I walked through the next door into a similar scene. Only this time a sickly man lay on one of the cots. His eyes were open but were covered with a thick, milky substance that looked dirty. When I made eye contact with the man, I got a feeling in my stomach that stayed with me until I left the building. Death would be best word to describe what I felt.

In the next room sat a teacher's desk and four chairs. One chair was behind the desk, two in front, and one up against the wall to my right.

"Have seat. I go tell the docta you here," the boy said.

As I sat alone in this room, I began to ponder the reality of the situation. Three doors deep I sat anticipating the arrival of a gangster who would probably just as soon kill me and take my money than sell me some

153

pills. The Mexican mafia runs the drug scene in Mexico. This was no secret. I understood my value to them but could not look past the reality that I was at the disposal of men who didn't value life. Business or no business, I was in an extremely dangerous situation dealing with extremely dangerous people, and my insides didn't let me forget it.

Moments later my little friend returned with two others. One of the two was dressed in scrubs. The hustler knew some English and worked as an interpreter for the boss, who conveniently spoke no English at all. When I looked into his eyes, murder jumped from his soul into my own. I immediately handed a five-dollar bill to the hustler who walked in with the "doctor" and told him to buy him and me a pack of smokes. I didn't smoke, but sure needed a cigarette.

"What medicine you like from docta," the boy asked.

"Xanax," I replied.

After he communicated my request to the "doctor," the boy said to me, "Two dollars and fifty cents each."

"What? No deal!" I said.

"This is best deal," he said.

"I'm ready to go to the next doctor," I said as I stood up.

After thirty minutes of negotiations—the doctor having left and returned several times—we agreed on a price and the helpers quickly un-bottled the pills and put them into two separate plastic bags and taped them up. I paid one hundred dollars to a one-legged Mexican in a wheelchair to smuggle the pills across the border. When we met just over the border, I gave him the rest of the money and he gave me the drugs.

Getting the drugs over the border was the hard part—so I was told. "Once you are over the border, you are home free," I'd heard. "The dogs will bump your car at the checkpoint just outside of Laredo, but dogs can't smell pills." It was common knowledge on the streets that dogs could not smell pills. With dogs being the only obstacle at the checkpoint, I had nothing to worry about.

When I saw the checkpoint in the distance, I was frightened a little. At the last minute I decided to hide the pills in the speaker box located under the backseat on the passenger's side of the truck. Then I drove up and it happened ...

"Unfortunately our dogs have alerted your vehicle for drugs and I need you to pull over and park so I can search," an officer at the checkpoint said to me after his dog bumped my truck.

Turned out that dogs do smell pills.

The Depth of Grace

What the man meant to say was, "Pull over so that we can find the pills hidden in your vehicle and arrest you for at least two felonies. You will get one felony for trafficking illegal narcotics and one for intent to distribute. The judge will decide for himself whether he wants to add a third felony for possession."

More drugs come through this particular checkpoint than any other in the United States. These dogs were no doubt the best in the world. The officers had every reason to be confident that I was up to no good.

So I pulled over, and one of the two officers asked me to walk with him about twenty feet away from the truck and stand with him while the other officer found the drugs.

"What are you doing here?" he asked as the other officer began the search.

"I came to town to bid on a job. I don't know why my boss sends me down here. He knows we can't compete with the cheap labor. I think he is just training me," I explained.

"Well ... we have heard it all. We just arrested a boy for steroids a few minutes ago." He apparently assumed I was there for steroids because of my athletic build.

"Sir, is there anything else that can alert the dogs other than drugs?" I asked, concerned to the point of death.

"Do you smoke marijuana?" he asked.

"No," I said.

"Have you loaned your car to anyone who does?" he asked.

"Well, my sister borrowed my car a couple of weeks back and she smokes," I told him.

He looked at me, paused for a moment, then said, "He will find the drugs and you will go to jail."

Ouch!

These officers worked their dogs for a living. The man was extremely confident that I had drugs and was certain that it was only a matter of minutes before his partner would find them.

I was relieved to a degree when the officer who searched the truck finished on the right side of my vehicle, after having pulled all the paneling and spending around twenty minutes doing so. I was sure I had just witnessed a miracle when he shut the door and proceeded to search the left side.

155

J. Bronson Haley

"Sir, he has been searching for around twenty minutes now. He isn't going to get mad at me after having wasted all that time, is he?" I asked, loud enough for the officer who searched to hear me.

"He will find the drugs," the man said.

When the search officer finished ripping all the paneling out of the left side of my truck and returned to search the right side, I began to dig my grave in my mind.

He figured it out, I thought.

He searched the right side for a few more minutes, and then the officer walked over to my new friend and me with sweat beaded up on his forehead. He looked as if he'd seen a ghost. I probably looked like I had seen a ghost as well.

"Well, here are your keys," he said.

It was obvious that this was an extremely rare occasion. The officer who stood with me didn't say anything.

Looking as if he didn't know what to say, the officer who searched my truck asked me, "Do you know that the speaker box under that backseat on the driver's side of your truck has a wire that is not plugged in?"

"No. I didn't know that. Thanks for telling me," I said.

"Does it need to be plugged in?" he asked.

"Yes, sir. It will not work if it isn't plugged in," I explained. (This was a very intelligent conversation.)

He walked with me to my truck to show me the problem and the other officer followed behind. The positive wire wasn't plugged into the speaker box behind the driver's seat, under the backseat.

"I wasn't aware of that, sir. Thanks again for telling me," I said, as I plugged the wire into the proper place.

"No problem," he said.

The mood between the officers was that of a state of shock. Actually we were all in a state of shock. This wasn't a normal conversation. It was as if we'd all seen a ghost, to be perfectly honest. The officer described shaking the speaker box, trying to hear something inside. It was almost like everything was happening in slow motion. I really cannot explain what it was like talking to the officers at this point.

As the officer who searched my vehicle shook my hand, he said, "We won't be taking you to jail today."

I apologized for the confusion as I climbed into the truck. I barely got the apology out of my mouth. I'm not sure if the cops noticed that my eyes were welling up with tears or not. The only place the cops did not

156

The Depth of Grace

search was the very speaker box the pills were hidden in. What were the chances?

This trip to Mexico was about trying to survive and live with who I was. I knew I couldn't live like this for long, but having those pills, I knew that for the next several months I would not have to deal with whom I had become. As I pulled away from the checkpoint, I cried and began trying to figure out how God might go about turning my life around if it indeed had been Him who saved me from getting arrested on this trip. These thoughts were soon drowned out by what I was going to have to do to support my habit. I would have to sell a fraction of these pills in order to pay for the next batch. I justified my actions because I knew whom I would sell them to and knew these people would get the drugs from someone regardless. I also justified my actions because I did not sell to kids. I sold to people my age in the bar scene. Most of them were my friends.

The hole I had been digging in my life for the past couple of years was getting deeper—and darker.

10TH REST STOP:
RECONCILIATION OF THE WORLD

I've been around people with phobias that they should be shot over. I don't care what is going on in one's central-nervous-forsaken system! Do not be more afraid of a bird than a rattlesnake! If I hear that one more time, I will be sure to prove the truth of why one should fear the snake. If I hear someone tell me they would rather be burned to death than drowned, I am going to torch them! I'm glad I saw you pick up that giant tarantula at the zoo. The next time you beg me to stomp on a roach because you are too afraid of him, I'm going to shove the prehistoric zero down your throat!

Do not judge me because I am having a bad day! Haven't you heard? "You, therefore, have no excuse, you who pass judgment on someone else, for at whatever point you judge another, you are condemning yourself, because you who pass judgment do the same things" (Romans 2:1). The Bible is a double-edged sword! Don't mess with me. I will cut you up.

No question about it, people are weird. And they don't care if people lie to make them feel better. Watch this: "I'm sorry for hurting your feelings. I share in this stupidity as well. I would rather scuba dive in a pond full of starving alligators than climb a radio tower with a safety belt. Now that you feel better, let's continue …"

As sure as every person has his or her own backward conglomeration of phobias, we all share one fear to some degree: rejection. Rejection is the most common fear among humans, and if we are rejected as Christians, that is good news!

"What? What do you mean 'good news,' Bronson?" you ask.

Yes—if you are rejected, that is good news.

The Depth of Grace

"What? If people fear rejection and it hurts, then why is it good to be rejected?" you ask.

Just because. This is my newest idea. Just accept the idea and go with it! Haven't I gained your trust by now? Glory to God! I can't even convince my own disciples to trust my ideas now. I have created monsters that eat the Bible. I know you eat it to scare off the Devil! I'm not making fun. But don't think that Pope Benedict wouldn't freak out as well if he walked into the heavenly sanctuary as you ravage the Holy Scriptures with your teeth.

As Christians we have joined with Jesus in an effort to bring home those who are lost. As Christians who are willing to speak of the Lord in public and to those who may not know Him, we will be rejected and sometimes hurt by what people do or say. Only one way exists to confront the fear of rejection. As believers we confront all challenges with the Word of God.

Now I will mention a man I hold close to my heart, one who helped me understand the truth hidden in the depths of rejection. Rejection actually opened the door for his ministry. His ministry was and is more powerful than any other. His name is Paul and he is the most powerful man of God mentioned in the New Testament.

First, let's take a look at the ministry of this man Paul, who had previously been known as Saul.

> In Lystra there sat a man who was lame. He had been that way from birth and had never walked. He listened to Paul as he was speaking. Paul looked directly at him, saw that he had faith to be healed and called out, "Stand up on your feet!" At that, the man jumped up and began to walk.

> When the crowd saw what Paul had done, they shouted in the Lycaonian language, "The gods have come down to us in human form!" Barnabas they called Zeus, and Paul they called Hermes because he was the chief speaker. [And, people say God doesn't have a sense of humor!] The priest of Zeus, whose temple was just outside the city, brought bulls and wreaths to the city gates because he and the crowd wanted to offer sacrifices to them. [What a bunch of lunatics!]

> But when the apostles Barnabas and Paul heard of this, they tore their clothes and rushed out into the crowd, shouting:

J. Bronson Haley

> *"Men, why are you doing this? We too are only human, like
> you. We are bringing you good news, telling you to turn
> from these worthless things to the living God, who made the
> heavens and the earth and the sea and everything in them.
> In the past, he let all nations go their own way. Yet he has
> not left himself without testimony: He has shown kindness
> by giving you rain from heaven and crops in their seasons;
> he provides you with plenty of food and fills your hearts with
> joy." Even with these words, they had difficulty keeping the
> crowd from sacrificing to them.*
>
> *Then some Jews came from Antioch and Iconium and won
> the crowd over. They stoned Paul and dragged him outside
> the city, thinking he was dead. (Acts 14:8-19, my comments
> added)*

What in the heck was that about? Why did they stone "Hermes"?
What could the men from Antioch and Iconium have said to the people
that could have possibly made enough sense to convince them all that the
apostle Paul came to harm them?

"Quick! Stone him before he heals another man!"

Huh? What made these people change from loving Zeus and Hermes
to the point of idiocrisy, then to hating someone to the point of murder?
The reason is that these people did not control their own desires. The men
in this town and the surrounding towns were under the power of the Devil,
and Satan grants his children the desires of their hearts. In their idolatry
they became blind to the point of absolute atrocity.

> *Therefore do not let sin reign in your mortal body so that you
> obey its evil desires. (Romans 6:12)*
>
> *Put to death, therefore, whatever belongs to your earthly
> nature: sexual immorality, impurity, lust, evil desires and
> greed, which is idolatry. (Colossians 3:5)*

Look at Paul's response to the abuse of these men: "But after the
disciples had gathered around him, he got up and went back into the
city" (Acts 4:20). Wow! They stoned him, and when they thought he was
dead, they dragged him out of the city so that the wild dogs and vultures
would have something to eat. But wait ... there is movement. Oh my! The
man—who had been stoned to death for his confession of Jesus Christ by

The Depth of Grace

the evil men of this city—jumped up and ran back into the city! Before we jump to conclusions and try to guess why Paul ran back into the city, let me explain. You see, the apostle Paul failed to clearly explain a couple of points before the larger of the rocks smashed his face in. He went back into the city to elaborate!

"But, Bronson! What happened to Paul that gave him this kind of boldness for Jesus?" you might ask.

That is a great question! Please welcome John Pollock, author of *The Apostle: A Life of Paul*, as he gives us insight into Paul's background:

> *Paul's parents were Pharisees, members of the party most fervent in Jewish nationalism and strict in obedience to the Law of Moses. They sought to guard their offspring against contamination. Friendships with Gentile children were discouraged. Greek ideas were despised. Though Paul from infancy could speak Greek, the lingua franca, and had a working knowledge of Latin, his family at home spoke Aramaic, the language of Judea, a derivative of Hebrew.*
>
> *They looked to Jerusalem as Islam looks to Mecca. Their privileges as freemen of Tarsus and Roman citizens were nothing to the high honor of being Israelites, the People of Promise, to whom alone the Living God had revealed His glory and His plans....*
>
> *By his thirteenth birthday, Paul had mastered Jewish history, the poetry of the psalms, and the majestic literature of the prophets. His ear had been trained to the very pitch of accuracy, and a swift brain like his could retain what he heard as instantly and faithfully as modern "photographic mind" retains a printed page. He was ready for higher education....*
>
> *But a strict Pharisee would not embroil his son in pagan moral philosophy. So, probably in the year that Augustus died, A.D. 14, the adolescent Paul was sent by sea to Palestine and climbed the hills to Jerusalem.*
>
> *During the next five or six years, he sat at the feet of Gamaliel, grandson of Hillel, the supreme teacher who, a few years*

J. Bronson Haley

before, had died at the age of more than a hundred. Under the fragile, gentle Gamaliel, a contrast with the leaders of the rival School of Shammai, Paul learned to dissect a text until scores of possible meaning were disclosed according to the considered opinion of generation of rabbis…. Paul learned to debate in question-and-answer style known in the ancient world as the "diatribe," and to expound, for a rabbi was not only part preacher but part lawyer, who prosecuted or defended those who broke the sacred Law.

Paul outstripped his contemporaries. He had a powerful mind which could lead to a seat on the Sanhedrin in the Hall of Polished Stones, and make him a "ruler of the Jews."

So, by the time Jesus began His ministry, Paul—at that time known as Saul—was highly respected by the Sanhedrin, the Jewish rulers of their people. He longed to take his seat in the "oval office" of that day and age. Saul was a teacher of the Law and actually anticipated the coming of Immanuel, which means "God with us." However, He didn't like the fact that Jesus was claiming to be Immanuel. Saul was likely in the same courtyard of the high priest as Peter when Jesus was mocked, spit on, and beaten as an innocent man. Certainly, Paul was one of the men who sneered at Jesus as He hung on the cross silent.

The people stood watching, and the rulers even sneered at him. They said, "He saved others; let him save himself if he is God's Messiah, the Chosen One." (Luke 23:35)

When the twelve apostles were reinstated after the resurrection and filled with the Holy Spirit, they began to minister the truth about Christ with great power and authority. The rulers and elders of the people did not respond well to the apostles' confession of the gospel of Jesus. These men of authority knew from the Scriptures that God would send a man to save them from their sins:

Therefore the Lord himself will give you a sign: The virgin will conceive and give birth to a son, and will call him Immanuel. (Isaiah 7:14)

The Depth of Grace

> *For to us a child is born, to us a son is given, and the government will be on his shoulders. And he will be called Wonderful Counselor, Mighty God, Everlasting Father, Prince of Peace. (Isaiah 9:6)*

The people of Israel looked forward to the day God would fulfill His Word and send them their personal savior. They knew the Scriptures and believed what they read. These men of authority did not like the fact that these followers of Jesus were telling Israel that they missed Immanuel when He came.

"Not only did you miss Him, but you mocked Him. You nailed the Son of God on the cross, you blind fools!" they said, in essence.

The apostles preached this truth, and the rulers and elders of the people hated them in return. Consider the incredible story of Stephen, who was one of the men chosen for responsibility in the early church. He was a humble man who loved Jesus and was willing to do anything necessary to spread the gospel to those who did not know Him.

> *In those days when the number of disciples was increasing, the Grecian Jews among them complained against the Hebraic Jews because their widows were being overlooked in the daily distribution of food. So the Twelve gathered all the disciples together and said, "It would not be right for us to neglect the ministry of the word of God in order to wait on tables. Brothers and sisters, choose seven men from among you who are known to be full of the Spirit and wisdom. We will turn this responsibility over to them and will give our attention to prayer and the ministry of the word."* ...
>
> *Now Stephen, a man full of God's grace and power, performed great wonders and signs among the people. Opposition arose, however, from members of the Synagogue of the Freedmen (as it was called)—Jews of Cyrene and Alexandria as well as the provinces of Cilicia and Asia—who began to argue with Stephen. But they could not stand up against the wisdom the Spirit gave him as he spoke.*
>
> *Then they secretly persuaded some men to say, "We have heard Stephen speak blasphemous words against Moses and against God."*

J. Bronson Haley

> *So they stirred up the people and the elders and the teachers of the law. They seized Stephen and brought him before the Sanhedrin. They produced false witnesses, who testified, "This fellow never stops speaking against this holy place and against the law. For we have heard him say that this Jesus of Nazareth will destroy this place and change the customs Moses handed down to us."*
>
> *All who were sitting in the Sanhedrin looked intently at Stephen, and they saw that his face was like the face of an angel.*
>
> *Then the high priest asked Stephen, "Are these charges true?"* (Acts 6:1-4, 8-15; 7:1)

In response Stephen preached a powerful sermon of truth to these men who falsely accused him in the same manner they accused Jesus. His conclusion was a perfect demonstration of the love he had for His Lord:

> *"You stiff-necked people. Your hearts and ears are still uncircumcised! You are just like your ancestors: You always resist the Holy Spirit! Was there ever a prophet your ancestors did not persecute? They even killed those who predicted the coming of the Righteous One. And now you have betrayed and murdered him—you who have received the law that was given through angels but have not obeyed it."*

When the members of the Sanhedrin heard this, they were furious and gnashed their teeth at him. But Stephen, full of the Holy Spirit, looked up to heaven and saw the glory of God, and Jesus standing at the right hand of God. "Look," he said, "I see heaven open and the Son of Man standing at the right hand of God."

> *At this they covered their ears and, yelling at the top of their voices, they all rushed at him, dragged him out of the city and began to stone him. Meanwhile, the witnesses laid their clothes at the feet of a young man named Saul.* (Acts 7:51-58)

And there he is—the very first mention of Saul who would become Paul!

The Depth of Grace

Saul was not yet a member of the Sanhedrin, but was highly respected by them. The Sanhedrin, as I mentioned earlier, served as rulers of the people and Saul was their perfect disciple.

While they were stoning him, Stephen prayed, "Lord Jesus, receive my spirit." Then he fell on his knees and cried out, "Lord, do not hold this sin against them." When he had said this, he fell asleep.

And Saul approved of their killing him.

On that day a great persecution broke out against the church at Jerusalem, and all except the apostles were scattered throughout Judea and Samaria. Godly men buried Stephen and mourned deeply for him. But Saul began to destroy the church. Going from house to house, he dragged off men and women and put them in prison. (Acts 7:59-60; 8:1-3)

Have you ever heard that Satan is like a roaring lion that seeks to kill, steal, and destroy everything in his path? "Be alert and of sober mind. Your enemy the devil prowls around like a roaring lion looking for someone to devour" (1 Peter 5:8).

Satan was outraged that the apostles proclaimed Jesus Christ with the boldness of Stephen and were clothed with this power from on high. The spirit of Satan took control of Saul and sent him on a murderous rampage.

Pastor and author Charles R. Swindoll gives a vivid description of the vicious hatred that arose in the life of Saul of Tarsus at the words of Stephen in his book, *Paul: A Man of Grace and Grit.*

The ninth chapter of acts begins abruptly. Saul's blood is boiling. He's on a murderous rampage toward Damascus. He charged north out of Jerusalem with the fury of Alexander the Great sweeping across Persia, and the determined resolve of William Tecumseh Sherman in his scorching march across Georgia. Saul was borderline out of control. His fury had intensified almost to the point of no return. Such bloodthirsty determination and blind hatred for the followers of Christ drove him hard toward his distant destination: Damascus. If you were a follower of Jesus living anywhere near Jerusalem, you wouldn't want to hear Saul's knock at your door.

J. Bronson Haley

People blinded by the Devil to the degree that they act in this same ignorance in different areas of their lives do so because they cannot see a foot in front of their face. "But anyone who hates a brother or sister is in the darkness and walks around in the darkness. They do not know where they are going, because the darkness has blinded them" (1 John 2:11). Consider what the Bible says about Saul …

Meanwhile, Saul was still breathing out murderous threats against the Lord's disciples. He went to the high priest and asked him for letters to the synagogues in Damascus, so that if he found any there who belonged to the Way, whether men or women, he might take them as prisoners to Jerusalem. As he neared Damascus on his journey, suddenly a light from heaven flashed around him. He fell to the ground and heard a voice say to him, "Saul, Saul, why do you persecute me?"

"Who are you, Lord?" Saul asked.

"I am Jesus, whom you are persecuting," he replied. "Now get up and go into the city, and you will be told what you must do."

The men traveling with Saul stood there speechless; they heard the sound but did not see anyone. Saul got up from the ground, but when he opened his eyes he could see nothing. So they led him by the hand into Damascus. For three days he was blind, and did not eat or drink anything.

In Damascus there was a disciple named Ananias. The Lord called to him in a vision, "Ananias!"

"Yes, Lord," he answered.

The Lord told him, "Go to the house of Judas on Straight Street and ask for a man from Tarsus named Saul, for he is praying. In a vision he has seen a man named Ananias come and place his hands on him to restore his sight."

"Lord," Ananias answered, "I have heard many reports about this man and all the harm he has done to your holy people

The Depth of Grace

in Jerusalem. And he has come here with authority from the chief priests to arrest all who call on your name."

But the Lord said to Ananias, "Go! This man is my chosen instrument to proclaim my name to the Gentiles and their kings and to the people of Israel. I will show him how much he must suffer for my name."

Then Ananias went to the house and entered it. Placing his hands on Saul, he said, "Brother Saul, the Lord—Jesus, who appeared to you on the road as you were coming here—has sent me so that you may see again and be filled with the Holy Spirit." Immediately, something like scales fell from Saul's eyes, and he could see again. He got up and was baptized, and after taking some food, he regained his strength. (Acts 9:1-19)

You see, Saul believed the Jewish leaders were right in crucifying Jesus for claiming to be the Son of God. And he believed he was right for trying to put an end to this rumor that Immanuel had already come. Saul believed Jesus was a mere mortal man who merely claimed to be the one God would send to His people, who suffered terribly because of their sin. However, at the moment Ananias prayed for Saul, the scales that kept him blind fell from his eyes. Not only was he able to see in the physical realm, but he could also see the truth in Jesus Christ. Saul began to realize that he had been wrong all along. This man called Jesus turned out to be the one spoken of by the prophet Isaiah, as we saw earlier in this Rest Stop.

Saul came to understand that God sent His Son just as He said He would, only he had missed Him. Not only did he miss Him, but he supported His crucifixion. Turns out Jesus was innocent after all: "He was oppressed, and he was afflicted, yet he opened not his mouth: he is brought as a lamb to the slaughter, and as a sheep before her shearers is dumb, so he openeth not his mouth" (Isaiah 53:7 KJV). Saul recognized that Jesus remained quiet during His time of suffering because of this day when Saul himself would have the opportunity to accept that the Lord had been crucified for him. Saul missed Jesus when He came, but did not miss his opportunity to come clean by His blood. Saul was terribly disturbed and surely experienced guilt that we cannot fathom. However, he was not able to tell Jesus that He didn't suffer enough to cover his sin. Saul began to ponder the details of the sins he had committed against those who had

167

J. Bronson Haley

accepted Jesus. He recalled the murders of men such as Stephen, whose "face was like the face of an angel" (Acts 6:15). Saul had murdered or taken part in the murders of these men because of their faith in Immanuel.

The blood of the men who suffered in Saul's hands, he could see on his hands. Saul knew the Scriptures better than most, but now the love of God engraved the Law on his heart as he later taught in 2 Corinthians 3:3: "You show that you are a letter from Christ, the result of our ministry, written not with ink but with the Spirit of the living God, not on **tablets** of stone but on **tablets** of human **hearts**" (my emphasis). This new heart pumped through his veins the blood Jesus Christ shed at Calvary. As a result the Lord took Satan's most dangerous weapon and turned it against him. The Lord took Saul's sin against Jesus and his sin against His children and created a lion of His own. The change was so dynamic that the Lord gave him a new name. This lion's mind was opened to the Scriptures and he was "clothed with power from on high" (Luke 24:49). Saul of Tarsus—now the apostle Paul—a product of the risen Lord, became a force to be reckoned with. It was the canceled debt of the apostle Paul that made Him a "prisoner of Christ Jesus" (Ephesians 3:1). The love of God took the man who called himself the "worst of sinners" (1 Timothy 1:16) and made Him a mighty warrior for the kingdom. His past sin was in direct correlation with how powerfully God later used him.

In Paul's ministry he learned what it meant to suffer for Jesus. No man has come into existence who understands what it means to share in the sufferings of Jesus better than the apostle Paul.

> *I have worked much harder, been in prison more frequently, been flogged more severely, and been exposed to death again and again. Five times I received from the Jews the forty lashes minus one. Three times I was beaten with rods, once I was pelted with stones, three times I was shipwrecked, I spent a night and a day in the open sea, I have been constantly on the move. I have been in danger from rivers, in danger from bandits, in danger from my fellow Jews, in danger from Gentiles; in danger in the city, in danger in the country, in danger at sea; and in danger from false believers. I have labored and toiled and have often gone without sleep; I have known hunger and thirst and have often gone without food; I have been cold and naked. Besides everything else, I face daily the pressure of my concern for all the churches. Who is*

The Depth of Grace

weak, and I do not feel weak? Who is led into sin, and I do not inwardly burn? (2 Corinthians 11:23-29)

For if, while we were God's enemies, we were reconciled to him through the death of his Son, how much more, having been reconciled, shall we be saved through his life! (Romans 5:10)

When Adam sinned in the Garden of Eden, man lost spiritual fellowship with God—and God lost spiritual fellowship with man. However, God said that through the seed of the woman He would regain this fellowship. As a result the Word of God became flesh and made his dwelling among us in the form of His Son, Jesus. Jesus suffered as He did because Israel was in the heart of His Father, which was His own heart. He wept for those who hurled insults at Him. His heart burned for those who mocked, spit on, and beat Him. Jesus continued to move forward quietly because He understood the truth in what was happening. "Father, forgive them, for they do not know what they are doing" (Luke 23:34). Jesus prayed this prayer for the guards who nailed Him to the cross just seconds earlier.

The Son of God was greater than Satan and the spirit of Satan that manifested itself within His people—within those who were in sin. The spirit of Satan is evil, and this evil is fueled by the lies he feeds his slaves. Satan was and is the father of lies. As a matter of fact, the rulers of the people didn't even know what truth was ... yet they knew the Scriptures.

Do you remember the day Jesus stood before Pilate and listened to the accusations of the rulers and elders of the people?

"If I said something wrong," Jesus replied, "testify as to what is wrong. But if I spoke the truth, why did you strike me?"
...

"What is truth?" retorted Pilate. (John 18:23, 38)

Pilate did not know what truth was because there was no truth in him. This man had not received Jesus. Jesus is "the way and the truth and the life" (John 14:6).

If a man or woman has not received Jesus, there is no truth in him or her.

"Oh, Bronson ... people can come up with truth if they do not know God."

J. Bronson Haley

Excuse me? You must not know what truth is. How can you understand the truth I speak of if there is no truth in you? Every believer reading this book knows what I am talking about. This is not a concept brought forth by some magnificent creation of the human brain. The Spirit of God understands this topic and those who have received His Spirit know that what I am saying is the truth—by the Spirit they understand. Many of the rulers and elders of the people had the equivalent of PhDs in the Holy Scriptures—yet they did not understand truth.

Rejection was and is man's most common fear. It is important that every man of God not overlook the power hidden in the depths of rejection. Jesus was sent to earth to redeem Israel. But at the desire of the Jews, Jesus was nailed to the cross. His death made forgiveness available to His people, the Jews. When Jesus rose from the dead, He made eternal life available to Israel. Glory to God! Israel has been redeemed through the death and resurrection of Jesus Christ! The Jews have hope in Jesus! But what about the rest of us? What about those who are not Jewish? What about the rest of the world—the Gentiles, as the Bible call us?

As Christians—believers united in Christ regardless of race, age, social status, or anything else—it's time for us to understand the power of rejection. "For if their rejection brought reconciliation to the world, what will their acceptance be but life from the dead?" (Romans 11:15). It was the rejection of Jesus Christ—a large portion of His sufferings—that made salvation available to Gentiles. "Now if we are children, then we are heirs—heirs of God and co-heirs with Christ, if indeed we share in his sufferings in order that we may also share in his glory" (Romans 8:17).

The rejection we experience because of Christ multiplies the power of our ministry just as His rejection made salvation available to the Gentiles. How much more effective is our ministry when we are able to reach more people through rejection? No apostle understood this concept better than the apostle Paul: "I ask you, therefore, not to be discouraged because of my sufferings for you, which are your glory" (Ephesians 3:13). The Lord sent Paul to the "dogs" of this world, at least in Jewish eyes: the Gentiles. It was the rejection of Jesus Christ that opened the doors to his ministry. Paul understood that, when he was rejected, his words became stronger. In turn the "dogs" were more likely to listen to him when he spoke. It was easier for me to confront this fear of rejection when I understood this concept. The greatest men of God in history were rejected. Jesus was rejected. We are not rejected because we are doing something wrong. Christians are rejected because they are doing something right. If we are not rejected, then the

The Depth of Grace

Devil is not threatened by us. If we go through life and are not rejected because of our faith, it is because people do not know what we believe. If people do not know what we believe, then we are not doing our jobs.

Don't forget the last part of Romans 11:15 above: "… what will their acceptance be but life from the dead?" The spirit in those who reject us is weakened by our obedience—if we are speaking the Word of God to them, that is. If those we reach out to truly reject us, we will be turned away because of our faith and that can sometimes hurt deeply, especially when the rejection comes from those we love and care about. Rejection can be painful! However, the truth we speak will stay with those who reject us. God will one day bring this truth to light and they will then understand. When God enables these people to see the truth, we may see them one day and notice that they acknowledge us with a different look in their eyes. If you notice this look, walk up and wrap your arms around these people. The deeper you have experienced the pain of being rejected, the more powerful that hug is. When you grab hold of them, you will take from them their sin against you, which has been a burden. They will never forget that hug. According to the Word of God, they will be raised to life. "… what will their acceptance be but life from the dead?"

To those who feel guilty because of the way they have treated certain people in the past because of their faith, take heart. A true man of God is a man of forgiveness. We must forgive in order to be forgiven ourselves. "For if you forgive other people when they sin against you, your heavenly Father will also forgive you" (Matthew 6:14).

The Word of God can overcome any fear, any phobia, even rejection.

> *For the word of God is alive and active. Sharper than any double-edged sword, it penetrates even to dividing soul and spirit, joints and marrow; it judges the thoughts and attitudes of the heart. (Hebrews 4:12)*

> *In his right hand he held seven stars, and out of his mouth came a sharp, double-edged sword. His face was like the sun shining in all its brilliance. (Revelation 1:16)*

CHAPTER 18

—

Officer "Abuse"

The snow began to fall late one evening while two friends and I headed home after a night of drinking and playing pool at a local bar in Denver, Colorado. This was my first night in town (a week after my adventure in Mexico), and I was excited about Denver and hanging out with my childhood buddies Mike Mertle and Jackson Hunter. On our way home I noticed a car with its rear tires spinning as it tried making its way up a highway ramp.

Mike got an astounding idea. "Let's make some money right fast!" he said.

After I pulled up to the ramp, Mike jumped out and approached the frightened girl.

"Hey, beautiful! We'll tow you up the ramp for twenty-five dollars," he said to the girl.

She accepted the offer, and after I secured the towrope to each vehicle, I pulled her up the ramp.

"Did you get the rope untied?" the girl asked, extremely concerned.

She must have been worried because, when I attempted to untie her end of the rope that was tied to her tire rod, I asked Mike to hand me my knife out of the glove box.

"Of course I did, sweetheart," I assured her.

Because I was not thinking clearly, I tied a slipknot when I secured the rope to her tire rod. Slipknots get tighter and tighter the harder the rope is pulled. I would have had better luck untying a pet rock.

173

J. Bronson Haley

Excited about the easy money, we headed to the next ramp in anticipation of our next victim. We saw a car at the bottom of a ramp on the other side of the loop, so I slowed down just enough to somewhat safely plow through the snow on the median. Now headed in the direction of the stranded car, I caught flashing blue and red lights in my rearview window. I knew I was soon to be robbed of my joyful and profitable good time with Mike and Jackson.

I wore camouflage pants with thermals that were tucked into my wool socks. I felt sure the officer would search my car, so I stuck my bag of approximately thirty Xanax pills between my thermals and underwear. As I stepped out of my truck, the drugs slid down my leg and stopped at the top of my socks where my thermals were tucked.

"That was stupid wasn't it, officer!" I said as I approached where he stood in the front of his vehicle.

"Okay, feet together, head back, eyes closed, right foot six inches off the ground, and say your ABCs," he said as if this was a joke.

"Sir! I couldn't even do that if I were sober! Wait! That's not what I meant. I'm not used to the altitude!"

Oops.

I continued to fail in my efforts to escape, once again, and finally was forced to refuse the Breathalyzer test. I was arrested for DUI my first night in Denver. As I sat in the back of the cop car, the officer searched my vehicle. I began to ponder the upcoming events. I had a decent argument. It was a full-fledged blizzard at the time of my arrest. I wasn't used to the altitude and the officer denied me the right to retrieve my jacket prior to the tests. I was wearing a Fruit of the Loom T-shirt, and it was around 25 degrees. Without my blood-alcohol record, the state would have a hard time getting a conviction given the circumstances. However, my real problem wasn't the DUI.

As I sat in the back of the car, I began to ponder the upcoming routine of being booked into jail. The officers would give me a final search at the station and find the Xanax.

Tonight's extravaganza will deal me a possible DUI, a felony for the pills, and a traffic violation, I thought.

It was hard for me to accept that I was defeated. By this time I'd escaped some pretty serious situations by what seemed like miracles. Due to what I'd already experienced, I believed that there might be a way out, but I was going to be a true believer if something got me out of this mess.

On the ride to the station, the officer mentioned that I would get one last chance to take and pass the breath test downtown.

"Thanks, but I'm not interested," I assured him.

"Are you sure? If you pass, you will be on your way home without the DUI you have at this moment," he said.

"I'm not taking the test."

Suddenly a lady addressed the officer on the radio. "Is the suspect willing to take the breath test?"

After he asked me again, he told the lady, "No."

"Give him one more chance," the lady asked.

I knew the scoop. My only chance was to refuse the test. They were really asking me to give them proof to convict me of the DUI.

"No, I'm not taking the test," I said again.

A moment later the lady told the officer that the jail was full and instructed him to take me to the detox center.

"Alleluia … I mean … where are we going?" I asked.

"The jail is full and you will be booked into the detox center until you sober up. You still have the DUI, so relax," he said, reaffirming his victory over me.

Yeah! But you got robbed of a felony arrest, I thought.

I couldn't believe what was happening right before my eyes. What were the chances of this? I'd never even heard of someone being taken to a detox center after getting arrested for DUI. This wasn't even an escape route I could have dreamed of. I was immediately comforted as the most severe of the potential violations had now been eliminated.

The officer gave me one last chance to take the breath test at the detox center and I refused. When the officer left the center, the lady at the desk asked me to take the test.

"No, thank you," I said.

"We cannot let you go until you blow a 0.0 on the breath test," she said. "Don't worry! By law the courts cannot obtain these records."

"No need for the test, ma'am. I'm not blowing a 0.0 right now regardless."

After I crammed my face full of food and waited around forty-five minutes, I blew a .032. At the time, that was three times *under* the legal limit for a DUI in Colorado. I was shocked that the test results were that low.

J. Bronson Haley

"You sure are pretty!" I said to the ugly woman. "How much time do the officers have to get a record of the suspect's blood alcohol level?" I asked her.

"Two hours. Don't worry. They will not know you had a drop to drink. They cannot get these records," she said in an effort to comfort me.

I slept—I am not sure how many hours—and then I blew a 0.0 as required and called a cab to take me to my truck. I guess you could say I had bad luck and extraordinarily good luck at the same time. Well, I definitely created the bad luck, but the good luck seemed supernatural.

That Monday morning, I made a few phone calls and retrieved my detox records. That was the easy part. Getting the proper documents rushed from the police station to the courthouse was a real pain. I didn't get anywhere over the phone so I decided to stop by the station. I didn't know what the deal was exactly, but the people at the station were downright rude to me. I think it was because they thought I was a redneck due to my accent.

"Hi, I got a DUI over the weekend. This has been one big misunderstanding, and I need you to rush the file to the courthouse for me this afternoon so I can get this taken care of," I said.

"Are you joking?" the man asked.

"No, I'm from out of town." I had a little attitude myself.

"I'm sorry, but you are going to have to wait for your court date," he said.

"That's impossible. I cannot make it back at that time, and I must catch a plane home in two days. I have to get his taken care of today."

"I apologize, but we are not allowed to do that," he said with a grin on his face that boiled my blood.

"That's no problem. I'm sure your boss can help me. I need to talk to him."

A few minutes later, as the man's boss came out to see me, I thought, *I know this woman isn't walking around the corner with a smirk on her face like this is funny.*

"Ma'am, there has been a mis—" and she cut me off.

"I know, he told me. We cannot do that," she said with a manly attitude and a prissy voice.

"Let's quickly review how ridiculous you are acting so that you can accurately communicate to your boss the details of your stupidity," I said. "I'm sure he is waiting right now in anticipation of being harassed by your ignorance. I live eleven hundred miles away. I have a plane to catch so that I can go home to my wife and kids and run the family business. Only I

176

have a ticket I need to take care of first. The courthouse is only couple of miles away, and be sure to give him the details of why you cannot drive my file down the street for me. I can assure you I will not have that problem when I talk to him," I explained.

I arrived at the courthouse at 9:00 a.m. the next morning. It took me around an hour to reach the DA's office. After waiting another thirty minutes, I sat down with the DA's assistant.

"I got a DUI over the weekend. I'm from out of town and I cannot return on the scheduled court date. This is a huge misunderstanding in the first place, and I'm certain you will recognize the truth in what I'm saying if you hear me out," I said.

"I'm listening," the lady said.

"I pulled through a median and was pulled over for the violation. Upon exiting my vehicle, I approached the officer, who was by then standing in front of his car. The officer proceeded to give me the standard field sobriety test. I'm not sure why I lost my balance. Maybe it was the altitude combined with the snow blowing in my face, I'm not sure. It doesn't make any difference either way—" and I was interrupted.

"What are you here for, sir?" she asked.

"To have the DUI dropped so I can go home to my wife and kids and go to work," I explained.

"That's not going to happen. You've been charged with a DUI. However, we can take care of this now if you'd like. Are you ready to make a plea? If you plead not guilty, we will have trial on the date written on the ticket," she said.

"There is no reason to plead guilty. This is a misunderstanding," I reminded her.

"You have every right to plead not guilty. If you do so, I'll see you in court next month. Understand?" she said. She was a nasty little assistant with an attitude.

"No problem. You simply do not understand my situation yet. Do you have my detox records?" I asked.

"The law will not allow us to retrieve them from the center," she explained.

"That's okay. I have them right here."

I handed them to her.

She began to review them and then said to me, "We can drop your charge to a .5 DUI. A DUI is given to those who read .10 or higher on the breath tests. A .5 DUI is issued when the suspect's breath test reads between a .05 and .10 on the test. From the looks of the records, you are guilty of a .5 DUI, and we can take care of it now if you'd like."

"This doesn't' make any sense to me. How can I be guilty of a .5 DUI when I blew a .032 at the detox center? I know you can see I'm innocent."

"Are you ready to plead, sir?" she asked.

"No, but I do want to talk to the district attorney," I replied, clearly conveying my frustrations.

"As you wish. But she's tougher than I, and you'll be better off with my proposal. We don't have to do anything here today."

"I'll be back in twenty minutes. I need to consult with my attorney to make sure I don't do anything stupid," I said.

After I climbed into my truck, I called a friend of mine back home to tell him what I had gotten myself into.

"You are doing what?" he asked in disbelief.

"I'm not kidding you! She thinks I'm on the phone with my attorney right now."

"Now I know you are crazy!" he said

"I'm very much aware of this. I'll call you when I get done."

I then walked back into the office and took a seat. After a few moments the DA walked in and sat down in front of me with an "I'm going to have you for lunch" look on her face. I'd thought I was going to get another shot at the assistant.

"Are you ready to plead, sir?" she asked.

"Have you reviewed the records, ma'am?" I asked.

"You have been charged with a DUI. You will either receive a DUI today or next month. Which would you prefer?" she asked.

"That doesn't make any sense. Obviously I wasn't drunk at the time I was arrested. Why can you not look at the records and see that I haven't broken any laws? Why would you ask me to plead guilty to something you can see I am not guilty of? I honestly do not understand the problem. If I were to come back next month, I would return with an attorney. You fully understand you would not get a conviction under these circumstances," I explained.

"I would not be able to convict you of a DUI. But based on your records, you are guilty of a .05 DUI. Your attorney cannot destroy proof you have submitted into evidence, and you will lose in court. And by the way, sir, the reading derived from the test you received from the detox center is proof only to a small degree. It gives the court a general idea of

The Depth of Grace

your condition when you arrived at the center. The test downtown is 100 percent accurate and decides whether you are innocent or guilty. You refused that test and it is now working against you."

"I have a real problem with that. The test at the detox center was the same test I refused while standing on the side of the interstate in a full-blown blizzard freezing my tail off because the officer would not allow me to grab my jacket prior to my willfully participating in the field sobriety tests. This is a serious issue. Are you are telling me that if I had taken the test the officer offered me on the road and passed that there is a chance I would have driven away legally drunk? Now that worries me."

The air was so thick by this point it could have been cut with a knife.

"Listen, I can prove based on your records that you would have blown a .05 or higher had you taken the test the officer presented you with on the road," she said. "You blew a .032 at the center, well after you were arrested. That will be easy to prove."

"With all due respect, what you have said is inaccurate. By law the officer has two hours to get my alcohol level on record in order for it to stand it court. It says right here that I took the test at the detox center exactly one hour and forty-five minutes after I was arrested. Will you please drop the charge so I can go home?" I asked with a humble attitude.

The DA then leaned back into her chair and gazed into my eyes with a cross-dressed spirit of both pride and respect. The air was thick and the moment very intense. This would have been a great scene for *Law & Order*. I felt like I knew what I was doing, but I had never done this before. It seemed as though I had more time to think than she, and more wisdom. I was more confident than I should have been, but at the same time, I was in shock. I can't really describe the feeling.

"I'll tell you what I'll do. The officer didn't ticket you for recklessly crossing the median. I'll drop the DUI to a reckless driving ticket. In doing this, you will receive just punishment for your violation and I will get a conviction. Deal?"

"Deal!" I said as I buckled in my chair and released several breaths at once.

"In a few moments you will stand before the judge and plead guilty to the DUI. He will then honor the plea of reckless driving and you will be on your way," she said.

It was strange how her attitude changed. It was almost as though we became friends all of a sudden.

J. Bronson Haley

As the district attorney left the room, she stopped, looked back, and after a brief moment, said, "You have a strong presence about you. Good luck on your journey and ... stay out of trouble."

I stood before the judge, pled guilty to the DUI, and was given instructions on how to take care of the reckless driving ticket. I then walked down the stairs and out of the building. I'm sure the judge and the others in the court wondered why I had tears in my eyes. As I walked down the stairs and into the parking lot, I pondered the details of everything that happened. There was no explanation for my getting away with the felony charge and the DUI. Halfway to my truck, I broke down and wept. I felt sure that God was with me.

"Why won't you just give up on me, Lord?" I asked.

It was almost like I felt He was protecting me because He had plans to use me again. I didn't understand because God knew better than I that I could not have been stronger for Him. I knew I did my best when I lived for Him, and I know that He knew, because He is all-knowing. I just didn't understand why He would keep me. One part of me wanted Him to simply let me go. One part of me hoped He would not.

CHAPTER 19

"Stoned" Cop

I choked as the glare of flashing blue lights bounced from my rearview mirror into my stomach. I coughed and coughed and coughed as the marijuana smoke exited my lungs. It was an unmarked narcotics unit that approached me from behind. In a panic I pulled over to face the music. I rushed to hide my pipe and bag of very expensive weed that I had picked up in Colorado. Of course, I was extremely paranoid. But what do you do? The real problem arose when, just as I got everything hidden, the officer tapped on my window, which is tantamount to an order to roll it down and talk to him. I slowly turned my attention from my console into the eyes of the officer who stood with his head half tilted like a curious puppy. After a brief hesitation—what seemed like an eternity to me—I forced a trembling hand to press the appropriate button on my door to lower the window down and allow a cloud of smoke to reach the narcotics officer. Now we were having fun! When the smoke hit the officer in the face, he withdrew a few steps. Nothing like a hit of secondhand marijuana smoke to jolt your senses, eh?

"Why don't you come back here with me and have a seat in the passenger's side," he said after a quick hand signal. "Do you have anyone who can come get your truck?" he soon asked as he climbed into the driver's seat of his car.

"Yes, sir. I can call someone," I said.

"Good, because you will not be driving away from here," he said.

181

J. Bronson Haley

I was shocked that he hadn't already arrested me. However, I didn't ask any questions.

"Okay, hand me your driver's license," he said.

"I don't have it on me, officer," I said.

"Did you know you were speeding?" he asked.

"I do now," I said, humble and defeated.

"Did you know it's against the law to drive without shoes?" he asked.

"No, sir. But I do now."

I was so high and paranoid, it wasn't even funny. He hadn't even mentioned the smoke yet. You could say I was in mild state of shock. At the same time, I had an extremely hard time thinking due to the cloud in my brain.

"Son, where are you going?" he asked.

Ouch! I was simply driving around getting high. I didn't even plan on stepping out of the truck. I was barefooted and wore shorts and a white T-shirt. I sat quietly for a brief moment and begged my poor brain for the right words. My response was very humbling. Many people who smoke marijuana argue that it doesn't hinder the thought process. Don't try and tell me that!

"You see, sir, I was headed up to the Highway 3 bridge to check the water level. If the water is just right, the fish will bite," I explained.

Whoops! In response to that statement, he slowly channeled his attention from the tickets he was writing into my eyes with a "What in the Sam Hill did you just say?" look on his face.

"I'm not kidding. If the water is just right, the fish will bite," I assured him.

Should the officer have suspected a joke under these circumstances? He shook his head and continued to write the ticket. I turned my head and looked out the window to my right in disbelief that I was able to come up with something so stupid to say at a time like this. He hadn't even mentioned the marijuana smoke yet. I wasn't sure why, but I knew it was coming.

He must be saving that for last, I thought.

"What do you do?" the officer asked.

I don't think he asked this question because he expected that I must have had a great career going. I felt like, by this point, I had become amusing to this cop.

"I'm a commercial diver and plan to go to work in South America within the next couple of months," I lied.

182

The Depth of Grace

"Well, that's good," he said.

"Yeah, it's the only thing good going for me at this point," I said.

I paid close attention to every shift in the officer's body language as we sat in the car. Moments after our brief conversation, I noticed him glance up at my truck for a second as if he pondered his next move. After two or three seconds of him looking at my truck, he turned his attention back to the ticket and continued to write. After around thirty seconds of complete silence, he glanced back up at my truck. I desperately wanted to know what he was thinking at this time, but was too nervous to say a word. In a silent gaze the officer pondered his thoughts and then continued with the ticket.

At this point I began to prepare mentally for the arrest. I was sure the officer was thinking about what he would do when he was done with the ticket. Usually they call in another officer for their own safety when drugs are involved. With a hint of frustration the officer quickly turned his attention from the ticket back to my truck.

Maybe he's trying to decide what to do with it? I thought.

It looked like he struggled with his thoughts. After moments of silence, with his eyes tightly fixed on the truck, he said to me, "Son, I don't know where you are going in life. I do know that if something gets in your way … it's not going to be me."

With his left hand he initiated a handshake. I shook his hand and he said to me, "Go home. Get your driver's license. Put your shoes on and drive wherever you would like to go."

"Yes, sir," I said, without knowing how to properly communicate my appreciation for his mercy.

Tears rolled down my face as I climbed into my truck. I pulled up around fifty feet and made a U-turn. When I passed by him, the officer gave me a big smile with a friendly wave. It was as though it made him feel good to let me go.

It was a few months later, on my fourth attempt to overcome my addiction, that I was going through withdrawals when I got the phone call from one of my best friends, Shawn, letting me know that Jackson Hunter had died from a drug overdose, as I related to you in the Introduction of this book.

And, as I said in the Introduction, that's when I dropped to my knees and begged God for forgiveness. I promised the Lord that, if He would restore me, I would tell the world about His Son. And that's why you now hold this book in your hands.

11TH REST STOP:
RIGHTFULLY INSECURE

I now bring you to a town called Ephesus. The people in this town worshiped an idol named Artemis—the Greek moon goddess. The apostle Paul had visited this town and convinced many of those who lived there to leave their sinful ways and worship the one true God. Well, this became a real problem. A man named Demetrius, who made silver shrines of Artemis, got ticked because his business was going downhill as a result of the ministry of the apostle Paul. People quit buying the idols he was in the business of making and selling.

> *[Demetrius] called [the craftsmen] together, along with the workmen in related trades, and said: "You know, my friends, that we receive a good income from this business. And you see and hear how this fellow Paul has convinced and led astray large numbers of people here in Ephesus and in practically the whole province of Asia. He says that gods made by human hands are no gods at all. There is danger not only that our trade will lose its good name, but also that the temple of the great goddess Artemis will be discredited; and the goddess herself, who is worshiped throughout the province of Asia and the world, will be robbed of her divine majesty." When they heard this, they were furious and began shouting: "Great is Artemis of the Ephesians!" (Acts 19:25-28)*

You and I know that Artemis is nothing more than a fallen angel. Who tries to put himself/herself above our Lord and Savior Jesus Christ other

The Depth of Grace

than Satan and his followers? Isn't Satan battling the Lord? Isn't the Devil trying to establish His throne above the stars? "You said in your heart, 'I will ascend to the heavens; I will raise my throne above the stars of God; I will sit enthroned on the mount of assembly, on the utmost heights of Mount Zaphon" (Isaiah 14:13).

In Ephesus the evil spirit Artemis had convinced the people in the town that she was great, and had established a military post in this city that had been longstanding and very structured. However, the apostle Paul strolled through with a couple of helpers and all hell broke loose. As a result the men who lost work began to campaign for Artemis. "Soon the whole city was in an uproar. The people seized Gaius and Aristarchus, Paul's traveling companions from Macedonia, and all of them rushed into the theater together" (Acts 19:29). The people grabbed Paul's disciples, but why didn't they go get Paul as well? And why did they all rush into the theater at one time? They did this because Paul caught wind of the chaos and was on his way to address the disturbance. Apparently the Devil was a bit intimidated by a man of real faith in Jesus Christ.

Okay, didn't God kick Satan out of heaven? And this man called Paul had the same authority because Christ lived in his heart, right? Paul understood this authority that Jesus granted His followers, and when he arrived, he planned to confront the people who were so greatly disturbed by his ministry. "Paul wanted to appear before the crowd, but the disciples would not let him. Even some of the officials of the province, friends of Paul, sent him a message begging him not to venture into the theater" (Acts 19:30-31). Try and imagine this scene! This theater was packed full of extremely vicious individuals. This angry mob under the power of Artemis was all huddled into this one theater. And there was one man outside saying, "Let me at them! Let me go! I'll be fine! Is Jesus Christ not greater than this Artemis?" Is the beef not with Paul? Why did these people not go outside and kill him then? It's because they were under the power of Artemis. This spirit was extremely inferior to Jesus Christ, who walked in front of the apostle Paul. She got very insecure when the Son of God began to invade her space.

"The assembly was in confusion: Some were shouting one thing, some another. Most of the people did not even know why they were there" (Acts 19:32). Do you now believe me when I say they were under the power of the enemy? The only real tool the Devil has is that he is able to blind us. If we were not blind, we could see how stupid we are in our sin.

The show must go on!

185

J. Bronson Haley

> *The Jews in the crowd pushed Alexander to the front, and they shouted instructions to him. He motioned for silence in order to make a defense before the people. But when they realized he was a Jew, they all shouted in unison for about two hours: "Great is Artemis of the Ephesians!" (Acts 19:33-34)*

Are you kidding me?

"Oh no! It's one of God's chosen people! Who cares if he doesn't have any faith? God might be watching out for him! Don't let him speak! Shout! Shout! Shout!"

What a bunch of lunatics.

This next part is downright hilarious: "The city clerk quieted the crowd and said: 'Fellow Ephesians, doesn't all the world know that the city of Ephesus is the guardian of the temple of the great Artemis and of her image, which fell from heaven?'" (Acts 19:35). Now isn't that something? They all agree with you and me that Artemis is an angel who was booted out of heaven. What is so great about worshiping a "god" who was stupid enough to get kicked out of heaven? Because they were so blind, they didn't care.

> *"Therefore, since these facts are undeniable, you ought to calm down and not do anything rash. You have brought these men here, though they have neither robbed temples nor blasphemed our goddess. If, then, Demetrius and his fellow craftsmen have a grievance against anybody, the courts are open and there are proconsuls. They can press charges. If there is anything further you want to bring up, it must be settled in a legal assembly. As it is, we are in danger of being charged with rioting because of what happened today. In that case we would not be able to account for this commotion, since there is no reason for it." After he had said this, he dismissed the assembly. (Acts 19:36-41)*

Now that is funny! Okay, let's look at the big picture. If we turn this around, we can see how ridiculously blind the Devil can make his people. What if you walked into a church and the pastor and congregation were marching around the sanctuary screaming in unison, "Great is the Most High!"—all because one man stood outside the door with different beliefs? If my church started acting like that, I would go somewhere else. However,

The Depth of Grace

if I were blind enough, I might join the parade and even strip. The enemy has real power and only Jesus Christ can make the blind man see.

This last scene showed that one could reason with people under the power of the Devil, to a degree. However, look how ridiculously obvious the stupidity of these people had to be for them to listen. This campaign went on for hours without a single good reason. Could these people not see this? No, they could not. This wasn't a battle of flesh and blood. Artemis, the fallen angel, had power over these people. This campaign was nothing more than Artemis blinding her followers and stirring them into a riot in an attempt to win back those she'd lost due to the ministry of Paul. Also, all this clerk could do was shut them up and send them away. He could not convince them to worship the God of Israel. Only a man of faith in Jesus who understood how to speak to Artemis could enable the blind to see. Wasn't that why Artemis was ticked in the first place? Yes! She was mad because Paul took authority over her, and when she was forced to release her prisoners, their eyes were opened and they were able to believe in Jesus. In turn they quit buying those stupid little statues of deception and instead followed Christ.

So what was the primary reason for all of this chaos? It was because a man who walked under the resurrection power of the Holy Spirit came to town—a man who learned to trust in Jesus Christ the risen Lord. Paul was a man who put his faith in the One who sits at the right hand of God the Father with all authority. Artemis knew this and freaked out. That's how insecure the Devil is! Who is insecure in Christ? If you are insecure, it's because you do not know enough about your Savior and who you are in Him. If you knew more about Jesus, you would be more like the apostle Paul. "Let me at 'em! I can take 'em!"

Don't worry! You are already on the right track. In reading this book, you are seeking truth. When you read God's Word, you seek truth. Get in the Word of God! When you go to church, you are seeking truth. When you pray, ask for truth. And remember: "if the Son sets you free, you will be free indeed" (John 8:36). The truth will set you free!

CHAPTER 20

The Word "Restore"

Before we move on, it's important that you understand what I meant by the word "restore" in the vow I made to the Lord after Jackson's death. When I said that I would tell the world about the Son of God, I meant it. I admit that it was a bold call. However, I never intended to have to move forward with my end of the deal. I pretty much made it impossible for God to hold up His end. Yes, I needed to overcome many challenges in order for me to hold up my end. But I needed God to do much more. Let me give you an idea of what I meant by the word "restore" in the vow I made to the Lord:

I wanted proof that it was God who protected me over the years that I was away from Him. Most Christians would say that it was the Lord, for sure. A man of God would have told me, "Oh, my gosh, Bronson! I can't believe you would even question this!" But I wanted proof that it was He who protected me. I wanted Him to prove it to me.

I was not willing to risk causing others to struggle again. After all, I hadn't left church quietly. I fell back into my old sins with sound. I ran into many of the kids from my youth group while I was away from the Lord, and I knew I caused them to struggle. I ran into kids from the old Sold-Out Saturday prayer meetings many times while drinking and carrying on. Many times in my sin, I ran into the girl who sent me the instant message, "Are you the same Bronson that came to my church and changed our youth?" She worked as a bartender through school, and I ordered drinks from her bar at times. I pretended I didn't remember her

189

J. Bronson Haley

from Grace Methodist Church. However, I remembered her and hated myself more and more every time I saw her.

So I was well known for my skill in sinning. My sin carried a fragrance. My distinct name added to the aroma. My failures swept through Shreveport/Bossier with the heat and speed of a nuclear blast. Thus I just wasn't willing to risk causing others to struggle again. I knew that I had done the best I could do prior to falling into sin this last time. Did I need a man of God to comfort me? No! I needed God to prove to me that I could stay strong if I returned to Him.

I also needed proof that God wanted to use me again. I wasn't going to just step out and tell someone about Jesus without knowing for sure that He planned to use me. No! I wanted Him to prove it first.

It was going to take a miracle in itself for me to forgive myself for failing the way I did. I failed everyone I ever knew in some form or fashion. I hated myself for letting down everyone and especially those who did not live through the struggle. I knew that many were watching me closely to see if the things I witnessed to them about Jesus were actually true. I needed help forgiving myself. Forgiving myself for my failures was going to take a miracle.

I was too ashamed to return to the presence of God and ask for forgiveness. I was too ashamed to return to God in my condition with my failures and ask for anything. The Lord gave me more than I needed when I had lived for Him, and He never let me down. It was going take a miracle to give me the strength to return to the Lord and ask for forgiveness.

I wasn't willing to take the chance that Jesus would again be persecuted because of my failures. He suffered enough and did not need to suffer more persecution and shame because of me. I was not willing to take the chance of failing Jesus again.

Obviously it was going to take a miracle in order for me to overcome my addiction. However, that was the least of my worries. Rehab can get a man off of drugs. The real problem was dealing with why I got hooked on the drug in the first place. Freedom from the addictive personality was what I needed. Finding freedom from the pain that drugs drowned out was an additional request I made.

I needed something more powerful than my salvation experience alone. I was saved and still fell. I needed something more powerful than the presence of the Lord. I prayed and worshiped Him in His presence for hundreds of hours before I fell, and He knows that what I am saying is true. I didn't fall because I didn't pray enough. It was going to take something

The Depth of Grace

more powerful than prayer for me to hold up my end of the deal. It was going to take something more powerful than great leadership. I fell while serving one of the best churches around. I was very involved when I failed the Lord, so I didn't fall because I got bored. It was not going to be more service on my part that would enable me to stay strong in my faith.

I understood that, if all these things actually happened—with the chances of an icicle in hell—I was going to have no choice but to tell the world about Jesus. I had eliminated every possible way God could restore me. I had a hard time believing the far-fetched stories in the Bible and knew if I ended up having to tell the world about Jesus, I was going to get the information from the Bible, considering I had ruled out all other possible hope. All preachers tell people that the Word of God is alive. If I was going to tell the world that the Word of God was alive, He was going to have to prove it to me. I was not concerned about that because the Bible was the least threat to me having to hold up my end of the deal I made with God. I did not stress having to tell anyone anything.

The demands I made on God were high. I confess that my commitment to tell the world about Jesus was very bold. The bottom line was that, in order for me to fulfill my end of the deal, God had to do the impossible. I believed in miracles, but most miracles come when people have faith and give God a chance. I was not willing to give Him a chance. Can you see the extent of my demands? I was not willing to go to church, pray, go into His presence, or talk to a man of God. Yet I needed Him to prove He protected me, to prove I could stay strong in my faith, to prove He could and would use me, to enable me to forgive myself, to enable me to come into His presence and receive forgiveness, and to set me free of my addiction. Plus I needed something more powerful than my salvation experience, prayer, church involvement, great leadership, and His presence. And I needed Him to prove His Word was alive!

"Absolutely! Lord, if you do these things, I will tell the world about Jesus Christ."

One might ask, "Who do you think you are, demanding that God prove Himself to you?"

I was a drug addict who was going to die if He didn't. I was a drug addict who would be willing to die for His Son if He did—and He did. One way He did this for me was to make His Word come alive inside me and change my life while I spent time with Him through studying the Bible. Many of the Rest Stops you've already read came from these times that God proved Himself to me. (Remember "Jacob's Journey"? God used

J. Bronson Haley

the story of Jacob in a mighty way to prove to me that He did indeed protect me during my time of sin, just as he had done for Jacob.)

Along with proving Himself to me through His Word, He also showed His faithfulness to me in real-life situations with other people, giving me the chance to tell others about His love and grace, as you'll see in some of the chapters that follow.

Bottom line: God is God, and He'll have His way in our lives even when we think we are the farthest from Him—because as soon as we turn around and take one step back toward Him, we'll discover that He's been there all along, just waiting for us with open arms.

CHAPTER 21

Sniper: Part 2

Two and a half years after Jared Volp and I left Commercial Diving Academy, I stood on my front porch as he walked up to greet me. His face was sunken in and I quickly realized the severity of his sickness. Jared had called me the day before and mentioned that he was ill.

"I've dropped from 180 pounds to 140 pounds in just a couple of weeks," he'd said. He had been diagnosed with a hyperthyroid condition and couldn't keep his weight.

"Why don't you come up and stay for the weekend? It would be really great to see you!" I said.

I had a roommate named Art Colbert at the time. We had just moved into a new house and planned to have friends over for a home-warming get-together. So, Jared, my friends, and I cooked out and got in some good laughs. We all hung out and had a good time.

I rarely told people the stories about when Jared and I were in Jacksonville. I only told my closest friends about the night we got pulled over with Jared on the windshield of my truck—really for no other reason than it's just a little hard to believe. When either of us did tell the stories, they really came to life. Every story is true and, believe it or not, unembellished. The stories went over well with everyone as Jared and I exhausted the details of the events. Back and forth we went, offering our individual perspectives, and everyone laughed in disbelief.

After we ate, Jared and I went for a ride. It was strange for us to recall that we had only spent six weeks together prior to this point in our lives.

193

J. Bronson Haley

I felt like Jared had been my best friend since childhood. It didn't make any sense, but it was very real.

It was really good to hear him talk about his family and his son. Jared was now married and lived with his family in Lafayette, Louisiana, three hours south of my hometown and eighteen hours west of his. His boy's name is Stan. It was sad to see Jared attempt to hide his fear for his family during this conversation. Jared had no guarantee that he would live through his illness.

"Jared, tell me the truth! What was going through your head when you told that cop that the reason your pants were wet was because you peed in them?" I asked.

"I don't know," he said, laughing so much that he could hardly get a word out. "Bronson, why didn't you let me claim the pipe? I was going to jail anyway and the cops didn't care one way or another."

"I don't know, Jared," I said. "Probably a stupid sense of brotherhood! But, Jared, what was going through your mind while you rode on the hood of my truck as we traveled down Main Street with you making faces through the windshield? What were your thoughts when you looked over and realized you performed for a police officer?" I asked.

"What was going through your mind as the driver, Bronson?" he asked.

This went on for about thirty minutes and we laughed until we could no longer breathe. My heart began to swell as Jared talked about what our friendship meant to him.

"I'll never be able to repay you for the things you did for me in Jacksonville. I'll be in debt to you for the rest of my life," he said to me.

Of course, we were nothing short of two psychopathic lunatics while at school in Jacksonville. However, that's not what Jared was speaking of. He was talking about breakfast, lunch, and dinner every day of the week. Whatever I did, he did, and money wasn't an issue for me. I didn't do these things because I was such a great person. I was aware that I was a failure in just about every aspect of my life. I did it because my heart softened toward him, for whatever reason. (I didn't yet understand that God's gifts and His call in a person's life are irrevocable [see Romans 11:29]. I didn't realize at the time that God could still manifest His gifts through me.) I wanted to tell Jared about Jesus back then, but I couldn't because of who I was at the time. So I gave whatever I could to Jared instead.

"There is only one thing that can come between our friendship," I kept repeating to Jared during our time together in Jacksonville. "That would be

The Depth of Grace

if you didn't forgive me if I let you down ... because I'm going to forgive you every time." This is something else I offered my friends during the years that I was running from God and living in sin. Sometimes I felt like I benefited more than my friends.

As my heart continued to swell in the truck, I realized that I had no choice but to talk to Jared about Jesus. I was not going to make the same mistake I had made in the past.

"Jared, there's something I need to tell you." I explained that the reason he felt he couldn't repay me was because the gifts were free. "You were at rock bottom and very alone in Jacksonville. Many people in your life whom you loved deeply had failed you. Your meals were free. My friendship was free. My forgiveness was free. You didn't deserve the things I did for you, but you got them anyway and this love pierced your heart. You haven't forgotten those gifts because something real happened inside of you," I explained.

I told Jared about the time I accepted Jesus as my Lord and Savior several years before. "I was at rock bottom and very alone. I was a complete failure. I wasn't worth the pew I sat on. As my heart began to swell, I was able to believe that God loved me and I accepted that Christ died so that I could be forgiven. I didn't earn His forgiveness. I didn't deserve to be called a son of God. Jesus was and is a free gift from God. What can we do to repay the Lord for giving us His Son? God was able to love you through me in Jacksonville because the gifts were free. The love of God is free. The reason you feel you can't pay me back is because you can't. Could you have purchased what happened in your heart? God loved you in Jacksonville, for free. Isn't it amazing how much He loves us?"

The power of God filled the truck as we discussed these things. I then popped in a worship CD and played two of my favorite songs. The first song gave a wonderful description of Jesus, then the singer repeated the word "beautiful" over and over again. The second song's main chorus went, "I will hold on ... I will hold on ... I will hold on ... and I will trust in You." After the second song I acknowledged Jared's illness.

"I know you are very afraid for yourself and your family. Your illness is very serious and you could die. At the same time, you are in the best place you have been in a long time. Tonight it's easy for you to acknowledge that you need Jesus. You also know for sure that He loves you because He has used me to prove that to you, and your heart is swollen now like it was in Jacksonville. You are very humble because of your condition. The Bible

J. Bronson Haley

says that God opposes the proud and gives grace to the humble. Because of your humility you are able to receive a miracle in your life."

Jared called me shortly after he left the following day. "When I get home, I'm going to a local pastor to give my life to Jesus. And Bronson … I suggest that you do the same."

I began to weep as those words came out of his mouth. I had been waiting on God to prove to me that He could and would use me again. As we talked about God together in my truck, Jared hadn't known I was struggling in my own way and desperately seeking the Lord. God used me to prove His love to Jared. God used Jared to prove Himself to me. I knew what the Scriptures said. But I still needed proof that God would and could use me. Well, I got proof. I knew for sure that, if God was able to use me in the midst of my sin in Jacksonville, He could use me again. That is great example of the redemptive power of the blood of Jesus Christ. I will never be able to repay Jared for what he did for me that day. From the depths of my spirit, thank you, Jared, for what you did for me.

Many will say that it's ridiculous for me to think this experience was a miracle from God. Before these people rob Jesus of His glory, first understand what the Word of God says about giving:

> *Each of you should give what you have decided in your heart to give, not reluctantly or under compulsion, for God loves a cheerful giver. And God is able to bless you abundantly [to make all grace abound to you (NIV 1984)], so that in all things at all times, having all that you need, you will abound in every good work….*

> *You will be enriched in every way so that you can be generous on every occasion, and through us your generosity will result in thanksgiving to God….*

> *Because of the service by which you have proved yourselves, others will praise God for the obedience that accompanies your confession of the gospel of Christ, and for your generosity in sharing with them and with everyone else. And in their prayers for you their hearts will go out to you, because of the surpassing grace God has given you. Thanks be to God for this indescribable gift! (2 Corinthians 9:7-8, 11, 13-15, my emphasis)*

The Depth of Grace

I'm not sure what "all grace" means exactly. I am sure, though, that "all" means "all." Every amount of grace made available through the blood of Jesus Christ is included in this Scripture. It seems to me that Jared and I have experienced the full extent of God's grace in our friendship. God was able to make "all grace" abound to us through our mutual giving to each other. Jared didn't care about my sin. Jesus Christ is greater than my sin. God used me to prove His love for Jared. God used Jared to prove His love for me.

"All" means "all."

I would like to mention one more interesting story about this experience. Just before Jared and I got in all of that trouble in Jacksonville during those six weeks we hung out, we went to Tampa for the weekend. We arrived at a popular bar on the beach around 2:00 p.m. on a Saturday afternoon. We got acquainted with the bar by ordering Long Island iced teas—a "sour" drink with several clear liquors mixed together. During the daytime people would lay out on the beach—most of them just drank and had a good time.

By 9:00 p.m. everyone at the beach bar was nicely dressed. It was apparently a local custom for everyone to go home, dress for the evening, and then return when the sun went down. Jared and I were the only two at the club in our beach attire.

If I am ever caught dancing, it's one of the best indicators that I've had too much to drink. I think everyone on the dance floor that night was fully aware of this. Barefooted, in swim trunks, and shirtless, I pretended to be like them. Over the course of thirty minutes, while dancing, I took note of this beautiful blonde who sat by herself at the bar.

Why is this girl sitting by herself? I thought.

"Hi!" I said just prior to picking her up and placing her on my shoulder. "Relax! I won't hurt you!" I assured her. She could hardly hear me because of the loud music. "Do you like to dance?" I asked, as if she had a choice.

"What is your name?" she asked.

"Bronson!"

"Where are you from, Bronson?"

"Louisiana!"

"That makes sense!"

"What do you mean?" I asked her.

"You're crazy! Most people from Louisiana are crazy!" she said.

I took it as a compliment, considering she was smiling and laughing.

J. Bronson Haley

After I carried her back and forth from the bar to the dance floor on my shoulder several times, I sat her down at the bar next to Jared and introduced them.

"Jared, Danielle; Danielle, Jared," and I left them to figure out the rest.

By the end of the night, Jared and Danielle were in love. They exchanged numbers and continued to talk over the next several months. Today they are married with two kids, living in Lafayette, Louisiana.

"All" means "all."

12TH REST STOP:
THE MOUNTAIN OF THE LORD

Many mountains stood along the path in the lives of Abraham, Isaac, Jacob, Simon Peter, the apostle Paul, and all of God's chosen people as related in His Word. We will always face mountains, so ridding our lives of mountains is not what is important. What is important is how we react when the mountains appear. It's how we react to our problems that matters most.

One of our biggest struggles when dealing with mountains in our lives is a lack of understanding. Many times we think something is wrong when a mountain shows up out of nowhere. Sometimes we automatically assume that our trouble is a result of our mistakes, and we blame ourselves. Yes, oftentimes our trouble is from our mistakes! However, the source of the mountain is another topic. When a mountain presents itself, we have no choice but to confront and overcome. Every time! No questions asked! In order to overcome every mountain that enters into our lives, we must understand some important things.

We need to understand that of the mountain can come from a variety of areas: the Lord, our choices, or other people's choices. It's important to understand that our *approach* to the problem is not affected by the source of the problem. It doesn't make any difference who or what is to blame for the trouble. Should a child of God be defeated in any aspect of his or her life for any reason? To whom should we give control of our destiny? We may not always be clear on the source of the problem, so we need to understand that *all* mountains are "mountains of the Lord" for children

J. Bronson Haley

of God who walk in repentance and follow Jesus—because, when we are His, the mountains we face in life become His too.

If you have not accepted Jesus Christ as your Lord and Savior, then you are on your own. The mountain you walk up is a mountain from hell and Satan walks with you. You have no way to gain victory on the mountain from hell because Satan is stronger than we are—if we walk alone. "The reason the Son of God appeared was to destroy the devil's work" (1 John 3:8). You can go ahead and view the curse of sin as the greatest mountain in history—because it would be just that for all of us, except that Jesus took care of that mountain for us. Praise be to the Lamb of God that He came and destroyed that curse! Jesus Christ already walked the greatest mountain and walked the perfect walk so we wouldn't have to stumble into death—which is the walk of a sinner who never finds Christ.

The Devil grants his children short-term "victories" over the curse of sin in the form of more sin and destructive behavior that numbs us to our pain. The satisfaction we get from sin only provides a short-term feeling of relief from the curse, though. What's really bad is that the sin that helped provide what felt like relief in the short-term actually only makes the curse stronger in the long run. What a nasty scam! This long-term suffering, a life of sin, is what the Devil offers his children. The Devil grants short-term relief from the curse in the form of more sin—and long-term suffering as long-term reward for obedience to him. For those who do not seek and find Jesus before life is over, Satan grants them even longer long-term suffering, as in for eternity. So Satan offers us short-term "relief" from our pain in the form of sin in exchange for an entire life of suffering and possible eternal damnation. Not a good deal!

Children of God only suffer for a little while and experience long-term victory—in every circumstance. We suffer from the different attacks and trials of life, but according to God's Word, we have no choice but to be victorious in the long run on every occasion. Children of God are victorious at the foot of the mountain! Jesus Christ walks before us and has given us power and authority over all our enemies.

> *And the God of all grace, who called you to his eternal glory in Christ, after you have suffered a little while, will himself restore you and make you strong, firm and steadfast. (1 Peter 5:10)*

The Depth of Grace

> *Now if we are children, then we are heirs—heirs of God and co-heirs with Christ, if indeed we share in his sufferings in order that we may also share in his glory. (Romans 8:17)*

Suffering is a part of life. God made it clear that we would suffer, so we cannot blame Him. Suffering leads to glory! Now that we have established that, let's look at how Abraham approached the mountain of the Lord.

> *The LORD had said to Abram, "Go from your country, your people and your father's household to the land I will show you. I will make you into a great nation and I will bless you; I will make your name great, and you will be a blessing. I will bless those who bless you, and whoever curses you I will curse; and all peoples on earth will be blessed through you." (Genesis 12:1-3)*

The Lord spent decades proving himself to Abraham (then called "Abram") and forgiving his mistakes. Abraham often lied in fear that God would not protect him from kings who wished to have his wife because of her beauty. He went through many trials and tribulations and saw that the Lord was with him on every occasion. In other words the Lord proved himself to Abraham over and over again. Finally, it came time for Abraham's faith to be tested to the full extent so that God could take him to his next glory—through his own son—just as we all go from glory to glory in our faith. No greater test exists than the mountain of the Lord—one that He puts in our path to accomplish His purpose in our lives.

> *Some time later God tested Abraham. He said to him, "Abraham!"*
>
> *"Here I am," he replied.*
>
> *Then God said, "Take your son, your only son, whom you love—Isaac—and go to the region of Moriah. Sacrifice him there as a burnt offering on a mountain I will show you. (Genesis 22:1-2)*

Excuse me? Can you imagine receiving those instructions from the Lord? "My only son, whom you promised to me, whom I love—you want me to sacrifice?" It was a miracle that Abraham had Isaac in the first place! Sarah gave birth at over ninety years old! That was a test within itself!

J. Bronson Haley

Abraham was a man of God, but don't think he did not struggle with the same things we struggle with. Don't think it was easier for him to deal with losing someone he loved more than himself than it would be for us to lose someone. Not to mention having to kill him with a knife on a pile of wood. Try putting yourself in Abraham's shoes on this journey.

> *Early the next morning Abraham got up and loaded his donkey. He took with him two of his servants and his son Isaac. When he had cut enough wood for the burnt offering, he set out for the place God had told him about. On the third day Abraham looked up and saw the place in the distance. (Genesis 22:3-4)*

Ouch! For three days, Abraham hid his fear, sorrow, and the real purpose for this trip from Isaac. Then he looked up and saw the mountain where he would soon slay his beloved son. That mountain was beautiful for sure! However, this was no Kodak moment.

> *He said to his servants, "Stay here with the donkey while I and the boy go over there. We will worship and then we will come back to you."*
>
> *Abraham took the wood for the burnt offering and placed it on his son Isaac, and he himself carried the fire and the knife. (Genesis 22:5-6)*

What? You mean this journey could get even worse? Abraham wasn't strong enough to carry the wood or he would have surely carried it himself. He was forced to make Isaac carry the wood that would later burn his body after he had been bound, laid on the pile of wood, and killed by the hand of his father, whom he trusted.

> *As the two of them went on together, Isaac spoke up and said to his father Abraham, "Father?"*
>
> *"Yes, my son?" Abraham replied.*
>
> *"The fire and wood are here," Isaac said, "but where is the lamb for the burnt offering?"*

The Depth of Grace

Abraham answered, "God himself will provide the lamb for the burnt offering, my son." And the two of them went on together. (Genesis 22:6-8)

Abraham believed that God was going to provide a way out somehow. However, he also understood that God's ways were higher than his own: "As the heavens are higher than the earth, so are my ways higher than your ways and my thoughts than your thoughts" (Isaiah 55:9). No matter how we look at it, Abraham was in an impossible situation. Notice that there was one reason the two of them hiked this mountain, and that was to sacrifice something to the Lord. There was no room for coincidence to gain the credit for this upcoming miracle. God designed this test so that, no matter what He did for Abraham, His name would be glorified. If God didn't pull off something huge, this was going to be a bad day for Abraham and especially Isaac. A lamb was not going to jump out of the woods at the last minute and jump on the pile of wood. Sometimes we cannot see a way out, but it is important to understand who is with us on our journey up the mountain. It's important to understand that God's ways and thoughts are higher than our own. After all, He created the brains that we think with! For God to be able to prove Himself to us and increase our faith, we have no choice but to walk up the mountain. The bigger the mountain, the greater the miracle!

When they reached the place God had told him about, Abraham built an altar there and arranged the wood on it. He bound his son Isaac and laid him on the altar, on top of the wood. Then he reached out his hand and took the knife to slay his son. (Genesis 22:9-10)

If I were Abraham, I would have been crying by this point. He had no choice but to break the news to his son. "Isaac, my son. About the question you asked earlier … you are the sacrifice." Isaac loved his father too much to fight him. Isaac could have overpowered his father, who was over one hundred years old at the time. Instead Isaac allowed Abraham to tie him up, and he willfully lay on the wood. This was no pretty scene. However, there is nothing pretty about the people around us who are dying and going to hell because men of God don't have any faith. God needs people who are willing to walk up the mountain so that He can build our faith and build the kingdom through us.

203

J. Bronson Haley

> *But the angel of the LORD called out to him from heaven,*
> *"Abraham! Abraham!"*
>
> *"Here I am," he replied.*
>
> *"Do not lay a hand on the boy," he said. "Do not do anything*
> *to him. Now I know that you fear God, because you have*
> *not withheld from me your son, your only son." (Genesis*
> *22:11-12)*

I believe Abraham buckled at the words of this angel and collapsed
on top of Isaac, then wept uncontrollably. I believe that, when Abraham
untied Isaac, they clutched each other in their arms and wept together.

> *Abraham looked up and there in a thicket he saw a ram*
> *caught by its horns. He went over and took the ram and*
> *sacrificed it as a burnt offering instead of his son. So Abraham*
> *called that place The LORD Will Provide. And to this day it is*
> *said, "On the mountain of the LORD it will be provided."*
>
> *The angel of the LORD called to Abraham from heaven a*
> *second time and said, "I swear by myself, declares the LORD,*
> *that because you have done this and have not withheld your*
> *son, your only son, I will surely bless you and make your*
> *descendants as numerous as the stars in the sky and as the*
> *sand on the sea shore. Your descendants will take possession*
> *of the cities of their enemies, and through your offspring all*
> *nations on earth will be blessed, because you have obeyed me."*
> *(Genesis 22:13-18)*

It was important that Abraham pass this test.

"Why? He was over one hundred years old and would soon die."

There you go again trying to figure out God with the very brain He
created. Stop that! Remember what we just read: "As the heavens are higher
than the earth, so are my ways higher than your ways and my thoughts
than your thoughts" (Isaiah 55:9). I can tell you only what God has shown
me. I am very young in my faith. I only speak from what God has allowed
me to receive. He will not give me more than I can handle. Some teachers
can give us scholarly answers to all of our questions. That's great! However,
it is important to understand that we don't have to understand everything

The Depth of Grace

in order to walk with God. Part of growing in our faith is giving God time to blow our minds through His Word and His faithfulness!

Prior to this mountain God had already proven himself to Abraham time and time again. Abraham was a man of faith by this point. But faith alone was not enough. Abraham was obedient to the Lord, obviously. However, faith and obedience together were not enough. Abraham was complete when God saw that he was more afraid not to obey Him than to spare his firstborn son out of fear. Also, this test was not for Abraham exclusively. A true man of God is a builder of people. Isaac was chosen to father Jacob, also known as Israel. Abraham raised Isaac to be a man of faith and obedience. Only the Lord can teach a man to fear Him. It was on this mountain where Isaac learned firsthand what it meant to fear the God of Israel. And it is only in facing our own mountains in life with the Lord that we can come to fear Him and serve Him with our whole heart.

CHAPTER 22

—

Facing the Wind

I was sitting at my computer writing a letter when a minister from a local Baptist church called.

"I was just in the area and wanted to stop by and say hi," said Dr. Larry Williams, pastor of senior adults at Broadmoor Baptist Church in Shreveport. I had visited the church a few weeks back.

"Sure! Come on by. I'll see you when you get here," I replied.

When he arrived with a friend named Chet Arkin, we sat in my living room. Dr. Williams and Chet briefly discussed their own stories of faith and explained the ministry of their church. I was quiet for the first twenty minutes or so.

"Well, sometimes people are not comfortable talking about their faith," Dr. Williams said and then paused for a moment before he asked, "Do you have a relationship with Jesus?"

"Yes, sir. My life depends on Him. I can't live without Him," I said.

I was a little nervous because I had been alone in God's Word for two years at this point. I had talked to some people about the things God showed me in the Bible. Most of the time I received positive feedback from those I spoke with. Many who previously did not believe now did believe. Those who had known a few things about the Lord were inspired. However, I had never discussed these things with men of God who knew His Word.

"Would you like to know more about my faith?" I asked.

207

J. Bronson Haley

As I mentioned, when Dr. Williams had called earlier, I was in the middle of writing a letter—to the mother of one of my friends. I felt as though the Lord had prompted me to write this letter. My friend's name was Cassie and we had a couple of classes together at Louisiana State University in Shreveport, and I had known her for around a year at this point. She was very Christlike and I was fortunate to have had the opportunity to be around her. I had just been set free of my drug addiction when we met and was still very hardened. Also, the drugs made me numb to my surroundings. While coming back into reality, I realized I had developed a lot of bad habits that did not reflect my heart for God. I paid little attention to my communication with people and was careless with my words and body language. Cassie, though, was a pro! Her speech was so soft and kind that I found myself paying close attention to everything she said, and I learned a great deal. She was also super sweet and I began to make a conscious effort to be as kind to her as possible. The funny part was that she had no idea what was going on. She was breaking me like a wild horse, but didn't have any idea.

Cassie didn't know what to think about me for a long time. She would often get frustrated because I would sometimes tell her a story from my sordid past and then say, "Well, there is another side of the story, but I'll tell you later." The truth is that I didn't know the other side of the story, but was believing that God would take the bad and use it for good. That's what His Word said, so I was expecting it. For example: I remember telling Cassie about Commercial Diving Academy in Jacksonville one day. I discussed some of the hardships I experienced and mentioned that there was more to the story, but I'd tell her later. Jared had not yet come and visited me while sick, so God had not yet used Jacksonville for the good. After a few minutes she became frustrated with my negative talk.

Interrupting me, she said, "You're a scuba diver, right?"

"Yeah."

"Well ... I want to be a scuba diver," she replied.

That, my friend, is how to talk to people.

Back to the meeting with Dr. Williams and Chet—and the letter I was writing! Cassie's mother—Lynn— and her grandmother both had asked me once, "Where did you get your love for God?"

I didn't know how to answer them. "Uh ... He's had mercy on me?" I replied.

Well, duh. God has had mercy on us all. So, I decided to write a letter and try to explain that my love for God came directly from His Word.

The Depth of Grace

I didn't know how to communicate that, though, when they asked. It's a really funny story when it comes down to it: I spent a year and a half trying to communicate my love for Jesus to this family by way of letters I wrote them. I didn't write to this family because I thought they needed to hear everything I said in the more than twenty thousand words contained in letters I wrote them. They are leaders in the largest Baptist church in Shreveport/Bossier and have an incredible pastor, Dr. Fred Lowery, who knows how to teach and preach the Word of God. I didn't know what was up with all the letters—but I felt the Lord was speaking—so I kept writing. I am sure I have my own little place in their house set aside for my letters. I most likely have my own little filing cabinet, actually—maybe even my own room. At the time, I felt as though I may have been annoying this poor family to the point of disaster with all my letters to them.

Of course, it could also be that I have my own personal furnace at their home with my initials on it, I thought.

Not to get off track again, but this brings up one of my top ten favorite Scriptures! When you just don't have a clue about the purpose of what the Lord is doing in your life, quote this Scripture! "It is the glory of God to conceal a matter; to search out a matter is the glory of kings" (Proverbs 25:2). If you hang in there long enough, this verse can turn a lost cause into a soldier for the kingdom! Because of what this verse teaches, Cassie's family ended up receiving the foundation of the book you now hold in your hands, via my letters.

I searched God's Word so that I could clearly explain my love for Him and back it up with Scripture in the letters I continued to write. During this study God began to open my mind to receive His words in an amazing way. It was in these studies that I learned how to explain the truth that set me free. I also learned that explaining my love for God isn't so difficult after all. It was after writing all the letters that I understood from the Scriptures that my love for Jesus was in direct correlation to my debt to Him. You will see in the letter that follows that, at the time, I only suspected that Peter's love for Jesus was linked to his sin. I never shared my testimony with Cassie's family. Cassie was extremely sheltered from the world. I was afraid that, if I shared my testimony with her, she would be afraid of me, and I didn't want to lose her friendship. This brings up an additional funny part of this story (yes, I am getting to Dr. Williams, whom we left sitting in my living room with Chet … don't worry).

J. Bronson Haley

A few times at college I said certain things that threw Cassie for a loop. For instance: "Statistics was a nightmare! I came so close to cussing out the teacher after the final," I said.

"Bronson! You didn't want to cuss him out," she said.

"Yes, I did."

"Don't say that! You're going to burst my bubble," she replied.

I still get a kick out of those remarks.

Anyway, I felt that God spoke to me about writing a book soon after Jackson's death.

"Lord, why would they listen to me? What would I say?" I asked.

"Just tell them the truth," He said.

Leave it to God to conceal a matter. The Lord and I have had many knockdown, drag-out fights in my walk. This is a good example! Of course, I did not understand what He was saying.

The truth? I should display my wall of shame to the world? I thought.

At that time, I didn't understand what God meant when He said, "the truth will set you free" (John 8:32). In the letters that I sent to Cassie and her family, I began to share the *truth* that had set me free. In this book you are reading, I have shared this *truth*. I was *comforted* by this *truth*. When I share this same *comfort* with those who have *suffered* as I have *suffered*, they experience this same *comfort* "because we know that just as you share in our sufferings, so also you share in our comfort" (2 Corinthians 1:7). And "just as we share abundantly in the sufferings of Christ, so also our comfort abounds through Christ" (2 Corinthians 1:5). Jesus Christ is Lord!

Okay, finally back to the original story about Dr. Williams. I left Dr. Williams and Chet in the front room and retrieved what I had written to Cassie's wonderful family, for whom I have deep respect. As I printed the letter, I was briefly overcome with fear. These two men knew the Bible, and my life and ministry were dependent upon the truth in this letter. Negative feedback would have devastated me. It was the truth in the letter that had set me free and given me hope. However, as I mentioned earlier, I hadn't shared these things with ministers who had a close relationship with God and knew His Word. I even feared what Cassie and her family might think about my faith. Not that I doubted my faith, but as children of God, we battle the spirits of doubt and unbelief all the time. These two spirits had tag-teamed me relentlessly for what seemed like an eternity. Most of the time I felt like a blind sheep being led to the slaughter. However, it was the stories like the ones in this letter that gave me strength, and I felt as though it would be these stories that I may one day preach.

210

The Depth of Grace

Here is the letter to Cassie's mom that I printed off and read aloud to Dr. Williams and Chet that day:

When your mom [Cassie's grandmother] asked me where I got my love for God in the hospital that day, I really didn't know how to answer her. I didn't know how to respond to that same question when you asked me over the phone. I know that both of you are women of God and love God as much or more than I do. I know you two spend a lot of time in prayer believing God to meet the needs of those in need. Cassie mentioned you and your husband ministering at the altar of the Franklin Graham crusade. So you pray for people and you are there when God brings them into the family? Is there a greater service than that? Cassie mentioned that you all helped restore a couple of houses for the victims of Hurricane Katrina and that you all also volunteered time at LSUS [Louisiana State University in Shreveport] to help these suffering people. Is there a greater service than that? Cassie is more Christlike than I ever thought about being. Is there a better way to be? I was humbled when you two asked me about my love for God.

About two years ago I found myself in an extremely difficult situation. I had been away from God for around four years. God called me to the ministry not long after I was saved in January of '97. God completely restored me and changed me from the inside out. He gave me a home as well. I told people about Jesus every chance I got. When I fell away after God did all these things in my life, I didn't have any intentions of ever returning. It wasn't that I didn't love Jesus. It was the shame. It was the fact that I'd done my best as well. What would make me think I could be stronger the next time? Guilt played a huge role in keeping me away for so long. I didn't hang out with my old buddies much over those four years, but I kept up with them. It was really sad keeping up with my friends. Pete Holt, a childhood best friend, was murdered by his roommate after a heated argument. Nate Baldwin was stabbed in the chest after fighting another man over his girlfriend. He died in her front yard. Joel Finnegan died of a drug overdose. Cam Barton was blown out of the back of

211

a truck headed south down I-49. He was drunk and stood up to relieve himself and he died when he hit the concrete. Gus Blackman committed suicide after a night of drinking. This was very hard to watch, knowing that one touch from Jesus would have set them free from their addiction to alcohol and drugs.

I had a friend named Jackson Hunter who had been on drugs for seven years. His parents own a car dealership and an oil business. He had everything in this world going for him. He wasn't a bad person. There was simply a void in his heart that he could only satisfy by staying numb. I remember him telling me a story about getting arrested in Denver a couple of years ago. He described going through withdrawals while being chained to several other people for three weeks being extradited here to Shreveport because of a warrant. One touch from Jesus could have set him free. I knew because it happened to me. I wanted to tell him but I wasn't in a position in my life where I could. I thought about how sad it would be to live a life like that and then have a tragic ending. What a horrible ending to a horrible story that would be. One morning I got a call from another friend of mine named Sam Newton. Jackson, Sam, and a couple of other friends of mine went out the night before to celebrate Jackson's birthday. He was turning 24! They all crashed at Jeremy's house after getting in late from the casino. Jackson laid his head down that morning and never woke up. When I got the news, I fell to my knees and begged God for forgiveness. I told him that, if He would restore me, I'd tell the world about His Son.

I began to read my Bible and noticed in the Old Testament that, when people brought their sin offering to the priest, the priest only examined the offering to make sure it was perfect. He didn't examine the person. I knew that Jesus died on the cross for our sins so that we could be saved. But what I didn't realize was that, when we make mistakes and repent, God examines Jesus, not us, and sees that what He did for us is sufficient to cover our sin. It's not because we are worthy of forgiveness. It's because Jesus is worthy. Can we ever reach a place where we could tell Jesus that what He did for us wasn't

The Depth of Grace

enough to cover our sin? I understood that day what God meant when He said, "The truth will set you free." My shame could no longer keep me from repentance after understanding this principle.

Later I read a story about Simon Peter. He felt like he loved Jesus more than the other disciples. Kinda funny if you think about it. Jesus was always rebuking Peter for something. Peter was always getting into trouble. Jesus even called him Satan once. But he loved Jesus with everything inside of him. I think he loved Him so much because he experienced his forgiveness so many times. Jesus kept him anyway ☺.

Remember when Jesus predicted Peter's denial? "My children, I will be with you only a little longer. You will look for me, and just as I told the Jews, so I tell you now: Where I am going, you cannot come" (John. 13:33). Peter couldn't believe that Jesus wouldn't at least let him come, given that he loved Him more than any of the others. "I will lay down my life for you," Peter replied. Jesus said to Peter, "Will you really lay down your life for me? I tell you the truth, before the rooster crows, you will disown me three times!" What were Peter's emotions when Jesus responded to him like that, I wonder? Peter probably felt bad when he was found asleep three different times while Jesus prayed at Gethsemane. Jesus had already mentioned to him that He was "distressed to the point of death." Peter wasn't the only disciple on watch, either. But Jesus rebuked Peter and not the others. He rebuked the one that loved Him the most.

When the soldiers came to take Jesus away, Peter drew his sword and cut one of the soldier's ears off. He was rebuked for that, too. The disciples scattered, but Peter and one other disciple followed behind at a distance. I wonder what was going through Peter's mind? I'm sure he wanted Jesus to know for sure that he loved Him, and felt Jesus still thought that he would deny Him three times. Peter did indeed deny Jesus three times. It's the third denial that gets to me. "Peter replied, 'Man, I don't know what you are talking about!' Just as he was speaking the rooster crowed. The Lord turned and looked straight at Peter." Their eyes made contact! "Then Peter remembered the word the Lord had spoken to him: 'Before the rooster crows today, you will disown me three times.' And he went outside and wept bitterly." I can't imagine what that experience was like for Peter. He ended up not only denying Jesus three times, but he also "began to call down curses on himself, and he swore to them, 'I don't know this man you're talking about'" (Mark 14:71), in the presence of Jesus being mocked, spit on, and beaten. This took place immediately after Jesus was betrayed by one of His own disciples whom He had spent much time with. His other disciples deserted Him moments before as well. Now Simon denied Him three times not too far from Him.

Peter wasn't around when Jesus was on the cross either. As far as I know, John was the only disciple there: "The one whom Jesus loved." I'm sure the following three days were the hardest days of Peter's life. A long three days for the others as well.

I don't like to think about how bad Jesus suffered too often. But it is the reality of His suffering that gives me strength when I need it most. "But he took our suffering on him and felt our pain for us" (Isaiah 53:4 NCV). "He was beaten down and punished, but he didn't say a word. He was like a lamb being led to be killed. He was quiet, as a sheep is quiet while its wool is being cut; he never opened his mouth" (Isaiah 53:7 NCV). It's amazing to me that He remained quiet because He was thinking about you and me. Who is like our God?

It must have been a humbling experience for the disciples when they saw Jesus after the resurrection. Especially humbling to Peter.

When they had finished eating, Jesus said to Simon Peter, "Simon son of John, do you love me more than these?" "Yes, Lord," he said, "you know that I love you." Jesus said, "Feed my lambs." Again Jesus said, "Simon son of John, do you love me?" he answered, "Yes, Lord, you know that I love you."

The Depth of Grace

> *Jesus said, "Take care of my sheep." The third time he said to him, "Simon son of John, do you love me?" Peter was hurt because Jesus asked him the third time, "Do you love me?" He said, "Lord, you know all things; you know that I love you." Jesus said, "Feed my sheep."*

Simon struggled more than any of the other disciples. When Jesus took him back this last time, Peter went out and died for Him. He was crucified upside down because He didn't want the honor of dying like Jesus died. They all died for their Savior. It comforted me to see that Peter struggled as well. It helps to know that other men of God struggled. When I saw how powerfully God used these men of God when they were reinstated, I knew that God could use me, too. Look at the apostle Paul. He murdered Christians for believing in Jesus, for crying out loud. And he wrote thirteen books of the New Testament? Can we fathom the power of God, really?

When I finished reading the letter to Dr. Williams and Chet, silence filled the room. I felt the glory of the Lord, but heard only silence.

"Glory!" Dr. Williams said to break the silence. He then looked over at Chet and said, "Halleluiah!" Then Dr. Williams looked back at me and said, "Glory to God!"

The power of God manifested itself in the room, and in a single instant these two men and I had everything in common. One of us a pastor, one a godly businessman, and one who tightly gripped a promise that God had made him two years ago.

"Son, have you ever thought about full-time vocational ministry?" Dr. Williams asked.

"I feel like God wants me in ministry to some degree. I have been alone in God's Word for two years. I don't have any training," I said.

"Well, you are doing a good job!" he said. Then he asked, "Do you know how the eagle responds when a storm blows in?"

"No, sir," I answered.

"When the storm blows in, the eagle faces into the wind," Dr. Williams said. "As the wind continues to blow, the eagle continues to rise. The harder the wind blows, the faster he rises. When his time has come, the eagle rises and soars above the storm. I see you as an eagle that has faced into the wind. The winds have blown and you have continued to rise. And Bronson … you will rise above the storm."

That story blew me away. His words went deep my heart. It was comforting for a man of God of his stature to confirm to me that I was

J. Bronson Haley

on the right track. The storm was still strong and the winds continued to blow. However, I knew how to follow Jesus Christ, and God used these men to confirm to me that I would soon rise above the storm. We talked for around an hour and a half total. We talked about Jesus, and He was the only thing in the world that was important during this conversation.

They left, and when I walked into my room, I collapsed on my bed and wept. I needed that visit more than those two men knew. I had been alone for a long time and for two prominent men of God to say such great things about my faith and me gave me strength. The story about the eagle found a place in my heart and I will never forget the story. I will never forget that day. God met me in my home and spoke to me through these two men. It didn't make any difference where we had been in life. We were all three sons of the living God. When we talked about Jesus, we had everything in common, just as the Scripture said we would.

In my spirit I had already faced into the wind. However, on this day I learned an extremely valuable lesson regarding the trials of life. We often create our own storms. But storms will blow in regardless of how careful we are. Life can deal a bad hand of cards and repeat the process without asking questions. Some people do not rest until they twirl in and out of the life of an innocent person with the devastation of a Hurricane Katrina. However, the source of the storm is not important when we smell the rain. Our fate is not determined by the lightning and hail. The wind does not decide whether we rise or tumble. It's the knowledge of truth that secures our destiny. Our victory is always found above the clouds. The thunder only draws attention to our destination. At the most crucial moment, we think about those we love most. They need us to survive. With this understanding we turn and face into the wind.

And no one but the eagle himself decides how to respond when the storm blows in.

CHAPTER 23

The Road to Emmaus

Every year UPS hires driver helpers during the holiday seasons to help deliver packages to customers. During the Christmas season of 2005, I needed some extra money and managed to land a job as a driver helper. I also worked pre-load from 4:00 a.m. to 9:00 a.m., Monday through Friday. My job was to load and unload trucks.

My second driver and I got comfortable with each other quickly. I guess you could say we had a lot in common.

"This job is absolutely killing me!" Rex said with obvious frustration.

"There is no doubt about that!" I replied. "This is the hardest job I've worked, and I poured concrete for several years in summertime—for four dollars and twenty-five cents an hour!"

This is how our conversation went for most of the first day. For me it was simply the hard work that I was consumed with. Twelve-hour-plus workdays were common for drivers during the Christmas holidays. I climbed into the truck after spending five hours loading delivery trucks like a madman. Although working for UPS is not easy, I realized that Rex's frustrations were much deeper than simply physical exhaustion. It was evident to me that his troubles surfaced from deep within.

Drivers work long hours and get home late in the evenings throughout the year. Rex told me about nearly having lost his marriage twice because of his job.

217

"I don't get home until 9:00 or 10:00 p.m. during the Christmas season, and it's tough on my wife and kids. It's even tougher on me," he said.

I worked with Rex four days during this holiday season. The first day he was very bitter and talked about the root of his bitterness the entire day: his job. The second day was a little better. We talked about God some, and Rex actually knew a lot about the Bible. It was evident to me that he believed in and loved the Lord. It was also clear that his hope and freedom were somewhere far off in the distance. The third day we talked about God all day long. We talked about Jesus and many of our heroes of faith in His Word. As we discussed the sufferings of these men of God, Rex began to lighten up a bit. It comforted us to discuss that our heroes in God's Word screwed up in their lives as well. They faced tough times and life wasn't easy. As a matter of fact, they suffered much worse than what most Christians experience today. Much of their suffering took place while walking with God. Most of our suffering takes place while rejecting His Son.

We also talked about the world and how screwed up it had become over the years.

"Bronson, we are fortunate that we didn't get caught up in drugs and things like that," Rex said. "I don't know why people do drugs. That's something you and I will never understand, I guess."

I mentioned that I worshiped the Lord at Shreveport Community Church in Shreveport. Rex was Baptist. It didn't make any difference on this trip. We were both comforted by the Word of God when we talked about the Scriptures.

One day Rex's boss called him and mentioned that we needed to meet a customer with a package. We decided to meet him at Wendy's during our lunch break.

"Rex, do you feel like God meant for our paths to cross?" I asked.

"I'm not sure, but it seems that way, doesn't it?" he said.

Somehow the fellow's package was loaded onto the wrong truck during pre-load. He desperately needed this package considering the following day was Christmas. We waited in the parking lot of Wendy's for the man to arrive. Within just a couple of minutes a car pulled up to our UPS truck. None other than Pastor Mark Donahue from my church exited the vehicle. I wasn't involved in church at the time, and it was good to see Mark. We were very close before I fell away from the Lord.

"Can I buy you two lunch?" he asked right off the bat.

The Depth of Grace

"Sir, you don't have to do that," Rex replied.

"I want to," Mark said.

Pastor Donahue stood with us in line as we ordered our food. He didn't order when his time came. He paid for the meals and left after a brief good-bye.

Rex was blown away. "Bronson, God must have brought us together," he said. He went on to tell many customers as we delivered their packages that day, "We had lunch today compliments of Shreveport Community Church!"

Rex was filled with joy and we had a blast for the rest of the day.

By day four Rex and I placed Jesus at the center of every conversation. We felt strongly that the Lord was with us. We couldn't be certain, but something was happening, and it was good. Around mid-afternoon on this last day that we would work together, I began to open up to Rex and shared my testimony. When I spoke of my past failures, he was blown away. He had no idea where I had come from.

"The Word of God says that we walk in a robe of righteousness made available to us upon the acceptance of Christ. What a great example," I said. "You would have never dreamed I used to be a drug addict and the most violent man in town. I didn't earn this robe I wear. It was a gift. People just don't know about it or don't believe. It's our job to tell them and God's job to save them."

That was a powerful conversation between the two of us.

I didn't speak to Rex as if he didn't understand the Bible or he needed me to preach to him. In my walk with Jesus, I shared revelations from God just as He shared them with me, whether I spoke with a man of understanding or a drug addict. I took Rex through many of the stories you have read thus far. They all floored him. After I discussed the details of the strongholds that kept me away from God for so long, I talked about my freedom. Rex knew the extent of my past shame by this time.

"I wanted another chance," I said. "I felt like God protected me while I was away. I felt like the Lord told me that he wanted to use me again. I knew it would take a miracle, but I believed in miracles. However, I didn't have the strength to return to His presence as a drug addict who took for granted everything His Son did for me. I was too ashamed to come to the Lord and ask for forgiveness. I didn't want Him to examine me in my condition, either. I needed to clean up first. Only I couldn't get clean."

Rex could see I was free of my shame. He listened eagerly as I approached my breakthrough.

J. Bronson Haley

"It didn't happen like the first time. Before, God touched me and I was set free instantly. My life changed when I accepted Jesus as my Lord and Savior. I wanted so desperately for that to happen again. Only it didn't happen like that."

I explained how it was the Word of God that set me free this last time. I briefly discussed how I just had to read God's Word, drug addiction and all. If Jesus is the Word of God in the flesh, and the Word of God is truth, and the Holy Spirit is the Spirit of truth, and it is by the Spirit that the sick man is born again, then why can't a sick man read God's Word? It's only because the Devil has lied to him, that's why. God doesn't expect us to overcome anything for any length of time without His Word.

"High on OxyContin, I noticed in the Old Testament that God's people brought sacrifices to the priest so that their sins would be forgiven," I said to Rex. "Most of the time it was a lamb. The priest would then examine the lamb and make sure it was worthy of their forgiveness. If the sacrifice was without defect, he would forgive them their sins. I took note that the priest never examined the person. He always examined the sacrifice. I wept as I recalled Jesus being referred to as the Lamb of God in the New Testament. Jesus Christ was sacrificed a perfect man. Three days later He rose again so that we could be born again and come into fellowship with Him. Today He sits on His throne at the right hand of the Father. When we bow before the Lord to repent of our sin, He doesn't examine us. He looks over and examines His Son. Jesus is found worthy ever time He is examined. No amount of sin can rob Him of this glory. Should we be too ashamed to bow before the throne and repent of our sins? Or should we be more ashamed to tell God, 'Thank you for sending Jesus to suffer such a horrible death. But He didn't suffer enough for me.' Because of this truth the Devil will never again keep me from repentance. The power of God can set you free. Only the Word of God can keep you free."

Rex counted my testimony as valid when my freedom came from God's Word. No one cares about our ideas on how wonderful God is. Neither does the Devil. If we want to change someone's life, we should speak God's Word.

I shared with Rex about the time God proved to me that He could still use me, which He was doing again at this point. When I mentioned the promises that came with giving, he received my testimony of Jared's conversion as being the work of the Lord.

The Depth of Grace

"I also needed to know I could stay strong in my faith," I said to Rex. "I didn't want to fail again. I later learned that, 'I have hidden your word in my heart that I might not sin against you' (from Psalm 119:11)."

I discussed how the Lord revealed to me that I have nothing to worry about as long as I stay in His Word, pray, worship, and adequately follow His Son. I shared many stories like these during this last day. I simply shared my *sufferings* and then the *comfort* I received through God's Word.

> *Praise be to the God and Father of our Lord Jesus Christ, the Father of compassion and the God of all comfort, who comforts us in all our troubles, so that we can comfort those in any trouble with the comfort we ourselves receive from God. For just as we share abundantly in the sufferings of Christ, so also our comfort abounds through Christ. If we are distressed, it is for your comfort and salvation; if we are comforted, it is for your comfort, which produces in you patient endurance of the same sufferings we suffer. And our hope for you is firm, because we know that just as you share in our sufferings, so also you share in our comfort. (2 Corinthians 1:3-7)*

With the end of our final day nearing, I asked, "Rex, have you noticed anything different about the way you feel now, compared to the beginning of the first day?"

Rex gazed off into the distance as he pondered his response to the question. His eyes filled up with tears as he sat for a moment in silence. He then slowly began to speak as a tear rolled down his face, "My heart … it … it's swollen. It burns inside of me," he said.

> *Now that same day two of them were going to a village called Emmaus, about seven miles from Jerusalem. They were talking with each other about everything that had happened. As they talked and discussed these things with each other, Jesus himself came up and walked along with them; but they were kept from recognizing him.*
>
> *He asked them, "What are you discussing together as you walk along?"*
>
> *They stood still, their faces downcast. One of them, named Cleopas, asked him, "Are you the only one visiting Jerusalem*

J. Bronson Haley

who does not know the things that have happened there in these days?"

"What things?" he asked.

"About Jesus of Nazareth," they replied. "He was a prophet, powerful in word and deed before God and all the people. The chief priests and our rulers handed him over to be sentenced to death, and they crucified him; but we had hoped that he was the one who was going to redeem Israel. And what is more, it is the third day since all this took place. In addition, some of our women amazed us. They went to the tomb early this morning but didn't find his body. They came and told us that they had seen a vision of angels, who said he was alive. Then some of our companions went to the tomb and found it just as the women had said, but him they did not see."

He said to them, "How foolish you are, and how slow to believe all that the prophets have spoken! Did not the Messiah have to suffer these things and then enter his glory?" And beginning with Moses and all the Prophets, he explained to them what was said in all the Scriptures concerning himself.

As they approached the village to which they were going, Jesus acted as if he were going farther. But they urged him strongly, "Stay with us, for it is nearly evening; they day is almost over." So he went in to stay with them.

When he was at the table with them, he took bread, gave thanks, broke it and began to give it to them. Then their eyes were opened and they recognized him, and he disappeared from their sight. They asked each other, "Were not our hearts burning within us while he talked with us on the road and opened the Scriptures to us?" (Luke 24:13-32, my emphasis)

I almost stroked out when I read this passage a couple of days after Rex said his heart was burning inside him. I immediately called Rex and we praised God for this time we'd had with Jesus. Experiences like this build our faith. "Then the disciples went out and preached everywhere, and the Lord worked with them and confirmed his word by the signs that

The Depth of Grace

accompanied it" (Mark 16:20). How can our faith increase if we do not get into His Word?

God further confirmed to me that He planned to use me again through my experience with Rex. Stories like this have helped to build my faith and give me strength. Even more, stories like this prove time and again to me that the Word of God is alive and well. Oftentimes God steps into our everyday circumstances when we least expect it. But that's because His Word comes alive inside of us as we read. Then He confirms His Word as we walk. Jesus Christ has not changed!

13TH REST STOP:
FLESH SEEKERS: PART 1

Those who do not believe in God have a good argument against living for Him. Most of the world argues the same argument, as most of the world does not believe in God. This is the foundation of the argument of nonbelievers: "It's hard to have faith in God. I don't understand how I could be happy living for Jesus. It's hard to imagine living an entire life without sin. And a life serving a church? That would be boring!"

This is the truth. Ouch!

"Bronson, stop telling people it's boring to be a Christian," one might say.

The problem is that nonbelievers feel this way and have a good argument against having faith in God and living for Him. Why should I not speak of this argument when it is a real issue? Let's get real! An entire life without sin? What a boring life (you'll see what I mean ... keep reading)! This is the truth and the Word of God. However, its only part of the truth. In order to understand why people feel this way, we need to understand more about where we have come from.

"The LORD God formed a man from the dust of the ground and breathed into his nostrils the breath of life, and the man became a living being" (Genesis 2:7). First, God created the human flesh. When God breathed life into Adam, birth was given to his spirit. "As the body without the spirit is dead, so faith without deeds is dead" (James 2:26). It was the Spirit of God that gave birth to the spirit of man—the life of Adam. It is our spirit that gives life to the body. It was Adam's spirit that had fellowship with the Spirit of God. It's by our spirit that we communicate with the

224

The Depth of Grace

spirit realm. Of course, in the beginning existed no desire to sin—to do evil. The reason is because Adam was not aware of evil. His spirit was in fellowship with God—not Satan. Adam desired only to please the Father and fellowship with Him. In the beginning Adam and Eve were under the protection of God. It was sin that gave Satan rights to have fellowship with man.

Adam and Eve were created in the image of God with the knowledge of good. Because they were in fellowship with the Father, their spirits were in communication with the Spirit of truth. They had no communication with the evil spirit of Satan because Satan had no rights to their lives—man was without sin. "Take delight in the LORD and he will give you the desires of your heart" (Psalm 37:4). The Lord breathed life into Adam so that He could have fellowship with him. If the Lord desires fellowship with man, then He must grant man the desire to fellowship with Him. There was no desire for sin in the beginning.

> How you have fallen from heaven, morning star, son of the dawn! You have been cast down to the earth, you who once laid low the nations! You said in your heart, "I will ascend to the heavens; I will raise my throne above the stars of God; I will sit enthroned on the mount of assembly, on the utmost heights of Mount Zaphon. I will ascend above the tops of the clouds; I will make myself like the Most High." (Isaiah 14:12-14)

As we saw earlier, Satan was cast out of heaven because of his pride—he wanted to be like God—he wanted His glory—Satan wanted to be worshiped like the great I AM. He was a beautiful angel and most likely the top angel. Based on the knowledge Satan had of himself and God, he felt sure he could overpower Him and become ruler of the heavens and the earth. Unfortunately for him the Lord had not made his manifold wisdom known to the angels and angelic beings in heavenly realms: "His intent was that now, through the **church**, the manifold wisdom of God should be made known to the rulers and authorities in the heavenly realms" (Ephesians 3:10, my emphasis).

If Satan had remained good, he could not have gone to war with God. Love cannot fight against love. Can good triumph over good? Can truth be any truer? "Every kingdom divided against itself will be ruined" (Matthew 12:25). The Lord gave the Devil a depraved spirit as a reward

J. Bronson Haley

for His pride. So that Satan could oppose God, he was made evil, which is in opposition to good. He is now the father of lies, which is in opposition to the God of all truth. He traded eternal glory for eternal damnation. Without understanding what would result from his rebellion, Satan traded long-term peace for long-term torment, and he has been ticked ever since. The war is now over you and me. Because Satan could not reach the Father in heaven, he met His children in the garden.

Satan immediately approached humankind and began to deceive them into becoming like him. Only they did not desire to be like him. They wanted to live. They desired to fellowship with God. What person who is truly alive desires death? Satan didn't know what God had planned for him before he desired to be like Him. The Devil lacked the wisdom of God. In his attempt to be like God, he deceived himself. The Devil so screwed himself that he knew just how to screw over man.

> *He said to the woman, "Did God really say, 'You must not eat from any tree in the garden'"?"*
>
> *The woman said to the serpent, "We may eat fruit from the trees in the garden, but God did say, 'You must not eat fruit from the tree that is in the middle of the garden, and you must not touch it, or you will die.'"*
>
> *"You will not certainly die," the serpent said to the woman. "For God knows that when you eat from it your eyes will be opened, and you will be like God, knowing good and evil."* (Genesis 3:1-5)

Just as Satan deceived himself in his quest to be "like God," he deceived man in the same manner: "… and you will be **like God**" (my emphasis). But man was already like God—created in His image! "So **God** created mankind in his own **image**, in the **image** of **God** he created them; male and female he created them" (Genesis 1:27, my emphasis).

Sin is the act of being disobedient to God. When we are disobedient to His Word, the Devil gets rights into our lives. The wages of sin is death: "You must not touch it, or you will die." Just as the Devil fell because of his pride, he deceived man into acting out of pride. "God opposes the proud, but shows favor to the humble" (James 4:6). The Lord is also bound by His Word: "God is not human, that he should lie, not a human being, that he

The Depth of Grace

should change his mind. Does he speak and then not act? Does he promise and not fulfill?" (Numbers 23:19). So ...

> To Adam he said, "Because you listened to your wife and ate from the tree about which I commanded you, 'You must not eat of it,' cursed is the ground because of you; through painful toil you will eat food from it all the days of your life. It will produce thorns and thistles for you, and you will eat the plants of the field. By the sweat of your brow you will eat your food until you return to the ground, since from it you were taken; for dust you are and to dust you will return." (Genesis 3:17-19)

Because of sin, man went from blessed to cursed. From children of light to children of darkness (see 1 Peter 2:9). From peace to torment. We were spiritually separated from God. Our spirit no longer had fellowship with the Spirit of truth—but rather a spirit of lies. It was no longer God who granted man the desires of his heart—but Satan. Today, because of this truth, we are born with a sinful nature—a relentless urge to commit sin.

> There is no difference ... for all have sinned and fall short of the glory of God. (Romans 3:22-23)

> All have turned away, all have become corrupt; there is no one who does good, not even one. (Psalm 14:3)

God also cursed the Devil on that darkened day when Adam fell into sin. At that time, the Lord mentioned to Satan that from the offspring of the woman would come an "enmity" who had not yet been spoken of—a messenger from God who would crush the head of the Devil (see Genesis 3:15). Do you see what I mean when I say that the angels—good and fallen alike—did not understand God's love or redemption? We can see from Genesis 3:15 additional proofs that God did not make his manifold wisdom made know to the rulers and authorities in heavenly realms. If Satan only knew then what he knows now! Without understanding what this curse meant, the Devil began a desperate attempt to intercept this "enmity" and destroy it.

Since God did not make His manifold wisdom known to the rulers and authorities in heavenly realms when he created them, they did not understand His love or redemption. Neither was redemption available

J. Bronson Haley

to them. Satan has no chance of coming back into fellowship with God and will spend eternity in hell. From the moment man fell into sin to the resurrection of Jesus Christ, the Devil had his way with man and appeared to be victorious on every occasion. So where was the God of love? It appeared as though Satan were winning the war between good and evil. The angels in the heavens watched as their opposition continuously ravaged God's people. But what is love? The angels who did not rebel against God were obedient to His Word. God made many promises to His chosen people we read about in the Old Testament. The good angels fought for Abraham, Isaac, Jacob, and all of God's anointed. They fought for Israel, but Satan continued to rule over mankind and inflict suffering beyond our imagination. God's angels were aware of the promises He made to His people concerning His love and their day of redemption. The promises were made to the patriarchs and they heard God speak to them. But they couldn't see the promises in their own lives. They never saw these promises. "These were all commended for their faith, yet none of them received what had been promised" (Hebrews 11:39). God is love. But what is love? Who can understand?

Israel continued to rebel. God's people continued to allow their pride and sinful lusts to destroy them and their children. For over four thousand years the heavenly angels observed a cursed generation suffer at the hands of Satan. To the angels of God it seemed impossible to tame these wretched people. There were none who did good. Not even one. They were slaves to the sin and were destroyed daily. Without understanding God's love, day and night the rulers and authorities in the heavenly realms never stopped saying, "Holy, holy, holy is the Lord God Almighty, who was, and is, and is to come" (Revelation 4:8). Though death continued to reign on earth, they never stopped worshiping Him in heaven. All awaited this promised "enmity" that would crush the head of the evil one.

Certainly the angelic army of God longed for the day when this "enmity" would rule God's people and put an end to the suffering. The angels didn't know what God was up to exactly. They had heard His words of love and redemption, but lacked understanding. To mention a few Scriptures …

> *Therefore the Lord himself will give you a sign: The virgin will conceive and will give birth to a son, and will call him Immanuel. (Isaiah 7:14)*

The Depth of Grace

Rejoice greatly, Daughter Zion! Shout, Daughter Jerusalem! See, your king comes to you, righteous and victorious, lowly and riding on a donkey, on a colt, the foal of a donkey. (Zechariah 9:9)

For to us a child is born, to us a son is given, and the government will be on his shoulders. And he will be called Wonderful Counselor, Mighty God, Everlasting Father, Prince of Peace. Of the greatness of his government and peace there will be no end. He will reign on David's throne and over his kingdom, establishing and upholding it with justice and righteousness from that time on and forever. The zeal of the LORD Almighty will accomplish this. (Isaiah 9:6-7)

Today in the town of David a Savior has been born to you; he is the Messiah, the Lord. (Luke 2:11)

And unto us a child was born. Satan had been anticipating this day for a long time. This was He who was sent to crush his own head.

This was the critical point in history for earth and heaven. And we'll pick up with the rest of this amazing story in the 14th Rest Stop! Until then, how about a visit with my old friend Mike Mertle?

CHAPTER 24

Mike Mertle

I picked up my phone and dialed. "Mike! What's up, man? This is Bronson!"

This is the same Mike with whom I had broken into Broadmoor Middle School. We were still best friends but had gone separate ways our senior year of high school. When Mike graduated, he packed up and moved to Denver, Colorado. Our friend Kasey was in Denver going to school at the time so Mike lived with him until he could get on his feet. Mike's father sent him some money when he arrived in Denver so that he could buy a bicycle to get around on. Mike is naturally and hysterically funny—plus, he's scary skinny with short blond hair. It cracks me up to picture him riding his bicycle around Denver like Pee-Wee Herman, looking for a job. Anyway, not too long after Mike got on his feet, his girlfriend from Shreveport moved in with him. A year later they had a baby and named him Kenny.

Over the next seven or eight years, Mike struggled with addiction. At the time of this particular phone call with him, he lived in Fort Worth, Texas. By this time he had developed a severe addiction to Xanax and sold drugs to support his habit.

During this phone call I began to share with Mike the things God was teaching me in His Word and the things He was doing in my life. I shared with him the story of Simon Peter, Jacob, and many of the others. I explained that God had protected Jacob even when he was away

231

and explained why I felt that way. I used God's Word to confirm my suspicions.

"You can look at your life and see that God has kept you as well," I said.

Mike was blessed with wonderful parents who prayed for him throughout his entire life. He, too, had many close calls and it was obvious that the Lord protected him through the years.

"People have prayed for you your whole life and God has heard them. He has big plans to restore you and use your testimony to bring people to Jesus," I explained.

Mike agreed that God had protected him. He believed the things I said. However, he could not comprehend how God could use him, given his condition and the mistakes he had made.

"You can't see it now, Mike, because you have been blinded. Trust me!" I said. "It's not about who you are right now. We are not called according to who we are. We are called according to the foreknowledge of God. It's not about you anyway. It's about Jesus Christ who walks before you. It's not up to you to change, so don't worry about that. It is up to you to learn how to follow the Son of God. Only He can change you, so relax."

It's not important that people are set free when we speak with them, although it is wonderful when they are. It is important that we get the truth inside of them. Once they have heard the truth, the Lord can confirm His Word to them at a later time and bring this truth to light. Their faith will grow as a result of God confirming His Word.

It's hard to imagine life without the easy money that comes from selling drugs once someone starts making some money. It's easy and profitable. At this time Mike had three cars with fancy rims and stereo systems. He had a house and life was good. However, the profits really amount to nothing in the long run. I experienced this myself, and I explained this concept to Mike on the phone that day.

"It's impossible to profit from selling drugs, Mike. God will not allow it. Proverbs 10:2 says, 'Ill-gotten treasures have no lasting value.' Proverbs 1:19 says, 'Such are the paths of all who go after ill-gotten gain; it takes away the life of those who get it.' The Word of God will hold true in every circumstance and God will prove this to you. If you decide to continue to sell drugs and live that lifestyle, be sure to remember the things I have said to you today. You will not profit. God will not allow it."

One year later Mike called me.

"Bronson! I'm in town and I need to talk to you."

The Depth of Grace

I picked him up within ten minutes and we talked. He described his experience over the past year. The details were explicit.

Once, Mike and his partner were led down some stairs into a basement where an illegal gambling operation was run. At the foot of the stairs two men stood outside of the door that led into the casino and a table sat off to the right. These men were Asian gangsters in dress suits.

"We know you have guns. Place them here on the table," one of the men said to Mike.

This wasn't Mike and his partner's first trip to this casino. Mike met his partner, who was in his mid-thirties, through one of his bookies who worked for a legal casino. This bookie had a hookup on pills for a good price. The fellow finally got tired of making the trips back and forth to and from Dallas, and introduced Mike to his connection. This connection was in business with the Asian mafia, which owned this particular underground casino.

So Mike and his partner placed the guns on the table, the men opened the door, and they entered. The casino was closed down to the public for the drug deal. Ten men, wearing suits and smoking cigars, sat in the room.

"Have a seat," one of the Asians said, implying that Mike and his partner sit at a poker table.

After they took a seat, Mike and his partner ordered the usual from a girl who was there to serve them.

"A Bud Light for him and Crown on the rocks for me," Mike's partner said to the waitress.

After five minutes a man called Jonny Linn entered the room. This was the man in charge of the underground operation. He was the boss. Jonny sat down at the dealer's slot and the two who entered the room with him stood behind—one to his back right and one to his back left.

"We have the money of thirty-two thousand dollars?" Jonny Linn asked.

"Of course as long as you have the goods," Mike's partner said.

Jonny spoke in some Asian language to the men who stood behind him. They both responded by heading in different directions into other rooms. One came back with a money counter and the other with two duffle bags.

"Give me the money," Jonny said.

233

As they handed their share of the money to Jonny Linn, the two duffle bags were placed on the table. The man pulled a bundle of one thousand Lortabs out of one bag and one thousand Xanax pills out of the other.

"There are thirty bundles in each bag," Jonny said.

By the time Jonny explained the transaction, the money counter had finished at twenty-nine thousand dollars.

"Where is the other money? You are three grand short!" Jonny said, with evident frustration. "We said thirty-two thousand! No money—no deal!"

At this point Mike pulled the other three grand out of his sock and handed it to one of the men who stood beside Jonny. He then put the money in the counting machine. This mistake was in direct correlation with how many pills Mike had taken before he walked in the building.

"Okay, good ... now we have a deal," Jonny stated and then walked out of the room.

The two men Jonny Linn had walked in with now stayed at the table, and another three men stood behind Mike and his partner. As Mike and his friend finished their drinks, Jonny reentered the room and spoke Asian to the two men who stood at the table. At that time, the three guys behind Mike and his friend pulled out pistols.

Jonny Linn said, "You try to short me this time! This is the last time!"

"What do you mean the last time?" Mike's partner asked.

"No more business! I am done with you two! I take your money!" Jonny said.

"Hey, man, come on ... the money is here. Let's do the deal and call it a day," Mike said out of desperation.

With his men's guns still drawn, Jonny again spoke to his boys in Asian. He then left the room. The two men who came in with Jonny grabbed the money counter and the duffle bags and left. At gunpoint my friend Mike and his partner were escorted out of the casino, up the stairs, through the kitchen, and out the back door of the restaurant. That was the last time they did business with the Asian mafia. When they got into the car, Mike was pistol-whipped by his partner.

Three months later the Dallas police raided the restaurant and the casino. Jonny Linn and many of his people were arrested. Mike's partner showed up at Mike's house shortly after he heard about the raid.

"My name is on the list. The cops will soon come to my house and search for drugs. I'll be back to get the pills in a few days," he told Mike.

The Depth of Grace

He left Mike with twenty thousand pills. After the cops searched Mike's partner's house, he came back and retrieved his pills.

"I sent my wife and kid to California," his partner said. "I'm not sure what will happen to me. I'll be in touch."

And he left. I would guess that the Asians suspected that Mike's partner turned them in. A couple of weeks later Mike called his partner, but his cell phone had been disconnected. He then called the partner's house, but his home phone had been disconnected as well. Mike never heard from his partner again. He owned an eight-hundred-thousand-dollar house and had a wife and a son. Today Mike's partner is either in jail or dead. "Such are the paths of all who go after ill-gotten gain."

A couple of months later on a cold and rainy night, Mike and a friend of his entered a strip joint to celebrate the fact that they had just made good money on a drug deal.

"So we went inside the strip club, sat down, and ordered a couple of beers," Mike told me. "Before the cocktail waitress returned with the beer, I got up and began to tip the girls left and right. I was very excited about the money I just made. My friend then encouraged me to come sit down and put my wallet up."

By this time Mike's friend had noticed that a group of Hispanics across the bar watched him closely.

"By the time I sat down and grabbed my beer, my friend got struck in the head with a beer bottle," Mike continued. "I went to swing at the dude that hit him and missed. A man then picked up my beer from the table and cracked it across my jaw. I immediately fell to the floor. After I shook it off, I stood up and got hit again in the exact same place. My buddy screamed, 'Get out! Get out! They're trying to rob us!' I was the first one out of the door of the club. My buddy ran out and screamed, 'Get in the car! Get in the car!' We both got in the car and my friend pulled out his gun.

"After he rolled my window down and pulled in front of the bar, he began to fire off rounds out of my window into the glass windows. At the first stoplight he looked at me and said, 'Damn, dude ... you got hurt.'

"'My jaw hurts bad,' I told him. Then he said, 'I'm going to have to take you to the hospital and drop you off. You're in bad shape.'"

Mike had surgery on his jaw and to this day he cannot fully open his mouth.

Two months later on a hot summer day, Mike made a phone call to Little Ned—one of his drug dealers—in desperate need of some pills. I know, it seems ridiculous, doesn't it? However, it's no fun when pills run

J. Bronson Haley

your life. Mike had an addiction and these pills made life bearable. He had previously attempted to get off of the drug and went into seizures.

"Hey, man, can you really get these pills or not? I heard that you couldn't," Mike said to Little Ned.

"Yeah, I can get the pills. Come pick me up," Ned said.

"Are you sure? I don't want to waste my time," Mike told him.

"I'm waiting on you."

After Mike picked up Little Ned, they lit and shared a blunt (a cigar filled with marijuana), and drove to the apartment to meet with the man who had the pills. Little Ned knocked on the door of the apartment. A Hispanic man opened the door and let them in. Mike and Little Ned sat down on the couch and the Mexican asked for two thousand dollars.

"I want to see the pills," Mike said.

"Okay, one second, let me go get them," the man said.

He returned moments later with two ziplock bags of pills and threw them on the table. One thousand pills were sealed in each bag. Mike threw the money on the table and the man counted it. At this moment Little Ned got up and went to the bathroom, and the dealer left the room as well.

"Get the @#$% up," said one of two men who walked out of a closet from behind.

They stuck their guns to the back of Mike's head.

"Whoa—wait a minute! What in the hell is going on here?" Mike asked in a panic.

"You are a salty-a$$ white boy who is getting robbed! Now get the @#$& out of here before I put a bullet in your head," one of the men said.

As he told me this story, I could hear in Mike's voice just how tense this moment had been for him. "I stood up and turned around to two black men who held pistols in my face," Mike continued. "They escorted me out of the apartment and that's the last time I saw Little Ned."

All three of these cataclysmic events had taken place since the last time I spoke with Mike a year ago.

"Well, are you ready?" I asked him.

"I don't have any choice," Mike said.

"I couldn't have said it better myself."

Over the next several days I poured into Mike many of the things you have read in this book. He believed me. God moved powerfully in several conversations we had. When I spoke the Word of God, Mike listened.

236

The Depth of Grace

Mike, his father, and I sat in the Mertles' home to discuss Mike's path to freedom. Mr. Mertle suggested that Mike go through an inpatient rehab program to get off the drugs.

"Dad, I don't need that," he said. "The Lord is with me and I don't need any help. God has moved in my life in the past several days, and Jesus is with me."

God had moved in Mike's life for sure. However, Mr. Mertle and I had a conversation with Mike's pride on this occasion.

"Mike, you are opposed in your pride," I said. "If you think you can overcome on your own, God will be sure you see that you cannot."

"Jesus is with me, and like you said, all I need to do is follow Him," he said with arrogance.

"That is true, Mike. We follow Him through prayer, reading the Word, assembling together with other believers, and things like that. The Word of God says to stay clear of the Enemy's campground. If you move back into your house in Fort Worth, you will be moving into the Devil's camp and you cannot overcome living there. (His roommate also had drug problems.) That would be disobedience to God's Word and He will have no choice but to show you that you cannot disobey Him and find freedom. When we are disobedient, we are no longer adequately following Christ. Jesus was obedient to the will of the Father. He knew His Father's will because He was the Word of God in the flesh. If we are disobedient to the truth, we are subject to the lies of the Enemy," I said.

Mike also struggled submitting to authority. His father spoke during most of this conversation. Reverend Mertle is a man of God who runs the Shreveport/Bossier rescue mission here in Shreveport and chose to give his life years ago to those who are in desperate need—mostly homeless people. He is a wonderful man and Mike was a prideful, arrogant son who didn't want to hear his father's opinion. My stomach turned as Mike responded to the things Reverend Mertle said to him. He was disrespectful and did not have a clue what it meant to honor his earthly or heavenly father.

Interrupting the conversation, I said, "I don't think there is anything left to talk about. God will not allow you to get anywhere in your pride. You can take your father's advice or see for yourself that the Lord is finished with this nonsense."

That was the end of the conversation.

Mike went back to his home and soon moved in with another friend of his. This was a better environment, but Mike still had access to the drugs.

J. Bronson Haley

Again, he went his own way. Mike was disobedient to God's Word and didn't honor his father.

Two months later Mike called. "Bronson, I lost my boy! I went to court today and I cannot see Kenny or talk to him for at least one year!" he said.

My friend was a total wreck.

"Mike, I want to discuss with you something the Lord spoke to me through his Word just today," I said.

I had recently begun to study the prophet Isaiah. In chapter 9, I read of God's anger and wrath against Israel. God was angered because of Israel's pride. He proceeded to humble His people. I related this message from Isaiah to Mike:

> *The Lord has sent a message against Jacob; it will fall on Israel.*
>
> *All the people will know it—Ephraim and the inhabitants of Samaria—who say with pride and arrogance of heart, "The bricks have fallen down, but we will rebuild with dressed stone; the fig trees have been felled, but we will replace them with cedars."*
>
> *But the LORD has strengthened Rezin's foes against them and has spurred their enemies on. Arameans from the east and Philistines from the west have devoured Israel with open mouth.*
>
> *Yet for all this, his anger is not turned away, his hand is still upraised.*
>
> *But the people have not returned to him who struck them, nor have they sought the LORD Almighty. So the LORD will cut off from Israel both head and tail, both palm branch and reed in a single day; the elders and dignitaries are the head, the prophets who teach lies are the tail. Those who guide this people mislead them, and those who are guided are led astray. Therefore the LORD will take no pleasure in the young men, nor will he pity the fatherless and widows, for everyone is ungodly and wicked, every mouth speaks folly.*

The Depth of Grace

> *Yet for all this, his anger is not turned away, his hand is still upraised.*
>
> *Surely wickedness burns like a fire; it consumes briers and thorns, it sets the forest thickets ablaze, so that it rolls upward in a column of smoke.*
>
> *By the wrath of the LORD Almighty the land will be scorched and the people will be fuel for the fire; they will not spare one another. On the right they will devour, but still be hungry; on the left they will eat, but not be satisfied. Each will feed on the flesh of his own offspring: Manasseh will feed on Ephraim, and Ephraim on Manasseh; together they will turn against Judah.*
>
> *Yet for all this, his anger is not turned away, his hand is still upraised. (Isaiah 9:8-21)*

"We know God when we know His Word," I said to Mike. "We understand what He will and will not do as we read what He has done in the past. According to the Scripture, things will continue to get worse until you humble yourself. Things are extremely tough right now. However, according to God's Word, His hand is still upraised."

I did not enjoy that conversation with my best friend. I wanted to tell him that everything was going to be okay and that life would only get better. I wanted to say, "Keep your head high. Everything will work out." However, that is not love. Love speaks the truth in every circumstance—even if the truth hurts deeply.

Everyone has heard people say, "The Lord giveth and the Lord taketh away." And this is true. However, don't give a man only part of the truth! That is not love. The truth is that God's hand will remain upraised unless we humble ourselves. We are opposed in our pride. This is true. However, there is more truth than that. Jesus Christ came and died for our sins for sure. He also came to heal the brokenhearted. Jesus also came to destroy the work of the Devil. The Son of God is our healer and deliverer. Jesus Christ is also our redeemer. The Lord will humble us in our pride. The Son of God will redeem our losses in our humility. It may look bad in the heat of the moment. Do not be discouraged! Humble yourself and allow God to prove to you the power that raised Jesus from the dead. It was the love of God that brought Jesus out of the tomb after He was crucified. The love

J. Bronson Haley

of God made available to all believers everything that was accomplished through the blood of Christ. Redemption can be found in the blood of Jesus Christ. God only needs someone to trust Him. The Lord only needs a chance to prove Himself.

Mike finally decided to humble himself and honor his Father in heaven and his earthly father. He humbled himself and confessed that only Jesus could restore him. My friend honored his father, having asked him to offer him three options for his recovery.

"I will pick one and trust you," Mike told his father.

One of Reverend Mertle's options was for Mike to do nothing and continue on his own path. Mike chose to detox and signed up for a three-month inpatient rehabilitation program.

If we speak the Word of God, God will confirm His Word.

14TH REST STOP:
FLESH SEEKERS: PART 2

Okay, picking up where we left off in the last Rest Stop, Jesus is now on the scene. He is the "enmity" that all of heaven had been waiting for the Father to release against the kingdom of darkness. Of course, the Devil wasn't going to go down without a fight. From the time Jesus was born, Satan launched attacks in an effort to kill Him. From town to town, the Son of God was guided to safety by the angels of heaven. More than thirty years from the time He was born, Jesus began His ministry and Israel began to mistreat Him. The Lord allowed Jesus to be abused. As Jesus continued to minister the truth about Himself and His Father in heaven, opposition became more and more fierce. Jesus didn't do any wrong, but many people began to hate Him. They also made up lies about Him in an effort to destroy His credibility. Later, the hate grew to a point where they sought His life. Why? Why were they so angry with Him? It was because Jesus was sent to destroy the work of Satan, as it is written in 1 John 3:8: "The reason the Son of God appeared was to destroy the devil's work." Satan sought to kill this "enmity" sent by God to crush his head. It was Satan who granted these people the desires of their hearts.

Along with the rulers and authorities in heavenly realms, Jesus' disciples watched as He was betrayed with a kiss by one of their own.

> *While he was still speaking, Judas, one of the Twelve, arrived.*
> *With him was a large crowd armed with swords and clubs,*
> *sent from the chief priests and the elders of the people. Now*
> *the betrayer had arranged a signal with them: "The one I kiss*

J. Bronson Haley

> *is the man; arrest him." Going at once to Jesus, Judas said, "Greetings, Rabbi!" and kissed him. (Matthew 26:47-49)*

Is that love?

> *In that hour Jesus said to the crowd, "Am I leading a rebellion, that you have come out with swords and clubs to capture me? Every day I sat in the temple courts teaching, and you did not arrest me. But this has all taken place that the writings of the prophets might be fulfilled." Then all the disciples deserted him and fled. (Matthew 26:55-56)*

Jesus did have understanding. They were not able to harm Him in the temple courts. These men only seized Jesus because the Lord allowed them to. He knew these men were deceived. The very men who plotted against Jesus anticipated the arrival of Immanuel—the Savior of Israel—Jesus Himself. Because they were not in fellowship with God, they were not able to recognize Him. They didn't understand the Scriptures because truth was not available to them at this point.

The people so hated Jesus that they did not care that He had never done anything wrong. They wanted Him dead. Yes, man was in opposition to good. As Satan so deceived himself, he deceived man and they rallied with him against the Most High. "Woe to those who call evil good and good evil, who put darkness for light and light for darkness, who put bitter for sweet and sweet for bitter" (Isaiah 5:20).

Then Jesus was unfairly tried before various councils.

> *The chief priests and the whole Sanhedrin were looking for false evidence against Jesus so that they could put him to death. But they did not find any, though many false witnesses came forward. Finally two came forward and declared, "This fellow said, 'I am able to destroy the temple of God and rebuild it in three days.'"*
>
> *Then the high priest stood up and said to Jesus, "Are you not going to answer? What is this testimony that these men are bringing against you?" But Jesus remained silent. (Matthew 26:59-63)*

The Depth of Grace

Jesus' heart burned for His people. Several days earlier, "As he approached Jerusalem and saw the city, he wept over it and said, 'If you, even you, had only known on this day what would bring you peace—but now it is hidden from your eyes'" (Luke 19:41-42). It was because of this understanding that Jesus remained silent before His accusers. He knew they were not able to receive Him.

"What do you think?"

"He is worthy of death," they answered.

Then they spit in his face and struck him with their fists. Others slapped him and said, "Prophesy to us, Messiah. Who hit you?" (Matthew 26:66-68)

Recall these words from Isaiah the prophet: "He was oppressed and afflicted, yet he did not open his mouth; he was led like a lamb to the slaughter, and as a sheep before her shearers is silent, so he did not open his mouth" (Isaiah 53:7).

Meanwhile Jesus stood before the governor, and the governor asked him, "Are you the king of the Jews?"

"You have said so," Jesus replied.

When he was accused by the chief priests and the elders, he gave no answer. Then Pilate asked him, "Don't you hear the testimony they are bringing against you?" But Jesus made no reply, not even to a single charge—to the great amazement of the governor.

Now it was the governor's custom at the festival to release a prisoner chosen by the crowd. At that time they had a well-known prisoner whose name was Jesus Barabbas. So when the crowd had gathered, Pilate asked them, "Which one do you want me to release to you: Jesus Barabbas, or Jesus who is called the Messiah?" For he knew it was out of envy that they had handed Jesus over to him.

While Pilate was sitting on the judge's seat, his wife sent him this message: "Don't have anything to do with that innocent man, for I have suffered a great deal today in a dream because of him."

But the chief priests and the elders persuaded the crowd to ask for Barabbas and to have Jesus executed.

"Which of the two do you want me to release to you?" asked the governor.

"Barabbas," they answered.

"What shall I do, then, with Jesus who is called the Messiah?" Pilate asked.

They all answered, "Crucify him!"

"Why? What crime has he committed?" asked Pilate.

But they shouted all the louder, "Crucify him!"

When Pilate saw that he was getting nowhere, but that instead an uproar was starting, he took water and washed his hands in front of the crowd. "I am innocent of this man's blood," he said. "It is your responsibility!"

All the people answered, "His blood is on us and on our children!"

Then he released Barabbas to them. But he had Jesus flogged, and handed him over to be crucified.

Then the governor's soldiers took Jesus into the Praetorium and gathered the whole company of soldiers around him. They stripped him and put a scarlet robe on him, and then twisted together a crown of thorns and set it on his head. They put a staff in his right hand and knelt in front of him and mocked him. "Hail, king of the Jews!" they said. They spit on him, and took the staff and struck him on the head again and again. After they had mocked him, they took off the robe and put his own clothes on him. Then they led him away to crucify him.

The Depth of Grace

As they were going out, they met a man from Cyrene, named Simon, and they forced him to carry the cross. They came to a place called Golgotha (which means "the place of the skull"). There they offered Jesus wine to drink, mixed with gall; but after tasting it, he refused to drink it. When they had crucified him, they divided up his clothes by casting lots. And sitting down, they kept watch over him there. Above his head they placed the written charge against him: THIS IS JESUS, THE KING OF THE JEWS. Two rebels were crucified with him, one on his right and one on his left. Those who passed by hurled insults at him, shaking their heads and saying, "You who are going to destroy the temple and build it in three days, save yourself! Come down from the cross, if you are the Son of God!"

In the same way the chief priests, the teachers of the law and the elders mocked him. "He saved others," they said, "but he can't save himself! He's the King of Israel! Let him come down now from the cross, and we will believe in him. He trusts in God. Let God rescue him now if he wants him, for he said, 'I am the Son of God.'" In the same way the rebels who were crucified with him also heaped insults on him.

From noon until three in the afternoon darkness came over all the land. About three in the afternoon Jesus cried out in a loud voice, "Eloi, Eloi, lema sabachthani?" (which means, "My God, my God, why have you forsaken me?")....

And when Jesus had cried out again in a loud voice, he gave up his spirit....

When the centurion and those with him who were guarding Jesus saw the earthquake and all that had happened, they were terrified, and exclaimed, "Surely he was the Son of God!" (Matthew 27:11-46, 50, 54)

Without understanding God's love or His plan of redemption, the rulers and authorities in the heavenly realm never stopped worshiping the Lord: "saying, 'Holy, holy, holy is the Lord God Almighty, who was, and is, and is to come.'"

J. Bronson Haley

I can remember wondering why the rulers and authorities in the presence of God only worshiped the Lord with their words. They say "Holy, holy, holy...." They never stop simply *saying* that the Lord is holy. It was because they did not fully understand Him. They did not yet understand His plan of redemption. They watched from the beginning of time, but lacked understanding. They didn't know why this and why that. But they worshiped Him, merely saying "Holy, holy, holy is the Lord God Almighty, who was, and is, and is to come." As they watched, they saw that not only did Satan continue to destroy Israel, but he crucified Jesus—the "enmity" that was to crush his head. Where was the love of God? What is love? The hope of Israel was tortured and murdered. This was the darkest day in history. Who could understand? Who understood the love of God? Who understood what Jesus spoke about just days before He was murdered? "'The Son of Man is going to be betrayed into the hands of men. They will kill him, and after three days he will rise.' But they did not understand what he meant and were afraid to ask him about it" (Mark 9:31-32).

I can tell you that, upon the resurrection of Jesus Christ, the love of God became known to the world, as we saw earlier in the Scripture, "His intent was that now, through the **church**, the manifold wisdom of God should be made known to the rulers and authorities in the heavenly realms" (Ephesians 3:10, my emphasis). When the angelic beings in heavenly realms witnessed what God did for His people through Jesus, they came to understand love and redemption. John the disciple was later allowed to witness this moment in the heavens. It was on this day that those in the presence of God went from just simply *saying* to lifting their voices in praises to the king:

And they sang a new song, saying:

"You are worthy to take the scroll and to open its seals, because you were slain, and with your blood you purchased for God persons from every tribe and language and people and nation. You have made them to be a kingdom and priests to serve our God, and they will reign on the earth."

Then I looked and heard the voice of many angels, numbering thousands upon thousands, and ten thousand times ten thousand. They encircled the throne and the living creatures and the elders. In a loud voice they were saying:

The Depth of Grace

> *"Worthy is the Lamb, who was slain, to receive power and wealth and wisdom and strength and honor and glory and praise!" (Revelation 5:9-12, my emphasis)*

In the Word of God, when a capital "S" is used in the word "Spirit," it signifies the Spirit of God. A lowercase "s" in "spirit" signifies the spirit of man. Because of Adam's sin, everyone is born with a sinful spirit, which is spiritually separated from God. The sinful spirit of man does not rest until our urge to sin in the flesh is satisfied.

Men and women can fight these sinful desires to a degree. However, human beings are sinful, and only sin can satisfy this relentless urge to be disobedient to God. The longer one who is not in fellowship with God is without sin, the more restless he or she becomes. So many people are hard on themselves because they know better than those around them how ugly they are on the inside. Do not be hard on yourself! Does God expect you to conquer the impossible task of putting to death this sinful spirit without Jesus? Of course He doesn't! God does not blame you for being born the way you are. He knows better than anyone that it's Adam's fault. Who, alive today, had the choice to be born without sin?

The Word of God says that, once we are born again, we are born of the Spirit of God: "Flesh gives birth to flesh, but the **S**pirit gives birth to **s**pirit" (John 3:6, my emphasis). When we receive Jesus Christ as our Lord and Savior, our old spirit dies (see Romans 6:6) and we receive a new spirit. This spirit is in fellowship with God. How can we be sure we are actually born again? People have many ways of explaining how someone knows if they are born again. I will mention two:

1. "The Spirit himself testifies with our spirit that we are God's children" (Romans 8:16). If we have been born again, we know that we know that we know we are children of God. If you do not know that you are a child of God, you have not been born again. If you are born of the Spirit of the living God, you will know it and there will be a distinct memory of that day when your life changed forever! The Spirit of God will say to your new spirit that is able to fellowship with Him, "You are my child."

2. "Those who live according to the flesh [sinful nature] have their minds set on what the flesh desires; but those who live in accordance with the Spirit have their minds set on what the Spirit desires" (Romans 8:5, my note added).

The reason nonbelievers have such a good argument against living for God is because of this constant temptation to commit sin. In them there

J. Bronson Haley

exists no desire to serve God or accept His Son as Lord and Savior. Only the first half of Romans 8:5 applies to them: "Those who live according to the flesh have their minds set on what the flesh desires." Only to those who have been born again does the second half of the Scripture apply: "... but those who live in accordance with the Spirit have their minds set on what the Spirit desires."

Nonbelievers have never once experienced an urge to satisfy the Spirit of God because they are not in spiritual fellowship with Him. They have not been born of the Spirit of God. To give up sin and try to satisfy the Spirit would be pointless because they would not benefit from it. Now do you see what I mean when I said that way back at the beginning of Part 1 of this Rest Stop? An entire life without sin? What a boring life! This is the truth for flesh seekers—those who do not know God or have His Spirit living within them. The argument of nonbelievers is in correlation with God's Word.

"Bronson, it's not fair that I was born this way and have had to suffer," you may say.

Listen ... I know! I was born that way and suffered greatly. It isn't fair. God took that into account. But remember: another man also received unjust punishment, more than we could ever experience. He endured the maximum amount of suffering without having ever committed a sin. Jesus Christ knows what it means to suffer because of someone else's wrong. However, we have a gift made available to us, which cannot be received by the human mind. This gift is much too glorious to share with the flesh of man. As it is written:

> *"What no eye has seen, what no ear has heard, and what no mind has conceived"—the things God has prepared for those who love him—these are the things God has revealed to us by his Spirit.*

The Spirit searches all things, even the deep things of God. For who knows a person's thoughts except their own spirit within them? In the same way no one knows the thoughts of God except the Spirit of God. What we have received is not the spirit of the world but the Spirit who is from God, so that we may understand what God has freely given us. This is what we speak, not in words taught us by human wisdom but in words taught by the Spirit, explaining spiritual realities with Spirit-taught words. The person without the Spirit does not accept the things that come from the Spirit of God but considers

The Depth of Grace

them foolishness, and cannot understand them because they are discerned only through the Spirit. (1 Corinthians 2:9-14)

> *The Father ... will give you ... the Spirit of truth. The world cannot accept him, because it neither sees him nor knows him. (John 14:16-17, my emphasis)*

However, satisfying the Spirit of the living God is truly satisfying—if we are born of the Spirit. The difference is that satisfying the Holy Spirit brings life instead of death. The wages of sin is death and only Jesus Christ can raise the dead.

> *The wind blows wherever it pleases. You hear its sound, but you cannot tell where it comes from or where it is going. So it is with everyone born of the Spirit. (John 3:8)*

> *As for you, you were dead in your transgressions and sins, in which you used to live when you followed the ways of this world and of the ruler of the kingdom of the air, the spirit who is now at work in those who are disobedient. (Ephesians 2:1-2)*

> *Therefore God gave them over in the sinful desires of their hearts to sexual impurity for the degrading of their bodies with one another. They exchanged the truth about God for a lie, and worshiped and served created things rather than the Creator—who is forever praised. Amen. (Romans 1:24-25)*

The choice to cross over from being a flesh seeker to a God seeker is ours and ours alone.

CHAPTER 25

—

Bullet

Having finished the rough draft of this book, I headed south to speak with my friend Jared in person. I couldn't wait to talk to him about the book. It was really good to see him as well. His wife and two kids were in Houston to visit her mother. Jared was on the phone when I arrived, so I took that time to walk through his house and look at pictures. Jared has a nice house, a beautiful wife, two beautiful kids, and is doing well.

We sat on his back porch for who knows how long talking about all the crazy things we did at dive school. We also talked about the twists of life we had experienced since we left dive school. We then talked about the future. It was during this time that I began to talk to him about this book.

"We have an opportunity to allow the Lord to take our failures and use them to help others," I told him. "We shouldn't be concerned about our past mistakes. The Word of God says that our call and our gifts are irrevocable (see Romans 11:29). If God ever planned on using us, He plans on using us."

I had arrived at Jared's on a Thursday afternoon. We planned to hang out for the weekend and spend some quality time together. Jared felt that he would have to return to work that Sunday. He worked for a large oil company and was spending from three to five weeks at a time offshore due to the destruction that resulted from Hurricane Katrina. He spent a week or less at home with his family in between workweeks. Jared got a call that Friday morning and the man instructed him to be on the boat by midnight.

J. Bronson Haley

"It's no fun offshore, Bronson."

Jared left around 8:00 p.m. that evening, and I hung out awhile with one of his neighbors who was also a good friend of Jared and his family. We talked and cut up until around 10:30 p.m. and he went home. I planned to leave the following morning. At 12:30 a.m., my phone rang. When I woke up enough to realize that it was indeed my phone, it quit ringing. I checked to see who it was and saw that I had missed nine calls back to back. One call was from my dad. One call was from the mother of my youngest sister and brother. Seven calls were from my youngest sister, Salina. Overcome with fear, I found myself too afraid to check my voicemail. I was too frightened to call anyone back. My stomach turned inside of me and I knew something wasn't right. Within a minute my phone rang again.

I took a deep breath and answered, "Hello?"

The shaky voice of my ex-stepmother's sister echoed in my ear. "Bronson, it's Michelle. Little Joe (my ex-stepmother's son and my little brother) has been shot in the back of the head. He is at LSU medical center. He has been given a one percent chance to live through the hour."

"I'm in Lafayette. I'm getting my car and will been there in four hours," I said, already up and moving.

Therefore I was left alone, and saw this great vision, and there remained no strength in me: for my comeliness was turned in me into corruption, and I retained no strength. Yet heard I the voice of his words: and when I heard the voice of his words, then was I in a deep sleep on my face, and my face toward the ground. And, behold, an hand touched me, which set me upon my knees and upon the palms of my hands. And he said unto me, O Daniel, a man greatly beloved, understand the words that I speak unto thee, and stand upright: for unto thee am I now sent. And when he had spoken this word unto me, I stood trembling. Then said he unto me, Fear not, Daniel: for from the first day that thou didst set thine heart to understand, and to chasten thyself before thy God, thy words were heard, and I am come for thy words. But the prince of the kingdom of Persia withstood me one and twenty days: but, lo, Michael, one of the chief princes, came to help me; and I remained there with the kings of Persia. Now I am come to make thee understand what shall befall thy people in the latter days: for yet the vision is for many days. And when he had spoken such words unto me, I set my face toward the ground, and I became dumb. And, behold, one like the similitude of the sons of men touched my lips: then I opened my mouth, and spake, and said unto him that stood before me, O my lord, by the vision my sorrows are turned upon me, and I have retained no strength. For how can the servant of this my lord talk with this my lord? for as for me, straightway there remained no strength in me, neither is there breath left in me. (Daniel 10:8-17 KJV)

When I got into my car, I turned up the volume on one of my worship CDs and began to sing to the Lord. I didn't do this because I was such a great man of faith. I sang to the Lord because the four-hour drive ahead of me was extremely dark. At the end of this long, dark tunnel was a dark room. In this dark room was my seventeen-year-old little brother with a bullet wound to the back of his head. He had been given a one percent chance to make it through the hour. Outside of that room was his little sister—my little sister—Salina, who had experienced more than her own share of suffering. At just fourteen years old, she had already lost five of her friends. She also lost her stepfather just a year before. He was a big part of her life and she loved him deeply. I sang to the Lord because I had no strength left in me.

I prayed intently for my brother. After around twenty minutes my father came to mind. With this thought came an increase in pain and fear. Dad had recently experienced a breakthrough in his life. He landed a great job four hours west of home. My little brother was my father's heart. Of course, Dad loves us all the same. However, my sisters and I did not live with him most of our lives. The love that my father was not able to give to his older children and youngest daughter, he gave to my little brother.

Dad had worked in northeast Texas for around six months. This time away from Little Joe was not easy for him. He had just received news that he would soon transfer to a local branch of the company and would move home. At that exact moment Dad was on a road similar to the one I was traveling. The road ahead of him was extremely dark. At the end of this long, dark tunnel was a dark room. In this dark room was his baby boy with a bullet wound to the back of his head. He had been given a one percent chance to make it through the hour. Outside of that room was his youngest daughter, Salina, who had already experienced more than her own share of suffering.

253

J. Bronson Haley

I picked up my phone and called my father.

"Dad," I said.

"Yeah?" he replied.

"Are you okay?" I asked

"I'm on the road," he said.

"I know ... I'll see you at the hospital."

It was impossible to find the words to say to him, and I know he struggled as well. It was hard to know what to think. It was difficult to drive. I could hardly breath. In the midst of my heart—already wrenched with grief and sorrow to the point of death—I heard a voice from within: "O Daniel, a man greatly beloved, understand the words that I speak unto thee, and stand upright: for unto thee am I now sent."

At that moment I turned the music up as loud as I could stand it. I sang to the Lord from the depths of my spirit, and prayed, "Lord, worst-case scenario, I ask that You draw my little brother to repentance by Your Spirit. Second, if you decide to bring him home, I ask that you give me the words to say to his family and friends at his funeral." I continued to pray for my brother and my family.

When I walked into the hospital and saw my little sister, I grabbed her and she grabbed me. We both understood the severity of Little Joe's condition. What do you say? I held on to her and she held on to me. Little Joe's mom, aunts, uncles, cousins, and friends were all there. Soon our older sister Shannon showed up. Minutes later dad walked into the building. His sister's husband was the hospital administrator and he provided us with a private room.

The news we received moments later wasn't good. The CAT scan showed that the bullet had gone into the back of Little Joe's head, through his brain, and lodged in his forehead. If he were to live through this, his quality of life would be limited. We were not able to see him because of his condition. Little Joe was not expected to live much longer. However, he was not supposed to live as long as he had.

Six hours and many miracles later, I was led down a long hall and into his room. My brother was in a medical-induced coma. His eyes were half opened and his body was cold. He had tubes in his throat, and attached to him were several machines. I walked up to him and stood to his left, placing my hand on his right arm. The nurses said that he might be able to hear, but they were not sure. Little Joe was saved years back at a local church, but didn't live for God. Some Christians believe in "once saved, always saved." Some believe that if a child of God dies in sin, they

The Depth of Grace

face eternal damnation. I have heard both arguments and everyone has Scripture that they feel backs up what they believe. I personally am not 100 percent sure one way or another. I can only be sure of the things I am sure of. I know that we are judged based on what we know. From what I understand, my Father is a just God. More importantly than what I am not sure of, I know that He pays close attention to every request I bring Him. I had already asked that He draw my brother to repentance by His Spirit. I made that request as I sang praises to His Son in my car. I knew that for sure.

"Little Joe," I said as I stood next to his hospital bed. "There is something you need to understand. The Lord is not concerned about the magnitude of your sin. The only thing important is that you accept the blood of Jesus as sufficient to cover your mistakes. The blood of Jesus is more powerful than your failures. I say to your oppressor: the blood of Jesus is against you. In the name of Jesus Christ, I rebuke you and command you to leave his mind, body, and soul. Father, I ask for the blood of Christ to wash my brother clean."

After I prayed for around ten minutes, I had to leave.

I am not sure about "once saved, always saved." I'm not sure that a child of God who dies in his or her sin will go to hell. I don't think so, but I do not know for sure. I am not sure that my brother was able to hear me when I talked to him in the hospital then. These issues are all debatable. We should not allow our attention to be kept by the things that we are not sure of. I was sure that God heard my plea in my weakest hour. I know He received my request as I sang to Jesus. Because of what I did know, I was not concerned about where my brother would spend eternity if he did not live through this struggle. Because of what I did know, his fate was not able to determine if I would see him again.

Around three hours after that point, the doctors brought Little Joe out of the medical-induced coma to show the family that he had no brain activity. My brother responded by opening his eyes and looking over at the doctor. This was a shocking moment for the MD. He then instructed Little Joe to move his fingers and toes, and he did. Then the doctor pinched him hard on the chest. Little Joe grabbed his hand and removed it from his chest.

The doctor then said, "I don't know what to say. According to the CAT scan, this boy should not have responded like this. If he is going to fight, we are going to fight."

The doctors then gave their best effort to keep him alive.

J. Bronson Haley

Three days passed, and my older sister, Shannon, and I sat in my brother's room in ICU. It was 5:00 a.m. and we hadn't slept. We sat in chairs at his feet and talked.

Weeks before, I had mentioned the heavenly sanctuary to my sister. Over these three days she came to fully understand this fellowship with God. When we left the hospital for whatever reason, we sang to the Lord in the car. It was our only sense of hope—our only relief from the pain. For the first time my sister and I acknowledged the presence of God together. We cried and sang and cried and sang. The Lord spoke promises to us in our most hurtful hour.

So at the feet of our brother, in his cold, dark room, I reminded my sister of a story that I had shared with her several months back.

"Jacob came to this same place in his life. His older, strong brother sought to kill him and his family, and he was hours away from meeting him. When his pain and fear reached a certain point, he sent his family across a stream and he was left alone. He was afraid for his family. He was afraid for his life. He was alone. Jacob was alone with God. He wrestled all night, and while he wrestled, he thought about all the mistakes he had made in his life.

"Jacob had run from God for over twenty years and doubted the Lord heard his cry in his most painful hour. During this wrestling match with the Lord, his hip was dislocated. At that point Jacob hit rock bottom. The pain and fear became unbearable for him. 'Then the man said, "Let me go, for it is daybreak." But Jacob replied, "I will not let you go unless you bless me."'"

At this time, my sister and I both cried. It was hard to speak the words and finish the story, but I did: "'The man asked him, "What is your name?" "Jacob," he answered. Then the man said, "Your name will no longer be Jacob, but Israel, because you have struggled with God and with humans and have overcome"'" (see Genesis 32:22-28).

My sister sobbed as she described the message coming to life during this meeting. "Bronson, I'm not sure how I know, but I know why God changed Jacob's name to Israel. I know what He meant."

The glory of God entered into the room with my sister and me, and we wept together at the foot of our little brother.

Two days later, on Thanksgiving Day 2006, Little Joe passed on.

Outside in the parking lot with me, Shannon rolled the window down as she sat in her Ford Expedition. "Bronson, can we borrow that CD?"

The Depth of Grace

During that five-day period of our brother fighting for his life, my two sisters and I got hooked on the song "Praise You in This Storm" by Casting Crowns. It was a dark Thanksgiving Day and my older sister Shannon and little sister Salina needed relief from their pain, as did we all.

From here two options lay before me. I could have joined those spoken of by the prophet Isaiah: "Distressed and hungry, they will roam through the land; when they are famished, they will become enraged and, looking upward, will curse their king and their God" (Isaiah 8:21).

I instead chose to follow Jesus.

Jesus lost one who was close to His heart in the same manner. He was doing the will of His Father, and John the Baptist—Jesus' cousin and the one whom Jesus placed above all other prophets with His own words—was beheaded by sinners for no reason at all.

> *Now Herod had arrested John and bound him and put him in prison because of Herodias, his brother Philip's wife, for John had been saying to him: "It is not lawful for you to have her." Herod wanted to kill John, but he was afraid of the people, because they considered him a prophet.*
>
> *On Herod's birthday the daughter of Herodias danced for them and pleased Herod so much that he promised with an oath to give her whatever she asked. Prompted by her mother, she said, "Give me here on a platter the head of John the Baptist." The king was distressed, but because of his oaths and his dinner guests, he ordered that her request be granted and had John beheaded in the prison. His head was brought in on a platter and given to the girl, who carried it to her mother. John's disciples came and took his body and buried it. Then they went and told Jesus. (Matthew 14:3-12)*

Jesus experienced the same pain and emotion on His walk as we experience. Because of His understanding, we know to do just as He did. "Return to your fortress, you prisoners of hope; even now I announce that I will restore twice as much to you" (Zechariah 9:12). Who understood this truth better than Jesus? "After Job had prayed for his friends, the LORD restored his fortunes and gave him twice as much as he had before" (Job 42:10). Who knew the character of the Father better than the Son? This same glory was passed on to God's children through the resurrection: "I

J. Bronson Haley

consider that our present sufferings are not worth comparing with the glory that will be revealed in us" (Romans 8:18).

According to the Word of God, if we choose to follow Jesus, we will not lose a single battle:

> *And the God of all grace, who called you to his eternal glory in Christ, after you have suffered a little while, will himself restore you and make you strong, firm and steadfast (1 Peter 5:10)*

> *"The glory of this present house will be greater than the glory of the former house," says the LORD Almighty. "And in this place I will grant peace," declares the LORD Almighty."(Haggai 2:9)*

I am sure that Jesus wished He had spent more time with John before his death. Naturally I felt the same way about my little brother. Also, it seemed as though there was no good reason for my brother to be hurt and suffer like he did, and finally to pass on. But John the Baptist was in prison and beheaded for no reason. John the Baptist was suffering when he died. I know Jesus felt this pain. Because of the knowledge I had of my Savior, I knew to do just as He did. Like the eagle we looked at earlier, I chose to face into the wind.

258

CHAPTER 26

The Celebration

Then there came again and touched me one like the appearance of a man, and he strengthened me, And said, O man greatly beloved, fear not: peace be unto thee, be strong, yea, be strong. And when he had spoken unto me, I was strengthened, and said, Let my lord speak; for thou hast strengthened me. (Daniel 10:18-19 KJV)

> *And he directed the people to sit down on the grass. Taking the five loaves and the two fish and looking up to heaven, he gave thanks and broke the loaves. (Matthew 14:19)*

During this time related in the book of Matthew, the Lord was grieving for John the Baptist. The bread He broke on this occasion fed many more than the usual. In the midst of His time of suffering, Father God placed before Jesus a crowd of people who were hungry.

My brother had gone home. Now, at Little Joe's funeral, I stood in front of a crowd of people who were hungry. Atop a stage that rose above the audience, I looked out at the faces of those who sat before me—and before Little Joe, whose body rested in a casket in front of the stage, just below me. Many family and friends had gathered to celebrate and memorialize the legacy that Little Joe had left during what seemed to be too short a life. Like me, these people were hungry for something that would satisfy their souls in this moment of pain and grief—I could see the hunger in their faces as I composed myself to speak in that moment. I knew that, within myself, I had nothing to offer these dear men, women,

259

J. Bronson Haley

and children. But, remember that, on my way to the hospital to see Little Joe, I'd prayed to God to give me the words to speak if He took Little Joe home. Now it was time to let those words flow out of the deepest places of my heart and spirit.

Everything that follows here is the message that God had given me for those hungry people that day. As you'll soon see, I shared some of what God had been teaching me in my study of His Word up to that point. And, yes, you've already read a little bit of what follows here. So I hope you'll please indulge me in allowing me to share this entire message with you.

Here's the message I gave on that day of celebration (please note that all the Bible verses I quote in this message are from the New International Version 1984 edition) …

Once, my little brother and I were at Black Bayou running yo-yos in the middle of the night. We were in an aluminum boat with a trolling motor and a one-million-candle spotlight. I shined the light on this stump that was about twenty feet away and there was a little baby nutria rat sitting on it.

Well, Little Joe loved animals, so after a brief disagreement between the two of us, he talked me into helping him catch it. We about ran the battery dead chasing the little rat through the water. Finally, we wore the little rat out and it slowed down enough so that Little Joe could grab it. When he had that rat in his arms, one would have thought he was holding a newborn baby. After about three seconds of comforting this terrified rat, Little Joe began to shake it violently and slammed it over and over again on the seat of the boat and finally he threw it in the water.

And I asked him, "Little Joe, why the change of heart all the sudden?"

And he said, "Well, he wasn't so nice after all."

When I shined the light on his hands, I could see that the rat had sunk his teeth into Little Joe's finger, and he was simply trying to make the rat let him go.

I told him, "Well, we can go back after him if you want."

He said, "You know what? I think I saw a fish on that yo-yo back there."

My brother had a heart for animals. He also had a heart for people. One morning he was taking my little sister Salina and a couple of friends to school and noticed a homeless man limping down the road. So he stopped and told him he would give him a ride and to hop in the back of the truck.

260

The Depth of Grace

The man pulled his pant sleeve up to show my brother that he had an artificial leg and could not climb into the back of the truck.

He told the man, "Stay right here. I'll be back."

He dropped off his sister and her friends at school, drove back, picked up the homeless man, and gave him the ride he needed.

My brother learned this from my father. My childhood is flooded with memories of dad stopping and giving rides to homeless people. He would often stop and buy them something to eat as well. Once, my father and brother spotted a homeless man on the side of the road standing in the rain in forty-degree weather. They couldn't stand this sight. They stopped and asked the man, "Where are you headed?" He was going to Texarkana. So my dad and my brother took the man to Texarkana.

The Lord does not take these acts of kindness lightly. My father and my brother loved these people when they couldn't love them back. Because this love was free, God was able to love them. The love of God has always been free, and there are many promises the come with loving people this way.

The Word of God says that:

> *Each man should give what he has decided in his heart to give, not reluctantly or under compulsion, for God loves a cheerful giver. And God is able to make all grace abound to you, so that in all things at all times, having all that you need, you will abound in every good work....*
>
> *You will be made rich in every way so that you can be generous on every occasion, and through us your generosity will result in thanksgiving to God.*
>
> *This service that you perform is not only supplying the needs of God's people but is also overflowing in many expressions of thanks to God. Because of the service by which you have proved yourselves, men will praise God for the obedience that accompanies your confession of the gospel of Christ, and for your generosity in sharing with them and with everyone else. And in their prayers for you their hearts will go out to you, because of the surpassing grace God has given you. Thanks be to God for his indescribable gift. (2 Corinthians 9:7-8, 11-15)*

261

J. Bronson Haley

The Lord was the first giver. He first selflessly gave Himself in the form of His Son, and we did not deserve this gift. God has not forgotten a single time my brother and father loved these people in need, and we now see and will continue to see the promises, that come with giving, come alive in our lives.

> *When the Son of Man comes in his glory, and all the angels with him, he will sit on his throne in heavenly glory. All the nations will be gathered before him, and he will separate the people one from another as a shepherd separates the sheep from the goats. He will put the sheep on his right and the goats on his left.*
>
> *Then the King will say to those on his right, "Come, you who are blessed by my Father; take your inheritance, the kingdom prepared for you since the creation of the world. For I was hungry and you gave me something to eat, I was thirsty and you gave me something to drink, I was a stranger and you invited me in, I needed clothes and you clothed me, I was sick and you looked after me, I was in prison and you come to visit me." (Matthew 25:31-36)*

If my brother were to pick one apostle for me to talk about today, it would be Simon Peter. Peter claimed he loved Jesus more than any of the other disciples. Kinda funny if you think about it. And Jesus was always rebuking Peter for something! Peter was always getting into trouble. Jesus even called him "Satan" once. But he loved Jesus with everything inside of him. Peter loved Jesus so much because he experienced His forgiveness so many times. Jesus kept him anyways.

Do you remember when Jesus predicted Peter's denial? "My children, I will be with you only a little longer. You will look for me, and just as I told the Jews, so I tell you now: Where I am going, you cannot come" (John 13:33). Peter couldn't believe that Jesus wouldn't at least let *him* come, given that he loved Him more than any of the others.

"I will lay down my life for you," Peter replied. Jesus said to Peter, "Will you really lay down your life for me? I tell you the truth, before the rooster crows, you will disown me three times!" What were Peter's emotions when Jesus responded to him like that, I wonder? Peter probably felt bad when he was found asleep three times when Jesus prayed at Gethsemane. Jesus had already mentioned to him that He was "distressed to the point of death."

The Depth of Grace

Peter wasn't the only disciple on watch either. But Jesus rebuked him and not the others. He rebuked the one that loved him the most.

When the soldiers came to take Jesus away, Peter drew his sword and cut off one of the soldier's ears. He was rebuked for that, too. The disciples scattered, but Peter and one other disciple followed behind at a distance. I wonder what was going through Peter's mind at this point? I'm sure he wanted Jesus to know for sure that he loved Him, and probably felt Jesus still thought that he would deny him three times. And Peter did indeed deny Jesus three times. It's the third denial that gets to me.

Peter replied, "Man, I don't know what you are talking about!" Just as he was speaking, the rooster crowed. The Lord turned and looked straight at Peter. Their eyes made contact! "Then Peter remembered the word the Lord had spoken to him: 'Before the rooster crows today, you will disown me three times.' And he went outside and wept bitterly." I can't imagine what that experience was like for Peter. He ended up not only denying Jesus three times, but he also began to call down curses on himself, and he swore to them, "I don't know this man you're talking about" (Mark 14:71), in the presence of Jesus being mocked, spit on, and beaten. Peter wasn't around when Jesus was on the cross either. As far as I know, John was the only disciple there—the one whom Jesus loved.

I always suspected that Peter loved Jesus so much because he experienced His forgiveness so many times. God confirmed my suspicion as I read His Word. Jesus had been invited to one of the Pharisee's house for dinner. While reclining at the table, a prostitute walked up behind Him, weeping. This woman had heard Jesus was changing the lives of many sick people. She heard about Simon the Leper being healed of his leprosy and given a new life. This story made history. Everyone who had ever been pronounced with leprosy lived a life of shame and seclusion and then died alone. The shame that came with this disease was very similar to the shame that came with prostitution. There was nothing this prostitute could do about her past. She was a whore and she was going to die a whore. When she approached Jesus, she was hoping in her heart that He would forgive her for her mistakes and give her a second chance. She was very ashamed and not sure of the outcome of her approach. What difference did it make? She lived a life of shame equal to death.

After she stood behind Jesus for a brief moment with tears rolling down her face, she knelt and wet His feet with her tears and washed them with her hair. Then she took an alabaster jar of expensive perfume and

J. Bronson Haley

poured it on his head. Jesus then explained this scene to the Pharisee, who was named Simon:

> *"Two men owed money to a certain money lender. One owed him five hundred denarii, and the other fifty. Neither of them had the money to pay him back, so he canceled the debts of both. Now which of them will love him more?"*
>
> *Simon replied, "I suppose the one who had the bigger debt canceled."*
>
> *"You have judged correctly," Jesus said. (Luke 7:41-43)*

Our debt is our sin that has been covered by the blood of the Lamb of God.

Many who were there were ashamed that this woman showed up. Some doubted Jesus because He allowed her to touch Him. Some rebuked her for the waste of perfume. Jesus said, "I tell you, her many sins have been forgiven—for she loved much. But he who has been forgiven little loves little" (Luke 7:47).

Simon Peter had the vision. He planned on being the "Rock" that Jesus would trust to establish His church. He was going to be great for God. He was in love with Jesus. God's call had nothing to do with Simon Peter, and Jesus had no choice but to be sure Peter understood that. Simon Peter was crushed when he was the strongest. He was crushed when His love for Jesus was at its peak. Jesus knew how much Peter loved Him but He still rebuked him and not the others at Gethsemane. Jesus knew how much Peter loved Him but He still referred to him as Simon when he messed up. Jesus was reminding him of whom he was before Jesus came into his life. That hurt Peter deeply. However, Peter was boasting after the Lord's Supper about how great he was going to be. That is pride. It doesn't seem like it, but it is. God opposes the proud and gives grace to the humble. Jesus had no choice but to humble Peter. He could not fail at that because He would have failed Peter if He had. God will be faithful for He cannot disown Himself. Jesus loved Peter too much not strip him of that pride. He did a perfect job even though it hurt Peter deeply.

Jesus reinstated his disciples during their last meeting after the resurrection. This meeting was different from that of the Lord's Supper. They had been hiding behind locked doors in fear of the Jews and were defeated. Now they sat humble before the Lord:

The Depth of Grace

When they had finished eating, Jesus said to Simon, "Simon son of John, do you truly love me more than these?"

"Yes, Lord," he said, "you know that I love you."

Jesus said, "Feed my Lambs."

Again Jesus said, "Simon son of John, do you truly love me?"

He answered, "Yes, Lord, you know that I love you."

Jesus said, "Take care of my sheep."

The third time he said to him, "Simon son of John, do you love me?"

Peter was hurt because Jesus asked him the third time, "Do you love me?" He said, "Lord, you know all things; you know that I love you."

Jesus said, "Feed my sheep." (John 21:15-17)

I was asleep in Lafayette when my phone rang and I received the news that my brother had been shot and that he had a one percent chance of living through the hour. When I got in my car, I turned on some worship music and began to sing to the Lord. And I prayed, "Lord, worst-case scenario I ask that you draw my brother to repentance by Your Spirit. Second, if you decide to bring him home, I ask that you give me the words to say to his family and friends at his funeral." My brother remained alive for five days. During this time my family and I received hundreds of text messages and phone calls assuring us that many prayers were being sent up for Little Joe and his family.

I tell you today that my brother has seen the glory of Jesus Christ. If he were to give me advice right now on what to do from here, he would say to me, "Bronson, you know what to do."

Simon Peter got a glimpse of the glory of Jesus Christ on the day of Pentecost. When he, the other disciples, and their followers were filled with the Holy Spirit, they flooded out into the streets. People then gathered around and began to mock them.

Then Peter stood up with the Eleven, raised his voice and addressed the crowd: "Fellow Jews and all of you who live in

Jerusalem, let me explain this to you; listen carefully to what I say. These men are not drunk, as you suppose. It's only nine in the morning! No, this is what was spoken by the prophet Joel: 'In the last days, God says, I will pour out my Spirit on all people. Your sons and daughters will prophesy, your young men will see visions, your old men will dream dreams. Even on my servant, both men and women, I will pour out my Spirit in those days, and they will prophesy. I will show wonders in the heaven above and signs on the earth below, blood and fire and billows of smoke. The sun will be turned to darkness and the moon to blood before the coming of the great and glorious day of the Lord. And everyone who calls on the name of the Lord will be saved.'

"Men of Israel, listen to this: Jesus of Nazareth was a man accredited by God to you by miracles, wonders and signs, which God did among you through him, as you yourselves know. This man was handed over to you by God's set purpose and foreknowledge; and you, with the help of wicked men, put him to death by nailing him to the cross. But God raised him from the dead, freeing him from the agony of death, because it was impossible for death to keep is hold on him....

"God has raised this Jesus to life, and we are all witnesses of the fact. Exalted to the right hand of God, he has received from the Father the promised Holy Spirit and has poured out what you now see and hear....

"Therefore let all Israel be assured of this: God has made this Jesus, whom you crucified, both Lord and Christ."

When the people heard this, they were cut to the heart and said to Peter and the other apostle, "Brothers, what shall we do?" (Acts 2:14-24, 32-34, 36-37)

That was a powerful sermon preached by Simon Peter. They accepted Jesus Christ as their Lord and Savior, and the church grew from one hundred twenty to over three thousand at that moment.

One day Peter and John were going to the temple at the time of prayer—at three in the afternoon. Now a man crippled from

The Depth of Grace

birth was being carried to the temple gate called Beautiful, where he was put every day to beg from those going into the temple courts. When he saw Peter and John about to enter, he asked them for money. Peter looked straight at him, as did John. Then Peter said, "Look at us!" So the man gave them his attention, expecting to get something from them. Then Peter said, "Silver or gold I do not have, but what I have I give you. In the name of Jesus Christ of Nazareth, walk." Taking him by the right hand, he helped him up, and instantly the man's feet and ankles became strong. He jumped to his feet and began to walk. (Acts 3:1-8)

At this:

The priests and the captain of the temple guard and the Sadducees came up to Peter and John while they were speaking to the people. They were greatly disturbed because the apostles were teaching the people and proclaiming in Jesus the resurrection of the dead. They seized Peter and John, and because it was evening, they put them in jail until the next day. But many who heard the message believed, and the number of men grew to about five thousand.

The next day the rulers, elders and teachers of the law met in Jerusalem. Annas the high priest was there, and so were Caiaphas, John, Alexander and the other men of the high priest's family. They had Peter and John brought before them and began to question them: "By what power or what name did you do this?" (Acts 4:1-7)

While these people were attempting to intimidate Peter, he began to think about the times these men did the same thing to Jesus when He walked the earth. He was thinking about the time he denied Jesus in the presence of Him being mocked, spit on and beaten in the hands of these men who questioned him. It was these men who had his Lord flogged and crucified as a perfect man whom Peter loved deeply.

Then Peter, filled with the Holy Spirit, said to them: "Rulers and elders of the people! If we are being called to account today for an act of kindness shown to a cripple and are asked how he was healed, then know this, you and all the people of

267

J. Bronson Haley

> *Israel: It is by the name of Jesus Christ of Nazareth, whom you crucified but whom God raised from the dead, that this man stands before you healed. He is 'the stone you builders rejected, which has become the capstone.'" (Acts 4:8-11)*

When my brother was shot, there were fallen angels who began to mock him. They made a big mistake in doing this. The death of Joseph Lane Haley, Jr., has sent a shockwave into the darkest corners of this city. The glory that Jesus Christ has received at this celebration has sent an earthquake across the United States of America that has been felt throughout the world!

The conclusion of this message is simple. If anyone has any hope, it is because of the words spoken by the prophet Isaiah: "The people walking in darkness have seen a great light; on those living in the land of the shadow of death a light has dawned" (Isaiah 9:2).

If anyone has peace, it's because, "In the beginning was the word, and the word was with God, and the Word was God. It was with him in the beginning" (John 1:1).

If anyone has learned anything, it is because, "The Word became flesh and made his dwelling among us" (John 1:14).

If anyone has been set free, it is because he that has been set free by the Son of God is "free indeed" (John 8:36). And, "The truth will set you free" (John 8:32).

Jesus Christ always walks in front. He never asked anyone to do anything other than follow Him—follow His lead. He didn't even ask them to change. Jesus took that burden upon Himself. We are opposed in our pride and granted grace in our humility. If we stand strong today, it's because of His mercy. When we are weak, He is strong. To God be the glory! The best is yet to come!

Thanks for letting me share this message with you. It means a lot to me to be able to share with you what God placed on my heart to share with my brother's family and friends that day.

15TH REST STOP:
HEAVENLY SANCTUARY

We now have a good idea about what it means to seek freedom and overcome our struggles by adequately following Christ. I have more good news! When I first faced into the wind and began to read my Bible, I was still screwed up and doubted that I would ever overcome, as you already know. Daily I heard lie after lie about how I would never be restored and that God would never use me again. I desperately wanted angels to meet with me and encourage me just as they did Jacob at Bethel during his journey. I needed God to talk to me and make me promises like He did Jacob. I wanted my Bethel! I wanted my angels! I wanted my stream and wanted a chance to wrestle with God and refuse to let him go. Well, like a foolish man, I asked for these things.

"Lord, where is my Bethel? Where are my angels? Where is my stream? Lord, I need these things and I ask You for them," I said. "I need You to talk to me. I need to know that I am going to be okay because I don't feel that I am going to be okay. I need to know I am going to make it because I do not feel like I'm going to make it."

I know this seems ridiculous. Remember, God was going to have to prove to me that the stories of the Bible were true and alive in order for me to tell people about it. I asked Him to prove the truth in the Scriptures concerning these powerful experiences with Him. I can tell you that I got more than Bethel. I got more than angels. I learned how to wrestle with God and refused to let Him go every day. I learned how to get relief at any time, and my sickness wasn't an issue. My failure could not keep me from meeting with the Lord.

269

J. Bronson Haley

One day back when my friend Mike Mertle and I were in high school, we walked into his house and his father, Reverend Hank Mertle, sat at the dining room table by himself. He was going through a midlife crisis. He played his guitar and sang to the Lord. He had tears rolling down his face. When Mike and I walked in the room, he stood up and gave his son a lengthy hug.

I thought, *What an incredible man of faith. He still believes after all this.*

I knew he was in pain then, just as I was in pain as I lay in my bed and recalled this day from high school.

I wish I had that kind of faith—that kind of strength, I thought as I contemplated that moment.

I had that same thought when I read about the time the Paul and Silas were imprisoned in Philippi. Paul had set a slave girl free from an evil spirit that enabled her to predict the future. The people who owned her got ticked because Paul and Silas robbed them of their monthly income. These two men of God were flogged and thrown into prison. When these men were in prison, they were in pain. Yet: "About midnight Paul and Silas were praying and singing hymns to God, and the other prisoners were listening to them" (Acts 16:25). In the midst of their pain, they prayed and sang to the Lord.

I wish I had that kind of faith, I thought as I recalled the story.

My pain caused me to doubt. My pain made me believe that God had given up on me. I wouldn't say that I was suicidal. However, thoughts came to mind and indicated that I would be better off dead. I knew this was a lie, but it is lies that we battle with. The Devil told me often to end my life so that I would not have to continue in such pain. Oftentimes people listen to Satan and end their lives.

At this time I had been reading God's Word for a couple of months and I still could not pray. It was so easy to doubt that God would hear me if I did pray. It was difficult not to believe the lies. I so desperately wanted God to come down and allow me to experience Him. Jacob had such moving experiences with the Lord while he was away that he often declared the places God met him as camps of God, and many times he built altars and set up pillars in memory of the powerful experiences he'd had with the Father. Jacob didn't do this because he wanted to be famous in God's Word someday. God really came to him and it was a powerful experience! I wanted that experience. In the Old Testament, God sometimes visited His chosen people in the form of angels, and we know He spoke to many

270

The Depth of Grace

others in the same way He spoke to Jacob at Bethel. Some had dreams and visions. People claim to have seen angels and I believe in them. I think it may have been an angel that spoke to my mother and told her about the white sheet I was wrapped in as I lay on the concrete after being ejected through the windshield that night.

The writer of Hebrews mentioned angels in human form once: "Do not forget to show hospitality to strangers, for by so doing some people have shown hospitality to angels without knowing it" (Hebrews 13:2). How do we know for sure if we have seen them? I am not certain that it was an angel who talked to my mother that day. I just don't know. Why get all bent out of shape because of the things we do not understand? When I was away from the Lord, I heard many people sit around and talk about the things they did not understand about God. Why this and why that? If God is this, then why did He do that? These same people lived in bondage every day of their lives. I never saw anyone get free by focusing on the things they did not understand. Instead let's ask: what *do* we understand? Let's focus on that!

> *[Jacob] had a dream in which he saw a stairway resting on the earth, with its top reaching to heaven, and the angels of God were ascending and descending on it. There above it stood the LORD, and he said: "I am the LORD, the God of your father Abraham and the God of Isaac." (Genesis 28:12-13)*

Later, God instructed His people to build a tabernacle, a dwelling place for the Lord—a place for God to dwell on earth. The Lord said to Moses, "Then have them make a sanctuary for me, and I will dwell among them. Make this tabernacle and all its furnishings exactly like the pattern I will show you" (Exodus 25:8-9). The Lord gave Israel strict instructions on how to build this earthly dwelling place.

The Lord assigned priests to serve in the tabernacle once it was built. They were the only people allowed in the Lord's dwelling place. And not even the priest could enter when the glory of God filled the tabernacle. When the people sinned, as we have already discussed, they presented a sin offering to the priest and he examined the offering to make sure it was without defect. If it was perfect, the blood of this offering covered the sins of the person or people.

Going back to the verse we looked at above, "[Jacob] had a dream in which he saw a stairway resting on the earth, with its top reaching to heaven, and the angels of God were ascending and descending on it. There

271

J. Bronson Haley

above it stood the LORD" (Genesis 28:12-13). *Shamayim* is the Hebrew word for *heaven* found in this Scripture. This word refers to the dwelling place of God. *Nasab* is the Hebrew word for *stood* in this Scripture. *Nasab* means "to set up, stand, station; to be firm, established, healthy; to plant; to establish boundaries." The Lord spoke to Jacob from the door of the heavenly sanctuary—His heavenly dwelling place. The Lord stood guard at the entrance of the heavenly place so that no unclean thing could enter.

The angels were ascending and descending on the stairway at Bethel. Only one other place in the Bible are angels mentioned ascending and descending, and that was where Jesus said, "Very truly I tell you, you will see 'heaven open, and the angels of God ascending and descending on' the Son of Man" (John 1:51). Jesus indicated in this verse that, through Him, God would open this door to heaven and allow men to enter into His presence.

We know that "Flesh gives birth to flesh, but the Spirit gives birth to spirit" (John 3:6), and when we are born again, we are born of the Spirit of God and become His children. Today Jesus Christ is our High Priest who serves day and night in the heavenly tabernacle. From the two above passages about angels ascending and descending, we understand now that Jesus was and is the stairway to heaven.

"Bronson, I know that no one comes to the Father except through Jesus. When we are saved and die, we go to heaven. But are you telling me that we can go to heaven now?"

"At once I was in the Spirit, and there before me was a throne in heaven with someone sitting on it" (Revelation 4:2). Here, John was called up to heaven because the Lord wanted to speak with him. Sure, John wrote the book of Revelation because the Lord spoke with him. Obviously it was pretty important that John write this book. So God called John into heaven to speak with him. John was able to enter into the dwelling place of the Lord because he was a born-again believer in Christ with the Spirit of the Lord inside of him. John was able to enter into the presence of God by his own spirit, which had been born of God. "Flesh gives birth to flesh, but the Spirit gives birth to spirit." It was John's spirit that entered into the heavenly sanctuary by the Spirit of God.

Someone might say, "God allowed John to come into His presence, but that doesn't mean we can go." That's a good point. However, I have noticed that, when the Devil attacks the Word of God, he never has truth to back it up. Or he has only part of the truth. But where in the Bible does it say we cannot enter the throne room of God? We know because of John's

272

The Depth of Grace

story that it is the character of God to allow His children to come into His presence through His Son. His Word also indicates that we should come into His presence in our time of need: "Let us then approach God's throne of grace with confidence, so that we may receive mercy and find grace to help us in our time of need" (Hebrews 4:16).

After this I looked, and there before me was a door standing open in heaven. And the voice I had first heard speaking to me like a trumpet said, "Come up here, and I will show you what must take place after this" (Revelation 4:1).

God had spoken to Jacob from the doorway of heaven. Here in Revelation we see this same doorway, but the Lord invited John to enter. John was able to go because He had accepted Jesus, who was and is the stairway to heaven.

At once I was in the Spirit, and there before me was a throne in heaven with someone sitting on it. And the one who sat there had the appearance of jasper and ruby. A rainbow that shone like an emerald encircled the throne. Surrounding the throne were twenty-four other thrones, and seated on them were twenty-four elders. They were dressed in white and had crowns of gold on their heads. From the throne came flashes of lightning, rumblings and peals of thunder. In front of the throne, seven lamps were blazing. These are the seven spirit of God. Also in front of the throne there was what looked like a sea of glass, clear as crystal.

In the center, around the throne, were four living creatures, and they were covered with eyes, in front and in back. The first living creature was like a lion, the second was like an ox, the third had a face like a man, the fourth was like a flying eagle. Each of the four living creatures had six wings and was covered with eyes all around, even under its wings. Day and night they never stop saying: "Holy, holy, holy is the Lord God Almighty, who was, and is, and is to come."

Whenever the living creatures give glory, honor and thanks to him who sits on the throne and who lives forever and ever, the twenty-four elders fall down before him who sits on the throne, and worship him who lives for ever and ever. They

J. Bronson Haley

> *lay their crowns before the throne and say: "You are worthy,*
> *our Lord and God, to receive glory and honor and power,*
> *for you created all things, and by your will they were created*
> *and have their being." (Revelation 4:2-11)*

I was often discouraged when I read the book of Revelation. But now I wept as I read this passage that I had read so many times before. The words were not just words. They came alive to me as I took note that everything in the throne room of God never stopped worshiping Him.

I desperately needed to get close to the Lord. I needed the Lord to talk to me. I wanted to hear Him tell me that I was going to be okay. I needed truth in my life. I needed a word from the Lord—a promise from God. I desperately wanted to wrestle with God and refuse to let Him go. I could see that the four beasts never stopped saying, "Holy, holy, holy is the Lord God Almighty, who was, and is, and is to come." The twenty-four elders of the church never stopped worshiping, saying, "You are worthy, our Lord and God, to receive glory and honor and power, for you created all things, and by your will they were created and have their being." Because my mind had been opened to the Scriptures, I felt that, if I did just as the four beasts, the elders of the church, and the angels, maybe I would get close enough to God to really hear from Him—and that maybe He would make Himself known to me like He did Jacob at Bethel.

Immediately I headed for the local Christian bookstore and bought some worship CDs. When I returned, I put a CD in my stereo, turned up the volume as loud as I could stand it, and turned off the lights. When I began to worship the Lord, I broke down and wept. I wept and I wept and I wept. I didn't see the throne of grace, as did John. I couldn't see the beasts, the elders, and the angels. I couldn't see God or Jesus. But I felt them. It was as though everything around me stopped. I no longer felt like a drug addict, but I felt like a child of God. For the first time in a long time, I knew that God loved me. I was in the Spirit of truth, and truth is what I got on this day. God began to talk to me about my future while I worshiped Him. Redemption seemed like reality at the moment. I didn't feel any pain. The torment was gone. For hours I worshiped the Father. During this time I began to better understand the man of God from Australia who had prayed with me in the upper room earlier in my life, as well as what was happening during the prayer meeting I had once led for the youth of my church. By His Spirit we entered into the heavenly

The Depth of Grace

sanctuary every Saturday night. Now, for hours, I wept and prayed in the presence of God.

I was surprised when I left my room that I was still hooked on OxyContin. I was still too ashamed to go to church and had the same problems. However, my life changed on that day. I listened to this music in my car. I worshiped Him at various times throughout the day—not because I was such a great man of faith, but because I was very sick, physically and spiritually. I needed to know I was going to be okay. I needed relief from my pain. I needed to be close to God. The Lord made me many promises even in my sickness: "I am with you and will watch over you wherever you go, and I will bring you back to this land. I will not leave you until I have done what I have promised you" (Genesis 28:15). I missed my church family and was too ashamed to return to them. I didn't know how the Lord planned on fulfilling these promises, but I didn't spend much time worrying about it. I spent as much time as I could in His presence. Every time I approached the throne of grace, I fell more in love with Jesus and my sickness was not an issue.

Throughout the days I was lied to and doubted God and myself often. When I turned on the music and worshiped the Lord, I knew who I was and knew that God loved me.

> *For those who are led by the Spirit of God are the children of God. The Spirit you received does not make you slaves, so that you live in fear again; rather, the Spirit you received brought about your adoption to sonship. And by him we cry, "Abba, Father." The Spirit himself testifies with our spirit that we are God's children. Now if we are children, then we are heirs—heirs of God and co-heirs with Christ, if indeed we share in his sufferings in order that we may also share in his glory. (Romans 8:14-17)*

It was the Spirit of God that testified with my spirit that I was a child of God. By Him I cried, "Abba (Daddy), Father." I couldn't see God, but my spirit responded to Him. I was in fellowship with my heavenly Father. The Spirit of God testified to the truth about Jesus, and I was able to believe because I had received God's Word. Who can understand this truth without the Spirit of the Lord? Who has known this freedom without having accepted the sufferings of Jesus Christ? Who breaks through the door of the heavenly sanctuary without permission? No peace can be found outside of God's Spirit.

J. Bronson Haley

So what do we do when we feel far away from God? What do we do when we feel like we can't pray or when we don't feel like praying? What do we do when we feel like we do not have the faith to believe God for a single thing? Maybe we are in a lot of pain and we are mad at God. Maybe we think we are going through things that we shouldn't have to go through and that God is mad at us. Maybe we are in a place where we are so alone and lost that we feel it's impossible to reach God. Maybe we are too ashamed because of the places we come up short in life. Maybe we are discouraged because God hasn't answered prayers we've been sending up for a long time. The truth is that we need to somehow get closer to God. If we actually get close to God, we will surely know it! If we come into the Spirit of truth, can the lies we are approached with throughout the day keep tormenting us? If we are lacking in faith, shouldn't our faith increase if we get closer to God? If we are really serious about something we are praying for, shouldn't we get as close as we can to God?

In our daily walk we can be lied to by the Devil. Thoughts can enter our minds that are not our own thoughts and surely are not God's thoughts. We know that in these last days there has been an increase in wickedness. We can see that when we look around and watch the news. Some struggle with things that doctors and psychiatrists can't really help with. When they cannot help someone, they write it off as a "disease" and then tell them things they can do to help them live with the "disease." Many of these diseases are nothing more than an attack from Satan. Can these struggles actually keep children of God bound? Can alcoholism keep prisoner a child of God who understands how to follow Jesus and draw near to the Lord who is in control of all things? Would God allow a spirit of addiction to keep His child a slave when this child continually approaches Him in a spirit of worship and follows His Son?

When I received this truth, I understood why Reverend Mertle worshiped the Lord in tears that day. He didn't worship because he was such a great man of faith, obedience, and strength like I first thought. He worshiped because he was hurting. He worshiped because he needed relief. Hank Mertle worshiped because he felt alone. This man of God drew near to the Father in his most painful hour. Reverend Mertle worshiped because he needed a promise from God.

Now I understand why Paul and Silas worshiped while they were in pain and in prison that day. They needed truth from the Father. These men of God needed relief, and in this case it was immediate: "Suddenly there was such a violent earthquake that the foundations of the prison were shaken.

The Depth of Grace

At once all the prison doors flew open, and everybody's chains came loose" (Acts 16:26). This took place after Paul and Silas began to worship God in prison on that darkened day. Sometimes the chains have no choice but to release God's children during worship. I was in pain and in my own prison when I received this truth. I knew that one day the chains would have no choice but to release me if I continually approached the Lord in worship, studied His Word, and adequately followed His Son.

Many would say, "How dare you pollute the throne of grace like that!" I don't know about you, but I've heard people say more stupid things than that. The Devil doesn't have any sense if you think about it. He was stupid enough to get kicked out of heaven. God gave him a depraved spirit and he doesn't even understand what truth is. Isn't Satan the father of lies? Oh, so he is everything but the truth? That makes sense. He is only able to feed our minds with lies that tempt us to sin, and if we sin, he keeps us bound by blinding us. God pays close attention when His children come into His presence to worship His Son in their sickness and pain, whether it be from drugs, cancer, divorce, or whatever.

"Yet a time is coming and has now come when the true worshipers will worship the Father in Spirit and in truth, for they are the kind of worshipers the Father seeks" (John 4:23). People have gone crazy lately and even nonbelievers agree. In other words a ton of lies are flying through the air and people believe them now more than ever! Children of God can buy into these lies as quickly as anyone. It's important to get into the Spirit of truth on a regular basis. Especially if you are sick—physically, mentally, emotionally, or spiritually! These are the worshipers the Father seeks!

"I was given a reed like a measuring rod and was told, 'Go and measure the temple of God and the altar, and count the worshipers there'" (Revelation 11:1 NIV 1984). I'm not exactly sure why the angel told John to do this. I do know that God was about to pour out His judgment just prior to the rapture of the church. While I'm still praying for my family and my friends, I know that I'm going to be counted there. When I need a word from God, I'm going to be counted there. When I need a breakthrough in my life, I will be counted there. When I believe God for a miracle in someone else's life, I will be counted there.

Have you ever noticed that, during the altar calls at Christian churches, there is always music? Have you noticed that the Lord often speaks to people during worship at church? Have you noticed that dead churches have dead music? Great churches have great worship!

277

People swear by someone greater than themselves, and the oath confirms what is said and puts an end to all argument. Because God wanted to make the unchanging nature of his purpose very clear to the heirs of what was promised, he confirmed it with an oath. God did this so that, by two unchangeable things in which it is impossible for God to lie, we who have fled to take hold of the hope offered to us may be greatly encouraged. We have this hope as an anchor for the soul, firm and secure. It enters the inner sanctuary behind the curtain, where our forerunner, Jesus, has entered on our behalf. He has become a high priest forever, in the order of Melchizedek. (Hebrews 6:16-20)

Now the main point of what we are saying is this: We do have such a high priest, who sat down at the right hand of the throne of the Majesty in heaven, and who serves in the sanctuary, the true tabernacle set up by the Lord, not by a mere human being. (Hebrews 8:1-2)

Let us then approach God's throne of grace with confidence, so that we may receive mercy and find grace to help us in our time of need. (Hebrews 4:16)

Many times I have extremely powerful experiences with God while worshiping Him. I never understood what was happening until I came across the Scriptures that told of similar stories. We know that the gift of the Holy Spirit was made available to all God's children on the day of Pentecost, and those present were filled with the Spirit. However, it didn't stop there. The followers of Jesus continued to be filled with the Spirit throughout the course of their ministry. "After they prayed, the place where they were meeting was shaken. And they were all filled with the Holy Spirit and spoke the word of God boldly" (Acts 4:31). This happened just after Peter and John were released from prison for preaching the gospel of Jesus with boldness that only the Spirit could have given them.

"And the disciples were filled with joy and with the Holy Spirit" (Acts 13:52). This happened just after a severe persecution broke out against Paul and Barnabas. They were expelled from the region where they ministered, and instead of allowing doubt, fear, and unbelief to set in, they were prayed for and refilled with the Holy Spirit.

The Depth of Grace

"Do not get drunk on wine, which leads to debauchery. Instead, be filled with the Spirit" (Ephesians 5:18). Obviously, getting filled with the Holy Spirit is a big deal. In this verse it's compared with getting drunk on wine. It wasn't until I was filled with the Spirit that I fully understood Ephesians 5:18. Nothing compares to the peace, joy, and every good thing that comes with being filled with God's Spirit. And we should be filled often—because our very own bodies become "temples" for the Holy Spirit to dwell in us. The heavens open inside of us, and we can enter into God's presence from within by way of His Spirit. And while we always have the Holy Spirit within us, we need to keep getting refilled as we pour out His love and mercy to others, and as the sin and filth of the world come against us.

Many times I am refilled with the Spirit during worship. Once, I was praying in my room when my longtime friend Parker Yalta came to visit me. He had been going to church with me sometimes by that point. When he walked into the room that day, I turned down the music.

He looked at me and said, "There's that look again."

"What look?" I asked.

"I don't know what it is, but your face looks different."

> *Then the Spirit lifted me up and brought me into the inner court, and the glory of the Lord filled the temple. (Ezekiel 43:5)*

The glory of God was upon me.

CHAPTER 27

—

Forget as God Forgets

Over are the days of having to memorize the Scriptures taught to us by men so that we may know something about God. We no longer need to depend on man in order to get a word from God and stay strong in our faith. Of course we need all men of God! Only we do not put them before the Word of the Lord and depend solely upon them. Have you not read that we serve a jealous God? "For the LORD your God is a consuming fire, a jealous God" (Deuteronomy 4:24).

And consider these words from the psalmist: "Since my youth, God, you have taught me, and to this day I declare your marvelous deeds" (Psalm 71:17). Notice that this man of God learned to hear from the Lord at an early age and continued on into adulthood. His faith stayed strong because He knew the Lord personally and knew how to get a word on his own. "It is written in the Prophets: 'They will all be taught by God.' Everyone who has heard the Father and learns from him comes to me" (John 6:45).

It is by the Holy Spirit that we receive from the Lord. It is by the Spirit that we receive anything from God, whether the word comes from the mouth of men or straight from the Scriptures. If we receive the truth in the word spoken, it is because the Spirit of truth enabled us to receive the truth.

"It's not that easy, Bronson," you may argue.

It's time we learn to ask for everything we need. As the apostle Paul wrote, "… in every situation, by prayer and petition, with thanksgiving,

281

J. Bronson Haley

present your requests to God" (Philippians 4:6). He is all-knowing for sure! However, His Word demands our attention and obedience. The Lord cannot go beyond what is written. He *is* the Word of God. Everything outside of His Word is in opposition to the truth. The opposite of the truth is the enemy's campground. Stay clear of the Devil's territory. "Do not go beyond what is written" (1 Corinthians 4:6).

"Because we know that just as you share in our sufferings, so also you share in our comfort" (2 Corinthians 1:7). Have you heard me quote this verse yet? Ha-ha ... More than a few times, right? Well, it's time to delve a bit further into this Scripture for better understanding. *Parakaleo* is the Greek word for *comfort* in this Scripture. It is used for every kind of call to a person, which is intended to produce a particular effect: "comfort, exhort, desire, call for, beseech." *Parakaleo* is derived from the word *paraklesis,* which means "an appeal, encouragement, exhortation, consolation, comfort." This *comfort* is received from the Father: "And I will pray the Father, and he shall give you another Comforter, that he may abide with you for ever; even the Spirit of truth" (John 14:16-17 ᴋᴊᴠ). This *comfort* is everything made available to us through the blood of Jesus Christ. When we share this *comfort* with someone who has shared in our *sufferings,* will they not be *comforted?* So when I suffer in an area and God *comforts* me, heals me, and sets me free, and I share this same *comfort* with you, you will be healed or set free in the same way I was *comforted.* "For just as we share abundantly in the sufferings of Christ, so also our comfort abounds through Christ" (2 Corinthians 1:5). If this is true, which it is, God who *comforted* me with the truth in this passage will *comfort* you.

> *I, even I, am he who blots out your transgressions, for my own sake, and remembers your sins no more. (Isaiah 43:25)*
>
> *As far as the east is from the west, so far has he removed our transgressions from us. (Psalm 103:12)*

If God forgets our mistakes, why should we keep bringing them to attention? Every man and woman of God in history has had to learn to forget as God forgets, and focus on the things God never forgets. I was *comforted* by this message.

God forgot about the time Abraham slept with the maidservant of his wife Sarah in fear that the Lord would not keep His promise. The Lord will never forget the day Abraham bound his son Isaac on a pile of wood and then raised his knife to slay him at His request.

282

The Depth of Grace

God forgot about the day Jacob deceived his father Isaac in order to receive the blessing of the Lord. The Lord will never forget the morning Jacob refused to let Him go at the stream—the ford of the Jabbok.

God forgot the sins of the prostitute who approached Jesus at the home of the Pharisee while Christ reclined at the table. God will never forget that she washed His feet with her tears and hair, that she anointed Him with expensive perfume from an alabaster jar: "Truly I tell you, wherever this gospel is preached throughout the world, what she has done will also be told, in memory of her" (Matthew 26:13).

God forgot about the time Simon denied His Son three times while in the very presence of Jesus being mocked, spit on, and beaten. God forgot that Simon left Jesus on the cross to be tortured without the support of the "Rock" whom He trusted to establish His church. The Lord will never forget the time he called Simon Peter to the ministry. He will not forget the day Peter dropped his nets and followed Him. God will never forget the day Simon Peter confessed His Son as his Lord and Savior. He will never forget the day He reinstated Peter. The Lord will never forget the day Peter addressed the crowd on the day of Pentecost and will never forget the day he confronted the chief priest and the teachers of the law to testify, "Jesus is 'the stone you builders rejected, which has become the cornerstone'" (Acts 4:11).

God forgot the time Saul of Tarsus threw His children into prison because they believed in His Son, Jesus. God forgot about the time Saul gave his vote in support of Stephen, whose "face was like the face of an angel," to be stoned to death for his confession of the glory of Christ. The Lord will never forget the letters of the apostle Paul and the churches he planted throughout the ancient Middle East.

God will forget the sins that Dr. Larry Williams and Chet Arkin will commit tomorrow. He will never forget the day these two men of God came to my home to tell me about the eagle: "When the storm blows in, the eagle faces into the wind. As the wind continues to blow, the eagle continues to rise. When his time has come, the eagle rises and soars above the storm. I see you as an eagle facing into the wind. The winds have blown and you have continued to rise. And Bronson ... you will rise above the storm." I will never forget those words and that day will never be forgotten.

God has forgotten my mother's mistakes. He will never forget the thank-you note she wrote as a prayer to God after my horrific wreck, which

J. Bronson Haley

I let you read in Chapter 6. The Lord will never forget that poem she wrote and neither will I. I love you, Mom!

God will forget the times we have come up short in life. The Lord will forget the times we have rejected Jesus and taken His sufferings for granted. He will never forget the day we renewed our friendship with His Son, who so patiently anticipated our arrival. The Lord will never forget the times we returned to His presence to confess that Jesus suffered enough for us.

Jesus said while He was with us on earth, "Whoever believes in me, as the Scripture has said, rivers of living water will flow from within them" (John 7:38). What does this mean? This speaks of the stream that flowed from within Jesus as He hung dead on the cross. We suffer in our flesh. Jesus suffered in His flesh so that we could be healed of our pain. Jesus' body was dead on the cross because in our sin we were all destined to die. However, the Word of God never died! The Word of God raised Jesus from the dead. Death could not keep its hold on the Son of God because the Word of God spoke against it. The love of God would not allow death to keep Jesus! The gift from God was raised to life! The Word of God speaks against the dead! Be raised to life in the name of the risen King!

When we receive Jesus Christ, a spring of living water is born inside of us. When we are healed or brought to life in an area we once suffered and overcame, God has *comforted* us. When we share this *comfort* with someone else who shared in our *sufferings,* they will be *comforted* in the same way. Therefore the streams of living water will flow from the life within us into the one who shared in our *sufferings.* "For just as we share abundantly in the sufferings of Christ, so also our comfort abounds through Christ" (2 Corinthians 1:5).

This book is made up of streams of living water I received from the Father through the Son during my *sufferings,* and I was set free and healed as a result. When I share these streams with someone who shares in my *sufferings,* they will be *comforted,* given that the Word of God sent a stream or streams of living water into their life. Right? Praise the Lord! How many streams of living water do you want? Get in the Word of God and get you some! "For the Lamb at the center of the throne will be their shepherd; 'he will lead them to springs of living water.' 'And God will wipe away every tear from their eyes'" (Revelation 7:17).

Jesus Christ suffered greatly for our sins, for sure. He died on the cross that we could be saved from death and receive eternal life through the resurrection. There also came an outflow of blood and water when the centurion withdrew the spear from the side of Christ as he hung dead on

The Depth of Grace

the cross: "one of the soldiers pierced Jesus' side with a spear, bringing a sudden flow of blood and water" (John 19:34). There is a never-ending supply of this blood and water. Because of the blood, we can forget as God forgets. Because of the living water, we can move forward under the resurrection power of our Lord and Savior Jesus Christ.

If you have not received Jesus, ask Him to draw you to repentance by His Spirit. When you are born again, you will be born of the Spirit of God. If we follow Jesus Christ, our sin cannot keep its hold on us. In your sickness and pain, follow the Son of God. Read His Word, pray, sing to Him, and assemble together with believers—follow Jesus Christ. If you follow Him, you will receive this never-ending supply of blood and living water. The Spirit of God comes when we have been washed clean of our sin. How do we believe this? "This is the one who came by water and blood—Jesus Christ. He did not come by water only, but by water and blood. And it is the Spirit who testifies, because the Spirit is the truth" (1 John 5:6). If only a man speaks of this truth, who can understand? If God speaks this truth to a man, how can he not understand?

The Word may come from our pastor. It may come from a friend. It may come from a book. God may speak to us directly from His Word as we read. Never stop asking—never stop believing—be forever receiving. Let us review:

> *For the Lamb at the center of the throne will be their shepherd;*
> *'he will lead them to springs of living water.' 'And God will*
> *wipe away every tear from their eyes.' (Revelation 7:17)*

> *He will swallow up death forever. The Sovereign LORD will*
> *wipe away the tears from all faces; he will remove his people's*
> *disgrace from all the earth. The LORD has spoken. (Isaiah*
> *25:8)*

And I pray that the Lord will speak into your life and bring freedom to you in every area of your life as you experience His love and truth. Thanks for joining me on this journey!

285

A FINAL NOTE FROM THE AUTHOR ...

Just a quick note to say that I appreciate you, the readers of this book, and I pray that God would use His Word to transform your life. Whether you're already a believer or not—and whether you're walking tall with God or you're so down and depressed that you can't imagine a way out—I hope you'll continue your own journey into the depth of God's grace by digging into His Word. In this book I've relied on the New International Version of the Bible, so if you don't own a copy of God's Word yet, maybe you can try this version, as it's very reader-friendly. And if you want to drop me a line, I'd love to hear about how God is working in your life. Just jump online and go to *www.DepthofGrace.com* to get in touch with me. Thanks again for spending some time with me!

— *J. Bronson Haley*

LaVergne, TN USA
24 February 2011
217783LV00002BA/1/P